Y0-CDN-347

THE PALATINE WRECK

SEAFARING AMERICA

Richard J. King, Williams College at Mystic Seaport, Editor

Seafaring America is a series of original and classic works of fiction, nonfiction, poetry, and drama bearing on the history of America's engagement with our oceans and coastlines. Spanning diverse eras, populations, and geographical settings, the series strives to introduce, revive, and aggregate a wide range of exemplary and seminal stories about our American maritime heritage, including the accounts of First Peoples, explorers, slaves, immigrants, fishermen, whalers, captains, common sailors, members of the navy and coast guard, marine biologists, and the crews of vessels ranging from lifeboats, riverboats, and tugboats to recreational yachts. As a sailor's library, Seafaring America introduces new stories of maritime interest and reprints books that have fallen out of circulation and deserve reappraisal, and publishes selections from well-known works that reward reconsideration because of the lessons they offer about our relationship with the ocean.

For a complete list of books available in this series,
see www.upne.com

The Palatine Wreck

THE LEGEND OF THE
NEW ENGLAND GHOST SHIP

JILL FARINELLI

UNIVERSITY PRESS OF NEW ENGLAND

HANOVER AND LONDON

University Press of New England
www.upne.com
© 2017 Jill Farinelli
All rights reserved

Manufactured in the United States of America
Designed by April Leidig
Typeset in Jenson by Copperline Book Services

For permission to reproduce any of the material in this book,
contact Permissions, University Press of New England,
One Court Street, Suite 250, Lebanon NH 03766;
or visit www.upne.com

Seafaring America is supported and produced in part by the
Maritime Studies Program of Williams College and Mystic Seaport.
Williams-Mystic empowers global, creative citizens while inspiring
an enduring relationship with the ocean. We create an open-minded,
interdisciplinary academic community, with experiential learning at
Mystic Seaport, along the coasts of America, and at sea.

Library of Congress Cataloging-in-Publication Data
available upon request

Paperback ISBN: 978-1-61168-705-7
Ebook ISBN: 978-1-5126-0117-6

5 4 3 2 1

This is for my husband, Seán Adam,
and our son, Rob.
I love you guys to the moon and back.

————————

In Travel, Pilgrims oft do ask, to know
What *Miles* they've gone, and what they have to go:
Their Way is tedious and their Limbs oppreſt,
And their Deſire is to be at reſt.
In Life's more tedious Journey, Man delays
T'enquire out the Number of his Days:
He cares, not he, how ſlow his Hours ſpend,
The Journey's better than the Journey's End.
—*Poor Richard's Almanack*, December 1739

CONTENTS

PART IV

The Legend

Seafaring America

The Inupiat of far northern Alaska have for centuries said that the bowhead whale lives two human lifetimes. In *Moby-Dick*, the primary entrepôt of all American literature of the sea, Ishmael yarns about a stone lance in an old whale: "It might have been darted by some Nor'-West Indian long before America was discovered." By studying amino acids in the eyes of legally killed bowhead whales and dating the old lances of stone, ivory, and steel found buried in the blubber, twenty-first-century researchers have confirmed that some individuals of this species might indeed live over two hundred years. A bowhead swimming around the thinning ice of the Arctic in 2015, when the Cuban-American poet Richard Blanco wrote, "we all belong to the sea between us," likely also swam in 1859 when Emily Dickinson penciled the lines: "Exultation is the going/Of an inland soul to sea"— and then put them in her drawer.

Since the first human settlement of our coasts, the voices expressing the American relationship with the sea have been diverse in gender, race, ethnicity, geography, and experience. And the study of maritime literature and history continues to converge and circulate with marine science and contemporary policy.

Seafaring America seeks to inspire and explore ocean study in this twenty-first century. The Taino chief Hatuey, James Fenimore Cooper, Harriet Beecher Stowe, Frederick Douglass, John Greenleaf Whittier, Winslow Homer, Alexander Agassiz, Joshua Slocum, Kate Chopin, Samuel Eliot Morison, Langston Hughes, Marianne Moore, Rachel Carson, Ursula K. Le Guin, Jill Farinelli, and generations of other American mariners, artists, writers, scientists, and historians have all known that the ocean is the dominant ecological, meteorological, political, and metaphorical force on Earth.

"The sea is History," wrote Derek Walcott in 1979, mourning the horrors of the Middle Passage and the drowned African American cultural memory. By the 1970s the sea was history in a new way. Americans began to perceive the global ocean as vulnerable to our destructive reach. The realization rolled in with the discovery of the dead zone off the Mississippi River delta, industrial overfishing off New England, and the massive oil spill that spoiled the same Santa Barbara sands on which Richard Henry Dana Jr. first landed his bare Boston Brahmin feet in 1835 after a passage of 150 days. Yet even today, the rising seas, floods, shipwrecks, and immutable tempests along the Great Lakes, the Gulf of Mexico, and America's Atlantic, Pacific, and Arctic coasts continue to remind us of an immortal and indifferent sea — a savage ocean that crashes and seeps over the transience of *Homo sapiens*.

Seafaring America is a series of new and classic works of fiction, nonfiction, history, poetry, and drama that engages with the country's enduring relationship with the oceans and coastlines. Seafaring America strives to introduce, revive, and aggregate a wide range of exemplary and seminal stories and verse about the American maritime heritage: to trace the footprints on the beach, the stone lances in the blubber, and the pearls in the drawer.

Richard J. King
Williams College–Mystic Seaport

ACKNOWLEDGMENTS

This project would not have been possible without the help of others. My sincerest thanks go to the following individuals:

To Dr. Esther Bauer, whose thoughtful translation of dozens of eighteenth-century letters and documents written in Old German script revealed details of the *Princess Augusta* tragedy that had been lost for more than 275 years. Not only did she squeeze me into her very busy work schedule, she and her husband took time out from a family vacation in Switzerland to drive to Schwaigern, Germany, where they spent two days at the city archives gathering information about the local families who traveled aboard the ship. I am profoundly grateful for their efforts.

To Gloria Hazard Miller ("Lady G"), sixth-great-granddaughter of Long Kate and New Port (Newport) Sands. We began corresponding in 2009, and over the past eight years she has generously shared her family stories and legends and taught me about the lives of free and enslaved Africans and Native Americans in colonial Rhode Island. Thank you for your friendship.

A number of individuals in Europe have done research for me when I was unable to travel overseas. In Germany, Uwe Schlund, Werner Clement, and Ralf Striffler from Schwaigern located documents in the city archives. Dr. Bernhard Weber, director of the Museum der Deutschen Binnenschifffahrt (German Inland Waterways Museum) in Duisburg, supplied information on travel aboard eighteenth-century Rhine River barges.

In the Netherlands, the staff at the Stadsarchief Rotterdam (City Archives of Rotterdam) could not have been more helpful. Christa Schepen searched the notarial records for charterparties and passenger contracts from Palatine ships of the era. Joop Verkamman also combed the notarial records and provided information on the

Kralingen holding camp and the route of the Palatine ships through the Rhine delta.

John Veerman, building historian and archaeologist at Veerman Bouwhistorie in Rotterdam, offered details about the residences of the Hope family of merchant bankers. He also translated several documents in Dutch related to the *Princess Augusta*'s companion ship, the *Oliver*.

Marc Mackenbach, a student from Amsterdam, along with his historian father and his grandfather, traveled to the Rotterdam Archives and pored through eighteenth-century Dutch newspapers for information about the ship's departure and its demise. Marc also helped pinpoint the location of the ruins of St. Ellebregt's Chapel in Kralingen, where the holding camp was established.

In England, Michael Hunt, director of the Ramsgate Maritime Museum, provided much of the information on the *Princess Augusta* and her owners. Genealogist and historian Duncan W. Harrington in Kent, England, located information on the Long and Brook families. Dr. Andrew Lewis, professional historical researcher, searched the National Archives in London for documents related to the merchant ship. Rhiannon Markless, lawyer, historian, and independent researcher at Remark Legal Archive Research in Kingston-Upon-Thames, answered my questions about charterparties and salvage law. Steve Holden, genealogist, historian, and former customs officer at Cowes on the Isle of Wight, shared his extensive knowledge of the inspection process in the eighteenth century.

In this country, Dr. Sherry Johnson, associate professor of history and director of academic programs at the Latin America and Caribbean Center at Florida International University, shared her research on the effects of environmental stress on historical processes. Tracy Bergstrom, in the Department of Special Collections at the University of Notre Dame, offered the services of a summer intern to read issues of the *Kentish Post* from 1739–40, looking for information about the wreck in the crew's hometown newspaper.

David Hauggard, director of research services at the Historical Society of Pennsylvania, and researcher Dana Dorman, located and sent me scans of the correspondence between Caspar Wistar and

Georg Friedrich Hölzer — not an easy task given that the centuries-old letters were handwritten in Old German script.

Pam Gasner, director of the Block Island Historical Society, took time to answer my questions about the island's early history and drove me out to the Palatine graves in her pickup truck. Millie McGinnes at the New Shoreham Town Hall cheerfully and speedily located the eighteenth-century wills belonging to the Sands and Littlefield families.

Dr. Marianne Wokeck, Chancellor's Professor of History at Indiana University–Purdue University Indianapolis, shared her expertise on the Palatine trade. I highly recommend her book, *Trade in Strangers: The Beginnings of Mass Migration in North America*, to anyone who has German or Irish ancestors who came to this country in the eighteenth century.

Closer to home, I am thankful to my lifelong friends, Anne Hunter and George Young, for introducing me to Block Island some thirty years ago. I first heard about the legend from them. I cherish the time we spend together on the island each summer. Heartfelt thanks also go to Jill Betz Bloom, who encouraged me to write this book and provided moral support during the process.

I owe a debt of gratitude to my agent, Janet Reid, and Fine Print Literary Agency. She was willing to take a chance on me, and were it not for her persistence and powers of persuasion, I might still be reading rejection letters. I am also grateful to Stephen Hull, acquisitions editor at University Press of New England, for agreeing to take this project on. I appreciate his guidance and his patience throughout the process. Thanks go to Dr. Richard King, research associate at the Maritime Studies Program of Williams College and Mystic Seaport, for his thoughtful comments on the manuscript, and to Peter Fong for his careful and thorough copyedit. And thanks as well to Patti Isaacs of 45th Parallel Maps and Infographics, who took my scribbled notes and turned them into gorgeous maps.

And finally, to my husband, Seán, and son, Rob: I am grateful for your love and support. Thank you for staying by my side during this sometimes challenging and uncertain journey we call life.

KNOWN CREW AND PASSENGERS ON THE 1738 VOYAGE OF THE *PRINCESS AUGUSTA*

Ages given in parentheses.

CREW

George Long, captain (20)
Andrew Brook, first mate (36)
George Brooks (age unknown)
Robert Hughson (age unknown)

PASSENGERS

Sebastian Dieter (32)
Catharina (Eberle) Dieter (32)
Johann Christian Dieter (5)
Maria Magdalena Dieter (3)
Maria Catharina Dieter (18 mo.)
Marcell Schneider (50)
Margaretha (Stumpf) Schneider (42)
Maria Catharina Schneider (11)
Maria Elisabetha Schneider (7)
Christoph Marcell Schneider (4)
Georg (Jerg) Gebert (31)
Elisabetha Gebert (maiden name and age unknown)
Johann Daniel Gebert (16 mo.)
Christoph (Stophel) Schaber (32)
Conrath Gehr (35)
"Long Kate" (name and age unknown)
"Short Kate" (name and age unknown)

A Maritime Mystery

Warren Ball peered through the window of his weather-beaten cottage atop a bluff at the southeastern end of Block Island. It was just past dark on December 27, 1912, and coastal New England was in the grips of an icy gale. The storm had blown in from the northwest earlier in the day, bringing heavy snow and seventy-mile-per-hour winds that howled down chimneys, rattled windows and doors, and churned the Atlantic into mountainous waves.

Scanning the horizon, he was startled to see a ship on fire far out at sea. Though visibility was hindered by the blowing snow, it appeared to be a three-masted schooner engulfed in flames from the waterline to the masthead. Ball watched as the blaze died down to a smudge of light and then shot upward in a spray of flame and sparks that lit up the underbelly of the sky. Telephone lines on the island were down, and the roads were impassable, so the fifty-eight-year-old fisherman pulled on his overcoat, wool cap, and boots and made his way on foot to the New Shoreham Life-Saving Station, about a mile north of his house.

Arriving at the boathouse winded and half-frozen, Ball told station keeper Amazon Littlefield about the burning ship he had seen southeast of the island. The heavy seas, bitter wind, and distance of the vessel from shore made launching the surfboat out of the question. Littlefield sent a wireless message to the superintendent of the Third Life-Saving District in Wakefield, Rhode Island, and two steam-powered revenue cutters were dispatched to the scene: the *Seneca*, a 1,200-ton, steel-hulled "derelict destroyer" stationed in New London, Connecticut, and the 800-ton *Acushnet* from Woods Hole, Massachusetts.[1] In the meantime, the surfmen from all three life-saving stations on Block Island and from stations along the Rhode Island coast patrolled the battered beaches with lanterns, looking for any survivors or bodies that might come ashore.[2]

When the *Seneca* got within four miles of the scene, the burning ship sank beneath the waves. The two cutters scoured the area through the night, hoping to find survivors in lifeboats, but their searchlights were clouded by the snowstorm. Nothing was found. The rescuers feared that the twenty-foot waves had made it impossible for the schooner to launch its boats, or if it had launched them, for those boats to remain afloat for more than a few minutes. The cutters put in at Martha's Vineyard at daybreak, then returned to the scene several hours later, expecting to pull frozen bodies from the water. But again, they turned up nothing. At nightfall the effort was called off.

Occurring just eight months after the *Titanic* disaster, the mysterious disappearance of the burning ship captured the public's imagination, as newspapers offered theories about what had happened. The *New York Evening Telegram* speculated that the schooner had been carrying explosives and that no survivors were found because the crew had either burned to death or, by some miracle, been picked up by a passing steamer.[3] The *New York Times* suggested that the illumination was not a burning schooner at all but the "burning out of a tug's smokestack."[4]

Warren Ball was unwilling to dismiss the spectacle as just another shipping accident, despite the fact that more than forty wrecks or strandings had occurred in the vicinity of Block Island in the past ten years alone.[5] What he saw that night matched descriptions of an alleged ghost ship that had haunted the waters surrounding Block Island for almost 200 years. Locals had long believed in a legendary apparition that resembled a three-masted vessel with sails set, completely enveloped in flames. Stunned witnesses of similar events over the years claimed that the raging fire seemed to have no effect on the hull, canvas, or rigging, nor did it produce any heat or smoke; and after the burning vessel sank beneath the waves, there were no bodies or debris left floating in the water, nothing to wash ashore. Like a phantom, it simply vanished.

The most famous and detailed account of the ghost ship had been written a century before Warren Ball's vision, by an island physician named Aaron Willey, who witnessed the phenomenon on two occasions in 1810. His report was published in the *Medical Repository* in 1813 and reprinted in numerous publications for years afterward. He wrote, in part:

> Its appearance is nothing different from that of a blaze of fire. It beams with various magnitude; being sometimes small, resembling the light of a distant window, at others expanded to the bigness of a ship with all her canvass spread. When large, it sometimes displays a pyramidical form, at other three coruscant [sparkling] streams. . . . It often happens that it is in a constant state of mutation, as it respects its bigness; decreasing, by degrees, till it becomes invisible, or resembles a lucid point; then shining anew, either, with a sudden flash, or gradual increment to its former size.[6]

The "curious irradiation" described by Willey had been linked to a shipwreck that occurred on the island on this very day — December 27 — in 1738. The story passed down through generations of Rhode Islanders was that a ship named the *Palatine*, transporting wealthy emigrants from Holland to Pennsylvania, had wrecked on Block Island under suspicious circumstances. What those circumstances were, however, depended on whom you asked.

According to the islanders, the crew murdered the captain, extorted money and valuables from the passengers by prolonging the voyage and withholding food and water, and then abandoned ship.

The vessel drifted ashore at Sandy Point two days after Christmas, whereupon the passengers were rescued by the islanders and nursed back to health, and then sent on to Philadelphia, their original destination. The damaged vessel was burned to prevent it from floating off and becoming a navigational hazard. A wealthy Dutch woman named Mary Vanderline, crazed by her ordeal and hiding in the ship's hold, became trapped and burned to death. This was the version passed down to Ball, whose ancestors had lived on the island when the wreck occurred.

In the version told on the mainland, the islanders lured the ship ashore with a false signal light — some say oil-soaked timbers set ablaze on a cliff, or a lantern hung from the neck of a grazing donkey — then robbed and murdered all on board. Afterward, they set fire to the ship to hide evidence of their crimes. As they rowed away, they cut off the arm of a drowning female passenger (or a crewmember, some sources say) who had reached for the gunwale of their boat.

That scenario seemed plausible to those on the mainland. In the eighteenth and early nineteenth centuries, Block Island farmers and fishermen earned part of their living from "wrecking"— salvaging cargo and equipment from the countless shipwrecks that happened there. It was a valuable service to grateful ship owners, but some landsmen mistook the term to mean the deliberate destruction of ships in order to plunder them. The islanders were also accused of sheltering pirates. In one year alone (1699), three notorious pirates, including William Kidd, stopped there, some say to hide treasure.[7] Paulsgrave Williams grew up on the island, but he left before his career in buccaneering began. Occasionally mutineers and sea robbers captured in the vicinity were jailed on the island while awaiting trial in Newport. In newspapers and court records these scoundrels were often referred to as "the pirates at Block Island."[8]

In December 1739, one year after the wreck of the *Palatine*, the crew of a merchant vessel passing through Block Island Sound spotted a tall ship on fire. They followed the burning vessel until it disappeared beneath the waves, but found no trace of the accident —

no survivors, no bodies, no debris. Because it appeared on the one-year anniversary of the wreck, the apparition became linked to the doomed ship and was nicknamed the Palatine Light.

According to local legend, the Palatine Light appeared annually at first. Later on, sightings happened at irregular intervals, during all seasons of the year, on calm, moonlit nights or in screaming gales. Ball recalled that the last cluster of sightings had occurred when he was in his twenties. In February 1880, a large ship on fire was seen off the eastern coast of the island at evening twilight, gliding swiftly north, toward Newport. The vision lasted about fifteen minutes before turning gray and misty and vanishing into thin air. More than fifty people claimed to have seen it that evening, including a U.S. senator.[9]

The light materialized several months later, and again in 1882. Its last recorded appearance that century was in 1885. The witness, a tourist from Philadelphia, told the *New York Times* it looked like a whitish flame, shaped like a pyramid, and about the size of a tall ship under sail. The flame shot up out of the water at the southeast end of the island and then moved north, toward Sandy Point, where it faded out of view.[10]

Block Island's ghost ship was immortalized by John Greenleaf Whittier in his famous poem "The Palatine," first published in 1867. Whittier, following the version popular on the mainland, blamed the islanders for the ship's demise.

> Into the teeth of death she sped:
> (May God forgive the hands that fed
> The false lights over the rocky Head!)
>
> . . . .
>
> Down swooped the wreckers, like birds of prey
> Tearing the heart of the ship away,
> And the dead had never a word to say.
>
> And then, with ghastly shimmer and shine
> Over the rocks and the seething brine,
> They burned the wreck of the Palatine.

> In their cruel hearts, as they homeward sped,
> "The sea and the rocks are dumb," they said:
> "There'll be no reckoning with the dead."
>
> But the year went round, and when once more
> Along their foam-white curves of shore
> They heard the line-storm rave and roar,
>
> Behold! again, with shimmer and shine,
> Over the rocks and the seething brine,
> The flaming wreck of the Palatine![11]

Whittier's poem spread the legend far beyond coastal New England, to the dismay of generations of islanders, who worried that as long as a volume of his could be found on a shelf, the stigma he cast upon them would never be erased.[12]

Throughout the winter of 1912–13, the main topic of conversation in C. C. Ball's general store, in Darius Dodge's drugstore, at the Baptist church, in the post office, on the docks, and at the ice houses was the burning schooner that the government's largest and most sophisticated rescue vessel could not reach and whose wreckage it could not find. Not just islanders, but mainlanders too wondered if the "waving brightness" described a hundred years earlier by Dr. Willey had been revived. Skeptics insisted there was a scientific explanation for the illusion, like the igniting of methane gas bubbling up from the ocean floor. The superstitious reminded the skeptics that none of their scientific theories had ever been proved, which was proof enough for them that the phantom vessel was real.

What all had forgotten by 1912 was the real identity of the ship. She was not named the *Palatine* but the *Princess Augusta*, an English cargo vessel chartered by a merchant banking firm in Rotterdam to transport several hundred German-speaking emigrants to Philadelphia in the summer of 1738. Most of her passengers were from the Palatinate and surrounding territories in what is now southwest Germany. Residents had begun fleeing the region in the late 1600s, driven out by religious persecution, political oppression, and eco-

nomic hardship. They were drawn to America by promises of freedom, peace, and prosperity. The British referred to these people as
Palatines, and the ships that carried them, Palatine ships. Because
the colonial newspapers that reported on the wreck never stated her
actual name, she came to be known simply as the *Palatine*.

Hers was a remarkably unlucky voyage in an otherwise successful, long-running business enterprise called the Palatine trade. In
the century before the Revolution, ships brought more than 110,000
Palatines to America (mostly to Pennsylvania), marking the first
mass migration of non-English-speaking Europeans to these shores.
The *Princess Augusta* was one of twenty-two Palatine ships that
sailed in 1738, one of more than 530 known voyages in all. She was
also one of only a handful of Palatine ships that never reached their
destinations.[13]

In her case, a combination of overcrowding, careless provision-
ing, disease, weather delays in the English Channel, horrific storms
at sea, and an unscheduled stop near the end of the voyage set up the
ship for disaster. Greed played a part in the passengers' suffering,
too, for at every stage of the Palatines' journey they encountered
people who made a living by preying on strangers in transit.

This book is the true story of the final voyage of the *Princess Augusta*, whose destruction on Block Island in December 1738 gave
rise to the legend of the ghost ship *Palatine*, later immortalized in
Whittier's beautiful and haunting poem. It reveals — for the first
time ever — the names of fifteen passengers, gleaned from letters
and town records written in Old German script nearly three centuries ago. These included several families from the medieval walled
town of Schwaigern, who chose to embark on the long and perilous
journey despite having very young children, as well as a man of ques-
tionable character who was hired by a merchant in the market town
of Neckargemünd to deliver a shipment of rifles to the merchant's
wealthy Quaker business partner in Philadelphia.

Also on board were two young women who chose to remain on
Block Island after the other castaways resumed their journey to
Pennsylvania. Who they were and where they were from remain a

mystery. According to island historians, one lived peaceably among her neighbors, while the other became notorious in the community for her bizarre behavior and belief in the supernatural. She has been blamed for conjuring up the ghost ship and for starting some of the rumors that haunt the ship's memory to this day.

The discovery of the passenger names occurred several years into the project. While reading about the Palatine trade, I came across references in two different sources to a letter written in October 1739 by a German immigrant named Peter Lohrman. Lohrman lived in Germantown, just northwest of Philadelphia. He had written home to Schwaigern to inform loved ones of the fate of several men from the town (including Lohrman's nephew), whose ship had wrecked the year before on its way to Philadelphia. He did not name the ship, but I knew that only one Philadelphia-bound Palatine ship had wrecked in 1738: the *Princess Augusta*.[14]

The Lohrman letter was written in Old German script, a late-medieval cursive handwriting style no longer used, and the ink on each surface of the centuries-old paper had bled through to the other side. Further, it was very poorly worded, and for that reason its meaning was unclear. All that probably explains why the two authors who had previously cited the letter interpreted it in different ways. According to one, everyone in the 1738 group had survived the wreck and arrived in Philadelphia. According to the other, all but one person in the group had died.[15]

I ordered a copy of the original letter from the Schwaigern City Archives and hired Dr. Esther Bauer, a translator specializing in Old German script, to decipher it for me. She confirmed that the men and their families had been on a ship that sank off "Rot-Eÿland," but the wording was confusing, so she was not absolutely certain of their fates. (To complicate matters, different passages within the letter contradicted one another.) I consulted two other translators and they said the same. Later, while visiting family in Switzerland, Dr. Bauer drove to Schwaigern and obtained copies of the families' estate inventories and examined the local church records. From these documents we learned the names of the wives

and children accompanying these men — fourteen people in all.
It would be several more years before I stumbled across a probate
document at Philadelphia City Hall that suggested the deadlier scenario was the correct one. That must have been why I could find no
record of the families in Pennsylvania (or in Virginia, where some
of their siblings had settled), nor locate any descendants.

I found the name of one more passenger while reading about the
smuggling that was rampant on Palatine ships. I followed a trail
of breadcrumbs that began with a customs dispute involving the
Princess Augusta in the port of Philadelphia in 1736; then led to a
wealthy Philadelphia merchant named Caspar Wistar, who had
smuggled goods on board the ship; and then to the loss Wistar
and his business partner in Neckargemünd suffered two years later
when the ship that carried their goods sank off the coast of Rhode
Island.[16] Once again, I knew that unnamed ship had to be the *Princess Augusta.*

Footnotes led me to Wistar's business correspondence housed at
the Historical Society of Pennsylvania. I ordered copies of twenty
letters he and his partner had exchanged in the 1730s and 1740s (all
written in Old German script). From Dr. Bauer's translations we
learned the name of the merchants' courier on board the *Princess
Augusta* in 1738 and about some of the precious items he carried in
his chests. One letter, written after the courier had landed in Philadelphia and spoken to Wistar, mentioned the horrifying conditions
below deck during the voyage and the desolation of Block Island at
that time. Unfortunately, part of this letter is missing, as is another
letter written several months later that apparently goes into even
greater detail about the voyage.

What follows is an uneven and incomplete story. Except for the
fifteen passengers I've discovered, and the ship's officers named in
the contemporary newspaper reports and the crew's depositions,
most of the people on board have yet to be identified. And we know
more about some stages of the journey than about others. Even
more frustrating is knowing what happened but not why. I have
tried to fill in the gaps by examining the shared experiences of other

Palatines who made the journey on other ships during that same time period — beginning with the *Oliver*, which set out across the Atlantic with the *Princess Augusta*. I have collected more than fifty travel accounts, most from the 1730s and 1740s. The letters, diaries, and journals were written both by ordinary emigrants and by prominent religious and political figures, most headed to Philadelphia but a few to other colonial ports. Their travel experiences are remarkably similar.

When I started this project ten years ago, I had already decided I did not want to simply regurgitate the legend and pass it off as fact, as so many articles have done over the years. I wanted to tell the true story of the voyage, and to do that I needed to be honest with the reader about what we know and what we don't know. I've tried my best to make a clear distinction between facts (based on primary sources), supposition, and legend. Because there are so many variations to the legend of this wreck, I've included only those elements that had a wide circulation and have stood the test of time.

Rewind to Block Island in the summer of 1913: Warren Ball had quite a story to tell the tourists, who arrived twice daily aboard the mail steamers from Providence and Newport. But as it turns out, he and his contemporaries didn't know the half of it. The wreck of the Palatine ship on tiny Block Island was not the criminal act it has been portrayed as all these years. Truth be told, the grounding might have been the least of the trials and tribulations the survivors experienced during their year-long ordeal. This is a tale not only of a shipwreck, but of the horrors that came before it.

PART I

The Old World

CHAPTER ONE

Leaving the Homeland

Sebastian Dieter's journey to America began in the fall of 1737 with a short walk from his father's house to the town hall. There he stood before the town administrator to declare his desire to move to the New Land. He was thirty-two years old, married, with three young children, and although he made a decent living as a weaver and a farmer, he worried about his children's prospects in a town with too many tradesmen and not enough land. He wanted more for his family than what lay within the fortified walls of their medieval German town.

The Dieters lived in Schwaigern (pronounced ˈshwī-gərn), a market town eight miles west of Heilbronn, in a region of rolling hills between the Rhine and Neckar Rivers. Several hundred people lived in this compact settlement. Some were tradesmen — tailors, shoemakers, carpenters, smiths, cartwrights, coopers, and butchers — who served the local community but not much beyond. Others were farmers who grew grain and vegetables and raised livestock for meat and milk. The small surplus they produced was sold in the *Marktplatz* in the center of town.[1]

Several blocks northeast of the marketplace was the palace of the local ruling family, the von Neippergs. Construction of the massive stone residence began in 1702, financed through heavy taxation and built in large part with mandatory labor. Next door to the palace was the tallest structure in town: the Evangelical Lutheran church. Dieter and most of his neighbors were members. The pastor was chosen by the current ruler, so the church served not just as the spiritual center of the community but as an extension of the state, monitoring the congregation's lawfulness and morality.[2] Together these three local landmarks — the market, the palace, and the church — controlled nearly every aspect of the townspeople's lives.

On the other side of the marketplace was the residential part of town, a densely populated area just a few blocks long and wide. Each block was divided into small lots. Standing shoulder to shoulder on the lots were half-timbered houses clad with wattle and daub. Some were single-family dwellings, while others had been partitioned to form "half-houses," usually the result of inheritance divisions.

The town was enclosed by a fifteen-foot-tall stone wall and a moat — a deep, broad ditch the earliest settlers had dug with shovels and pickaxes. Only a handful of houses stood outside this barrier. The wall and moat were built in the fifteenth century, not long after Holy Roman Emperor Karl IV granted the town its charter and the right to hold a weekly market. While the fortifications kept out vagabonds and thieves, they were no match for the armies of the great European powers — namely, France and Austria — which traversed the region during the bloody battles between Protestants and Catholics in the seventeenth century. The wall also could not stop the spread of plague. Hundreds of Schwaigern residents — in some cases, entire families — died from the disease in the 1630s.[3]

The entrance to the town was marked by a large gate and a circular watchtower that doubled as a prison. In 1713, Anna Maria Heinrich, wife of the town's locksmith, was charged with witchcraft and incarcerated in the tower. She and her two daughters were accused of "enchanting" the ruling noble's fourteen-year-old son, causing him to suffer episodes of anxiety and twitching, along with fits of convulsive laughter. Heinrich was tried, convicted, and condemned to death by fire. In a grisly plea bargain, the prosecutors offered to strangle her first if she confessed.[4] Sebastian Dieter was seven years old when Heinrich was burned at the stake and her two daughters forced to watch.[5] The sentence was carried out by the owner of a nearby slaughterhouse, who worked on the side as an executioner.[6]

Beyond the wall and moat was a dirt road that encircled the town. Beyond the road were the agricultural fields and the von Neippergs' precious vineyards. Several villages were located just a few miles away, inhabited by peasant farmers who grew and made what they needed with little to spare.[7] They lived in a precarious state, one hailstorm away from crop failure and famine, with little hope of ever owning the land they lived and worked on.

In general, the residents of market towns were more prosperous than their village neighbors. Dieter, a linen weaver by trade, had done relatively well. Although he and his wife and children lived in his father's house, he had acquired several farm lots where he grew peas, oats, vetch, wheat, and flax with the occasional help of hired labor. He also owned six parcels of vineyard, some meadowland, a vegetable garden, and a cabbage patch. In all, his real estate holdings totaled about fifteen acres.[8]

But not everything Dieter produced belonged to him. In Schwaigern, residents who cultivated parcels of vineyard were required to use Lord von Neipperg's wine press, located next to the town hall, and to pay him for its use in measures of wine. This was just one more reminder of the control the ruler had over the land and the population. Whether farmer or craftsman, tenant or landowner, burgher or serf, in early modern Europe the citizens were considered the wealth of the state, and their role was to support their ruler and the local church (in some places the ruler *was* the church) with heavy taxes, tithes, mandatory labor, and compulsory military service.[9] The financial burdens forced many families into debt, while those who had managed to accumulate some wealth worried that new fees and policy changes — and reignited war — could wipe it all away. It was an oppressive system that fostered great resentment. Dieter wanted to get out while he still had the means.

Sebastian Dieter and his wife, Catharina, were not alone. Two other families were planning to leave with them — Marcell and Margaretha Schneider and their three young children, and Georg (Jerg) and Elisabetha Gebert and their toddler son — along with the unmarried Christoph (Stophel) Schaber.[10] Sadly, only one of these would set foot in Philadelphia.

This group of fourteen would be following the more than 20,000 German-speaking emigrants who had already braved the Atlantic in search of a better life in America.[11] Most came from the southwest part of present-day Germany, in the region along the middle and upper Rhine River and its tributaries, the Mosel, Main, and Neckar. During the eighteenth century, this area — the Rhineland — was part of the Holy Roman Empire and consisted of a patchwork of more than 350 territories, each with its own government, laws, and religion (usually that of the local ruler), but all owing allegiance to the emperor. The boundaries of the territories constantly shifted with wars, treaties, and royal marriages, until the empire finally dissolved with the Napoleonic Wars.[12]

Schwaigern was a tiny parish situated at the juncture of three of the largest territories in the Rhineland: Baden, Württemberg, and the Palatinate.[13] All three contributed heavily to the German migration, but because so many people fled the Palatinate — a poor Protestant state ravaged by nearly a century of warfare with its powerful Catholic neighbor, France — all German-speaking emigrants came to be called "Palatines," even though many (like the Schwaigerners) came from adjacent territories, as well as from France and Switzerland.

At the root of the exodus were the religious wars that had devastated the Rhineland during the seventeenth century.[14] The Thirty Years' War (1618–48) began as a conflict between Catholics and Protestants in the Holy Roman Empire following the Protestant Reformation in the 1500s. Although it eventually spread all over Europe, most of the fighting occurred in the German states. More than 8 million people died in battle and from war-related famine and disease, making it the most destructive conflict in European history prior to World War I. Southwest Germany lost 40 percent of its population. Nearly a thousand Schwaigerners were killed during the war, and their ruler's palace was destroyed.

After several decades of rebuilding and repopulation (mostly by Swiss immigrants), war broke out again in 1688 when Louis XIV claimed the Palatinate and sent his army back into the Rhineland. During this conflict, the War of the Grand Alliance, French troops raided the Neckar Valley and burned much of it to the ground. Town after town was reduced to smoldering rubble, and the inhabitants were tortured and executed. When the war finally ended in 1697, southwest Germany had been laid to waste, and the recovery process had to begin all over again.

After enemy troops retreated, the local rulers sought to reassert their authority by regulating virtually every area of life, ranging from which trade a young man was allowed to practice, to whether a resident would be permitted to marry someone from outside the community, to how much wood a family could cut from the town forest. They were able to do this with the help of the local clergy, who functioned as both informants and enforcers.

Much was asked of the inhabitants. Men were required to serve in the military and could be loaned out as soldiers to other rulers. All adults had to provide their ruler with a certain amount of free labor each year. The work requirements usually were based on household means: the wealthier the family, the more days of labor they were expected to contribute.[15]

Among the most onerous burdens, however, were the exorbitant fees, penalties, taxes, tithes, and tributes people were required to pay. In some communities, the fiscal demands added up to half of a yearly income.[16] Much of the revenue was used for repairing public buildings and defensive structures after the wars, although these projects usually included a lavish new residence for the local ruler.

Land splintering was a problem in the region too. Inheritance laws required a landholder to divide his estate evenly among all his children, a practice called partible inheritance (*Realteilung*). Yet after several generations of subdividing, each plot was no longer large enough to support a family. The only way to increase one's holdings was to purchase small plots in other parts of town as they became available. Sebastian Dieter's fifteen acres were scattered in fourteen separate locations around the parish.

Combine overcrowding, competition for dwindling resources, and unfair regulation of those resources by the authorities with weather-related crop failures, high prices, underemployment in the trades, and indebtedness, and it is easy to see why so many people wanted to leave the Rhineland.[17] The only question was which direction to go.

Palatines had two choices: they could travel east and settle in Prussia, Austria-Hungary, or Russia (between 85 and 90 percent of all Palatine emigrants moved to Eastern Europe), or they could undertake the much longer, more dangerous, and more costly journey west, to British North America.[18] Despite the greater risk and expense, the Schwaigerners chose to go west — specifically, to William Penn's "island of Pinßel Fania," where most Germans in the New World had settled.

The land that drew these Palatines to America had been given to William Penn in 1681 by King Charles II as repayment of a debt to Penn's father. Penn wanted to create a safe haven for fellow Quakers, who were being harassed and imprisoned in England. But he also was a businessman and wanted to make money from the venture. To do that, he needed settlers to purchase and improve the land.[19]

He began publishing promotional tracts and distributing them in different languages across Europe. The first of more than a dozen was titled *Some Account of the Province of Pennsilvania in America.* The ten-page prospectus was meant to publicize the province and encourage people to "settle a free, just and industrious Colony there." In it Penn promised religious and political freedom to all who would come and participate in his "Holy Experiment." He also offered prospective settlers large tracts of land — larger than what could be had in Eastern Europe — at very low prices and "free from any Indian incumbrance."[20]

The earliest German immigrants to Pennsylvania had arrived in the late 1600s and were members of small religious sects. Most of the Germans who arrived in the eighteenth century, however, came for economic opportunity and political freedom. While open land was scarce in German territories, individual families could purchase hundreds of acres of field, forest, and meadow in Pennsylvania for just a few pounds. At the same time, a labor shortage offered jobs and good wages to both unskilled laborers and tradesmen of all kinds. And while the citizens of the Rhineland were ground down by heavy taxation and forced labor, the residents of Pennsylvania paid very little tax. Initially Penn charged them a quit-rent of one shilling per hundred acres per year, but most settlers didn't bother to pay it (a problem that eventually forced Penn into bankruptcy). Compulsory labor occurred only once or twice a year, when neighbors got together to fix the local roads.

As for the freedoms promised by Penn, the settlers enjoyed a "quiet" government that allowed them to work and pray as they wished, as long as they obeyed the law. "No one is here molested because of misleading principles or doctrine which he may follow," wrote a Swedish traveler in the province in 1748. "And he is so well secured by the laws, both as to person and property, and enjoys such liberties that a citizen here may, in a manner, be said to live in his house like a king. It would be difficult to find anyone who could wish for and obtain greater freedom."[21]

Not surprisingly, among the first residents to leave Schwaigern were the sons of accused-witch Anna Maria Heinrich.[22] Their two sisters had been imprisoned as well; in 1715 the older one was executed by sword and the younger one flogged and run out of town.[23] The following year the two young men fled to Pennsylvania, where the only woman ever tried for witchcraft had been set free. Even after she had confessed in court to riding a broomstick, Governor Penn, the presiding judge, dismissed the case, stating he knew of no law against it.[24]

Between 1715 and 1737, more than 130 Schwaigerners moved to America. Among them were Jerg Gebert's brothers, Michel and Friedrich; Sebastian Dieter's brother Georg, a cousin named Georg, and his aunt and uncle, Margaretha (Dieter) and Peter Lohrman; and Catharina Dieter's brother, Hieronymus Eberle.The Lohrmans and Eberle had set out in the spring of 1737, along with twelve others from the town.[25]

Sebastian Dieter had observed the process his family and friends had to follow in order to gain permission from Lord von Neipperg to leave. The person in charge of that process was the town administrator, Mattheus Böhringer.

On the day that Dieter met with him, Böhringer probably began by asking Dieter to state, for the record, why he wanted to leave. Choosing his words carefully, Dieter told the official that he wanted to move to Pennsylvania to make a better living for his family.[26]

Böhringer may have asked whether Dieter and his friends had been influenced by "newlanders," a term originally used to refer to emigrants who traveled back and forth between America and the Rhineland, transacting business for themselves or on behalf of others. Now the term also was being applied to the unscrupulous recruiting agents hired by Rotterdam shippers to travel the German countryside, enticing people to move to America. The agents received a bounty for each "freight" they secured, while the shippers gained a steady supply of human cargo to fill their vessels on the less profitable westbound leg of their transatlantic trading voyages.[27] They were usually easy to spot, dressed in their wigs and ruffles and jingling coins in their pockets. Horror stories abounded about newlanders who escorted emigrants to Rotterdam, then ran off with the travelers' money. Prospective emigrants were warned not to have any dealings with them, and town leaders chased them off or imprisoned them whenever they were found.[28]

The Inventories and Settlements records in the Schwaigern City Archives tell us that the authorities took the administrative procedure for emigration seriously. So even though Dieter was familiar with the process, Böhringer likely reviewed it with him anyway. First, Dieter was required to take all his dependents with him. That included his thirty-two-year-old wife, Catharina, and their children: Christian (five), Magdalena (three), and Maria Catharina (eighteen months).

Because Dieter and his wife were freemen and not serfs, they did not need to petition for manumission (freedom from bondage) or pay a manumission fee. However, they were required to have an inventory made of all their assets in order to calculate the departure fee: 10 percent of the value of their estate. This fee was to compensate the government for its loss of a taxpayer, laborer, and soldier.

Next, they had to sell their land and pay off all debts, allowing a two-month waiting period to give creditors time to make their claims. If they were to skip town without satisfying this requirement, any property they had left behind would be confiscated and sold off, and their inheritances seized. Further, remaining family members could be held liable for any outstanding debts.

And finally, by relocating to the British colonies, the Dieters would forfeit their citizenship in the parish of Schwaigern. If they changed their minds and decided to come home, they would be charged a steep readmission fee. Unless, of course, they had left illegally. Then they would celebrate their homecoming in jail.

Sebastian Dieter had no intention of stealing away like a thief in the night. And if what he had heard about America was true, he had no plans of returning.

On October 8, 1737, around the time Sebastian began making plans to leave Schwaigern, 109 bedraggled men crowded into the second floor of the courthouse on the corner of Second and High Streets in Philadelphia.[29] The immigrants had just walked from the waterfront, where their ship, the *Charming Nancy*, was docked. Under the command of Captain Charles Stedman, the ship had left Rotterdam in late June with 274 Palatines on board. Among them were Sebastian and Catharina's aunt and uncle, Peter and Margaretha Lohrman, and the Lohrmans' three daughters. Catharina's brother, Hieronymus Eberle, and twelve others from Schwaigern had traveled on the ship as well.[30] After a customs stop in England and nearly twelve weeks on the Atlantic, they had sailed up the Delaware River early that morning. Before the Palatines could be discharged from the ship, however, the men were required by law to pledge their loyalty to the British Crown.

This statute had been enacted by the Provincial Council in 1727, in response to growing concerns about the large influx of German immigrants "who being ignorant of our Language & Laws, & settling in a body together, make, as it were, a distinct people from his Majesties Subjects."[31] The law stated that within forty-eight hours of arrival, all males ages sixteen and older who were well enough to leave the ship were to appear at the courthouse and take an oath of allegiance to the British government and the Province of Pennsylvania, and an oath of abjuration (renunciation) of the pope and of all pretenders to the British throne. At this same time, the captain was to submit to government officials a list of all men, women, and children on board, the occupation of each head of household, and the immigrants' places of origin.

The men, filthy from their time at sea, stood nervously before the most powerful men in the province: the acting governor of Pennsylvania, James Logan, and Philadelphia's mayor, William Allen. Captain Stedman handed the mayor a large sheet of paper on which he had written the names of all the passengers on his ship. He did not list the twenty-five souls — mostly children — who had died en route, nor display much concern with accurate spelling.[32] (He recorded the Lohrman name as both "Lowman" and "Lorman.") He also did not include the occupations or hometowns of the immigrants. None of the captains did. In fact, Stedman was one of the few who bothered to include women and children in his manifest. Many captains turned in nothing at all.

Governor Logan spoke a few words of welcome to the Palatines, then read aloud the two necessary oaths. The oath of allegiance began like this: "We subscribers, natives and late inhabitants of the Palatinate upon the Rhine and places adjacent, having transported ourselves and families into this Province of Pennsylvania, a colony subject to the Crown of Great Britain, in hopes and expectation of finding a retreat and peaceable settlement therein, do solemnly promise and engage, that we will be faithful and bear true allegiance to his present majesty King George the Second, and his successors."[33]

The Palatines were instructed to sign their names to the oaths, each of which was written at the top of a separate sheet of paper. Two members of the Provincial Council, seated at separate desks, oversaw this process. Those Palatines who couldn't write drew an X and had their names written for them. Among these three lists — the captain's manifest and the two lists of signatures — an illiterate immigrant could have had his name spelled three different ways.[34] This was one method by which many German names became anglicized.

After the ceremony, the group made their way back to the *Charming Nancy*. Once the passengers had squared their debts with Captain Stedman, they were free to leave the ship. The Lohrmans had left home with 1,300 florins, more than enough to cover travel expenses.[35] Peter Lohrman would use the balance to buy a farm in Germantown, six miles northwest of Philadelphia, where a number of emigrants from Schwaigern had already settled. By this time next year, he would be in a position to help other newcomers in need. He would ride to Philadelphia each time he received word that a Palatine ship had arrived, and search for travelers from his hometown. He would loan them money to pay off their travel debts, and put them up in his home until they could find work and a place of their own. And he would continue to provide this welcome service every year for as long as he lived.[36]

Back in Schwaigern later that fall, court clerk Wendel Böger was sent to the Dieters' home to make an inventory of their estate. He began by itemizing the family's real estate holdings, by far their most valuable asset. On the basis of the location, size, and use of each parcel, Böger determined that the Dieters' fifteen acres were worth 570 florins.

Next, Böger examined the couple's "movable goods"— their housewares, furniture, clothing, tools, and livestock. He appraised each item on the basis of its condition and age: "1 bodice of blue cloth of average quality," "1 small melting pan of bad quality," "1 old candlestick," "2 very old woven bed linens." Böger missed nothing, not even the two cartloads of manure Sebastian had planned to spread in the fields. Including a small cash gift Catharina had received from her father, and some money owed to the couple by a woman in a nearby village, the Dieter family's total assets were valued at just over 678 florins.

The clerk then added up the family's debts, which totaled 123 florins. Half was owed to merchants and tradesmen in town, including a barber, a tailor, a shoemaker, a blacksmith, a cartwright, and a housepainter. The other half was owed to the government for wood cut from the town forest and to support two charities set up by the authorities to help local citizens in need. A small fee was also owed to the "Laudable Fiscal Authority of his Lordship." After subtracting debts from assets, Böger determined the Dieter family's net worth to be 555 florins. From this, 55 florins would be deducted for the emigration tax, leaving them with 500 florins.

The Dieters' traveling companions endured the same process. Marcell and Margaretha Schneider owned a half-house, a half-barn, and an assortment of land parcels, including fields, vineyards, and vegetable gardens. Like the Dieters, most of their wealth was in real estate. However, their debts totaled a third of their assets, leaving them with 415 florins after the emigration tax was deducted. Jerg and Elisabetha Gebert were of more modest means. They owned several parcels of vineyard but no house or fields. After the departure fee was paid, they would be left with an estate worth 63 florins, half of that given to them in cash by their parents. Schaber had even less. His estate, after the tax, would be worth just 30 florins.

Throughout the winter of 1737–38, Sebastian and Catharina Dieter and the other families made final preparations for the move to America. They obtained passports from the authorities, which vouched for their health and identified their hometown, and certificates attesting that they were not serfs. These documents were necessary to pass the numerous border guards on their way to Rotterdam. They also requested each child's baptism certificate, which provided proof of age, and a "certificate of character" from their pastor.

The Dieters had no trouble selling their land to other members of the community who were eager to consolidate their own splintered holdings. Likewise, they sold or gave away the household items they had decided not to bring with them. After paying off their debts, they were fortunate to have enough cash left over for traveling expenses. Ship's passage alone cost between 5 and 8 British pounds per adult (about 35 to 55 florins).[37] Both the Dieters and Schneiders would be able to pay the full fare up front in Rotterdam. The Geberts and Schaber would have to borrow money or travel on credit.

When it was time to pack up the household, the Dieters placed their pine table, two "arm chairs," canopy bed, and large farm implements into crates and nailed them shut. Hand tools and household items were placed in barrels lined with straw. Additional housewares, clothing, and linens were stored in chests with sturdy locks. (The legs were removed from the chests so they could be stacked during transport.) Their two feather mattresses and duvets were rolled up tightly, tied, and stuffed into linen sacks. Finally, a small chest was set aside for items to be used on board ship: a couple of cooking pots, some wooden bowls, a few utensils, a change of clothes for each person, the family bible and hymn books, medicine, and money. A separate basket would be used to carry food and drink.

In mid-March, after the departure fee had been paid and their estate settled, a summary of their material life was recorded in the town's book of Inventories and Settlements, preceded by the following statement: "Since [the] above mentioned Diether and his wife's appetite have also been whet to visit the Island of Pennsylvania in order to make a better living there, and to this end have given up their citizenship here entirely, his assets and those of his wife were sold off with prior knowledge of the authorities, and they have fully prepared themselves for the trip."[38]

That preparation had taken a good five months, but perhaps it had been a blessing to be so busy. It kept their minds from dwelling on their worst fears: disease, pirates, shipwreck, and drowning. When the couple's imaginations took a dark turn, they comforted themselves in knowing that friends and family were waiting for them on the opposite shore. After all, if God wanted to exact His revenge, He could do so just as easily on land as on water. The journey would be long and tiring and dangerous at times, but the Atlantic was not insurmountable. In fact, very few Palatine ships had wrecked.

The hardest part was leaving loved ones behind, whom they might never see again. Sebastian's sixty-two-year-old widowed father would be left in the care of Sebastian's younger brother, Matthäus. Catharina would bid farewell to her sixty-three-year-old father, also widowed, as well as five siblings.

As the days grew milder, the Dieters and their friends made final arrangements with a boatman in Heilbronn for passage down the Neckar and Rhine Rivers to the port of Rotterdam. In Rotterdam there would be a handful of Palatine ships headed to Philadelphia. Two of the shippers in particular had experience transporting Germans to America: the brothers John and Charles Stedman — who had a reputation for both competence and compassion — and the Hope family, led by Archibald and sons Isaac and Zachary. The best "season of going," wrote William Penn, was that which delivered you to the New World in early fall. It was best to arrive before winter, Penn advised, for during the coldest months the prevailing northwest winds that blow off the mid-Atlantic coast made it difficult for ships to enter Delaware Bay.[39] For the Schwaigern families, that meant leaving in early spring, soon after the ice had gone from the Rhine.

CHAPTER TWO

Down to the Sea

T he first leg of the Palatines' journey was the arduous trip by barge down the Rhine River to the port of Rotterdam. There British shipping firms were readying vessels for their annual trading voyages to the colonies. Most of the merchant fleet left the Dutch port in June and July, so to ensure a berth on one of the America-bound ships; the emigrants set out soon after the Rhine and its tributaries had thawed and the dangerous rapids from snowmelt had subsided.[1]

The Dieters, Schneiders, Geberts, and Schaber left Schwaigern in mid-April of 1738 to begin the six- to seven-week river passage.[2] Walking alongside two horse-drawn wagons heavy with crates, chests, and children, the group passed by the "witch's tower" on their way out the main gate. They crossed over the moat and the creek that powered the town's gristmill, before turning left onto the dirt highway that led to the city of Heilbronn, eight miles away.

Heilbronn is located on the banks of the Neckar River. By prior arrangement, a boatman would be waiting for the group to arrive. He had been hired to transport them down the Neckar to the Rhine, where they would have to switch boats twice before reaching the Netherlands. Stophel Schaber was single, poor, and traveling

The journey down the Rhine River to the North Sea.
Map: Patti Isaacs, 45th Parallel Maps and Infographics

light. Everything he owned — a hymn book, some clothes, and a few hand tools — fit in a single satchel. Like other men in his situation, he could have walked to Rotterdam to save on the boat fare. But for the Dieters, Schneiders, and Geberts, who had small children and bulky household goods, boat travel was the easiest and cheapest way to get to the seacoast.[3]

Several hours after leaving Schwaigern, the group arrived at Heilbronn, a thriving commercial center of 8,000 people. This was likely
the farthest some of the group had ever been from home. The city
proper was located on the east bank of the river. From across the
water, it was an impressive sight, with its twenty-five-foot-tall defensive wall crowned with ten evenly spaced towers, and the soaring
gothic steeple of St. Kilian's Church. On the west bank of the river
stood a wooden crane operated by two large, human-powered tread-
wheels. The crane was used to load stone blocks, slings of gravel, and
barrels of wine onto waiting barges. This unmistakable local land-
mark would have made a good meeting place for the luggage-laden
emigrants and their skipper.

The group had likely booked passage on a market boat, which
would take them as far as the city of Mainz, on the Rhine, a trip of
about two weeks. The boat would stop at several towns and cities
along the way, to sell goods and pick up and drop off passengers. At
Mainz the emigrants would switch to a boat operated by a member
of the Cologne boatmen's guild, which controlled the stretch of river
between Mainz and Cologne. At Cologne the travelers would have
to switch boats again, as traffic between Cologne and the Netherlands was controlled by the Dutch.[4]

With the help of the crewmen, the emigrants loaded their crates
and chests into the hold of the boat. At this point, they might have
wished they had gotten rid of their old household goods and carried cash to Rotterdam instead. They then could have purchased
new wares in the Netherlands, or in England, where all ships bound
for the British colonies had to stop for a customs inspection. They
could even have bought a few extra items to sell for profit in America, where manufactured goods were scarce and very expensive. A
lot of Palatines recouped part of their travel expenses this way. Emigrants had to be careful, though, as this was a violation of British
trade laws. Only British citizens were allowed to conduct transatlantic trade with the colonies. Customs agents at the English and
American ports could seize any property they deemed was for resale and not personal use.[5]

After the cargo was loaded, the emigrants walked up the wooden gangplank and stepped aboard. The craft that plied these inland waterways were sailing barges: long, narrow, flat-bottomed boats, with one or two masts for sailing and towlines for hauling upstream and when conditions downstream required it. Because the Rhine and its tributaries were so shallow — less than five feet deep in spots, especially in summer — only boats with a shallow draft could be used.

Most of the sailing barges were built to carry both cargo and passengers. On a market boat, the passengers sat on benches, under a tarp when it rained, and shared the top deck with cages of squawking poultry, baskets of eggs, tubs of butter and cheese, and piles of spring produce: white asparagus, mushrooms, spinach, and rhubarb. The fourteen Schwaigerners were probably joined on board by passengers from nearby towns. Some would have been traveling just a stop or two downriver. Others, like the Dieters and their friends, would be on their way to America.

When it was time to leave, the helmsman pushed off the riverbank with a long wooden pole and, with the help of several rowers, guided the boat into the channel. In no time, the vessel was drifting silently downstream.

Over the next several days, the barge made its way through the winding Neckar Valley. Around each bend in the river — every couple of miles or so — another ancient walled town or half-timbered village came into view. They traveled during daylight hours, stopping at towns to sell farm products and to load and unload passengers. Because the boat could not navigate safely after dark, and there was nowhere to lie down on the crowded vessel, the skipper would pull up to the bank or to an island at nightfall, so the passengers could disembark to cook meals over a campfire and sleep on the ground.

Traveling with children was made easier by the captivating sights and sounds on the river. The Neckar was crowded with heavily loaded barges moving in both directions. Vessels headed upstream were hauled by teams of horses or mules, their numbers ranging from two to twenty animals, depending on the weight of the boat and the swiftness of the current. The drivers banged pots and shouted profanity at the animals, to keep them plodding along the muddy towpath. The helmsmen of the towed boats had to keep a close eye on the current: a slight shift could pull the boat toward the opposite shore, dragging the draft team and driver with it.

The barges shared the river with long, narrow timber rafts built of oak, fir, pine, and spruce felled in the Black Forest, where the Neckar begins. The logs were lashed together and sent down to the Rhine, to join with other rafts to form enormous wooden platforms. These were destined for the sparsely forested Netherlands, to be broken up and sold for fuel and for building material.[6] Some emigrants — young, poor, single men — paid their way to Rotterdam by working on board timber rafts.

The adults were entertained by the stories told by the boatmen, most of whom had spent their entire lives on the water. They had transported many hundreds of emigrants over the years, and recounted tales of some of the more memorable characters they had met: a brother helping his sister escape her abusive husband, a family that became destitute after bailing their son out of jail, a minister and his family who left home in disgrace following his affair with a housemaid, and numerous young couples defying their parents by running off to elope.[7] The boatmen had often wondered what became of all these people: if they managed to find peace and happiness in the New Land or if their troubles, like shadows, followed them across the sea.

The Schwaigerners had their own tales of loss and disappointment. Fifty-year-old Marcell Schneider had buried his first wife and their two children, then lost two more children with his second and current wife. Their most recent child, a son named Michael, had died at birth, a year ago. Schneider may have decided that Schwaigern was not a lucky place to raise a family. Stophel Schaber, meanwhile, still single at the age of thirty-two, hoped he would have better luck — both financially and romantically — in Pennsylvania.

By late April, the Schwaigerners had passed Neckargemünd and the ancient scholastic center of Heidelberg and were approaching the city of Mannheim, at the confluence with the Rhine. It was here

that emigrants from the Neckar Valley joined with those from lands
along the Upper Rhine: not just fellow Germans, but French, many
Swiss, and a few resolute Italians too. Some had been on the river
for a month already; from Mannheim the emigrants had another
month of travel to reach the Dutch border. Those who fared best
had carried ample supplies of food and clean water and had the cash
to cover unexpected expenses. Even so, the journey down to the sea
could seem endless, for reasons that had little to do with distance.

A man named Conrath Gehr also has been identified as a passenger on the *Princess Augusta*. Not much is known about him, other
than that he was thirty-five years old, unmarried in the spring of
1738, and a carpenter by training. He had been to America once already, having signed a land warrant in 1734 indicating his intention
to purchase thirty-four acres of land in Salford, Pennsylvania, about
thirty miles northwest of Philadelphia.

Gehr's connection with the *Princess Augusta* begins in the market
town of Neckargemünd, fifty miles downstream from Heilbronn.
In early 1738, Gehr was hired by merchant Georg Friedrich Hölzer
to transport some rifles and other goods to Hölzer's trading partner in Philadelphia, a wealthy dry goods merchant named Johann
Caspar Wistar.[8] Each fall, Wistar wrote to Hölzer with a list of
goods he wanted Hölzer to send. Hölzer purchased the wares from
local craftsmen and at trade fairs, then shipped them via couriers to
Wistar the following spring. Gehr was one of several men Hölzer
hired to transport the goods.

Such couriers were crucial to Hölzer and Wistar's commercial
enterprise. The two merchants had begun conducting overseas
transactions on behalf of German settlers in Pennsylvania around
1730. Using the same ships that brought the Palatines to America,
they delivered letters and documents, transferred money, and re-
trieved inheritances. A large part of their business involved providing German transplants with the goods they longed for from home.

Among the items that Wistar ordered from Hölzer were brass

and iron pots and pans, scythes, and strawcutters. The list included scissors, sewing notions, fabric, stockings, and hairpins. Hölzer sent barrels of wine, wine glasses, whetstones, and side holsters, as well as saffron, borax, and ink powder. German bibles, hymnals, and spelling books also were in demand.[9] One shipment alone contained 10,000 large screws, 500 knives, 7½ dozen ivory combs, 6 dozen silk handkerchiefs, 13 dozen mirrors, 3 dozen eyeglasses, 15 dozen tobacco pipes, and 2 copper tea kettles, along with several long-barreled rifles.[10] Wistar was proud of his rifles, which he had custom-made for the American market. He knew that settlers on the Pennsylvania frontier preferred hunting rifles with extra-long barrels because of their accuracy and range. These well-crafted firearms were the precursor to the famed Lancaster and Kentucky long rifles.

In early fall of 1737, Wistar sent two lengthy letters to Hölzer, in which he ordered 20 long rifles with barrels 39 to 40 inches in length, 4 double-barreled rifles, and 1 "air rifle" that could shoot both pellets and bullets.[11] He gave detailed instructions on how the guns should be made (down to the trigger mechanism and the bore size and rifling of the barrel) and the particular gunsmith he wanted to make them.[12]

Hölzer did as his trading partner asked and filled the order, some of which was to be sent with Conrath Gehr. Hölzer packed several chests for Gehr. These contained some of the rifles Wistar had ordered (each gun placed in its own white flannel pouch), along with a few other items on his wish list: floral silk handkerchiefs, black silk handkerchiefs, small hand mirrors, and eyeglasses. Hölzer then added a few items of his own choosing. To judge by shipments from other years, these probably included pieces of red coral (popular in jewelry at the time), some unpolished brass sheets for Wistar's button-making business, and some copies of the Frankfurt newspaper for his friend. The foregoing goods were valued at almost 500 florins in all. In addition, one of the chests included some merchandise for Wistar's brother-in-law, Georg Hüttner.[13] All of this would end up in the hold of the *Princess Augusta*.

Wistar had become a naturalized British citizen in 1724 and could therefore legally participate in overseas trade. Even so, it was more expensive to import goods from Continental Europe than from England, as trade laws required that duties be paid on imported goods that were not British made. By identifying German emigrants and newlanders who were willing to stash small amounts of merchandise in their chests and pass them off as household goods — something these travelers were already doing on their own — Wistar and Hölzer devised a way to avoid the tax. Wistar would pay the couriers for their trouble when they arrived in Philadelphia.

The practice worked well while the number of Germans arriving in the colonies was relatively small. In those times, inspectors looked the other way or were easily bribed. But as the number of immigrants increased — nearly tripling at the port of Philadelphia between 1735 and 1736 — officials began to crack down.[14] In fact, Wistar nearly lost a bundle of wall mirrors in 1736, when the *Princess Augusta* was impounded by Philadelphia customs agents who accused the passengers of smuggling. One of Wistar's agents rowed out to the vessel at night and removed the mirrors before they could be seized.

Alarmed by the close call, Wistar instructed Hölzer to label the barrels for the following year's shipment so that when they arrived in Rotterdam, Captain John Stedman, "who is my good friend," could receive them and pay the appropriate duties.[15] For the 1738 shipment, however, the two merchants seemed to have returned to their old business practices. Wistar asked Hölzer to tell the gunsmith not to engrave the rifles with Wistar's initials — CW — so that if customs agents discovered them, they wouldn't know the guns were for him. He also reminded Hölzer to divide up the shipment among different people.[16]

Hölzer and Wistar typically relied on a small group of trusted newlanders. This was the first year they had used Gehr, and they probably knew as little about him as we do.[17] Shortly after April 20, Gehr and the chests were drifting down the Neckar toward the Rhine, en route to Pennsylvania.[18]

Both Hölzer and Wistar knew the risks of illicit transatlantic trade, which Wistar had spelled out in a letter early in their partnership: the "dangers are first in England, in that one is not supposed to bring such goods from other places, and secondly the great danger of the big sea."[19] The men would soon learn there was yet a third danger: that the people you hired to help you cheat the king of England might steal from you as well.

The Palatines' journey from the Rhineland to America typically lasted about six months from door to door, including the three-month voyage across the North Atlantic. After arriving in the colonies, however, many German emigrants complained more about the tiresome trip to Rotterdam than the frightful ocean crossing.

The Rhine River has its headwaters in the Swiss Alps, becoming navigable at the city of Basel on the German/Swiss border. From Basel the river flows 530 miles in a north-northwest direction before fanning out near Rotterdam and emptying into the North Sea. According to historian Charles Haller, it would take a free-floating barge about eight days to drift from Basel to Rotterdam (about five days from Mannheim to the Dutch port) on the modern Rhine.[20] In the eighteenth century, however, that same passage could have taken up to two months, as a result of numerous obstacles both natural and manmade.

The geography of the Rhine varies dramatically along its course. The Upper Rhine, from Basel to Bingen, is wide, meandering, and slow moving as it crosses a broad alluvial plain. Conditions change drastically along the Middle Rhine, from Bingen to Bonn. Here the current is fast as the river enters a narrow, twisting gorge. This is the most scenic part of the passage, with more than forty medieval castles and fortresses perched atop steep hills carved by terraced vineyards. Leaving the gorge at Bonn, the river once again enters a broad, marshy plain. Like the Upper Rhine, the Lower Rhine is wide and meandering, with a sluggish current. Just past the Dutch border, it divides into several channels, forming a delta before draining into the sea.

Before nineteenth-century engineering projects deepened, widened, and straightened the Rhine (cutting fifty miles off its length),
navigational hazards slowed boat traffic and occasionally even
brought it to a halt. The river was heavily braided in spots, with
thousands of small islands, shifting sandbars, and gravel beds clogging the channel. These obstacles became even more pronounced
during drought, when passengers and cargo would sometimes have
to get off and go around on land. At other times, heavy flooding
along the Upper and Lower Rhine could obscure the channel, stopping traffic until the water receded and the riverbanks reappeared.
During severe floods, the channel could change course permanently,
and a village would find itself on the opposite side of the river after
the water subsided.

The most dangerous part of the river passage was along the Middle Rhine, with its narrow channel, sharp turns, treacherous rapids,
and hidden reefs. At Mainz, emigrant families would switch to a
type of barge better able to navigate this part of the river, steered
by a skilled boatman with knowledge of local conditions. Then, at
Cologne, where the Rhine becomes wide and sluggish, the families
would switch boats again, to a two-masted barge 65 to 100 feet long
called a *samoreus*.

The guilds controlled shipping on their respective stretches of
the river by invoking the "right of compulsory transfer." That meant
all passengers and cargo had to be transferred to locally run boats.
Such monopolies were an economic windfall for the guilds and for
the local businesses that sold food, drink, and lodging to the detained passengers. These two transfers (and there may have been
others along the way) delayed the Palatines' journey, diminished
their supplies, and added to the expense of the trip.

Traffic congestion could further slow downstream progress.
Since Roman times, the Rhine has been a main trade and transport
artery through the heart of Europe. The emigrants shared the river
with barges loaded with Rhenish, French, and Italian wine; with
produce, grain, and salt; with coal, gravel, and blocks of sandstone
and basalt; and with cloth, iron goods, and weapons. Where the

channel was narrow, the barges traveled in single file, unable to pass slower boats or any boats moving in the opposite direction.

Then there were the timber rafts, which grew spectacularly in size as the river widened along its lower reaches. The largest rafts were more than 300 yards long and 50 yards wide and required upwards of 500 men to handle. With livestock aboard and small huts to house the crew, they looked like floating villages. The bargemen knew to stay clear of these wooden behemoths, as no boat would survive such a collision.[21]

The main causes of delay along the Rhine, however, were the dozens of toll stations set up by the rulers of the many territories through which the river flowed. Tolls had been an important source of income since the Early Middle Ages. By the mid-1700s — the height of the Palatine migration — there were up to forty-one toll stations between Basel and Rotterdam, with a heavy concentration along the Middle Rhine.[22] For the Schwaigerners, the first toll station appeared at Mannheim; they would pass through nearly two dozen more before reaching the Dutch border.[23]

The castles that line the banks of the modern-day Rhine mark the sites of former toll stations. The Pfalzgrafenstein (Pfalz) castle was probably the most memorable station the Schwaigern families passed on their way to Holland. Built in 1327 on an island in the Middle Rhine, the "bow" of the ship-shaped structure points upstream, to part ice floes and floodwaters. The castle's central tower was hung with a bell, to signal boatmen to stop and pay the fee, and a chain was hung across the water to prevent boats from passing. Merchant boats that tried to slip by without paying the toll would be seized. The crew would be thrown into the castle's dungeon, which consisted of a floating raft in the bottom of a well.

At each toll station, the boats were unloaded at the collector's leisure, and the cargo and passengers' luggage were inspected. Emigrants were required to present their travel papers and pay a fee, which the travelers often found to be arbitrary and excessive — more like a ransom than a toll.

Before 1789, there was no real regulation of the number and location of tolls or the amount that could be charged.[24] Toll stations would pop up unannounced and tolls increase without notice. Rates were not published, so travelers couldn't plan ahead. The term *robber baron* (*Raubritter*) originated in the thirteenth century to refer to toll operators—usually low-ranking nobility—who operated toll stations without permission or charged more than they were authorized to charge. To ease their passage at the toll station, some emigrants used agents to negotiate on their behalf; sometimes that role was played by the boatman or the tolls included in the price of the fare. Inclusive pricing (and bribery of toll collectors) made the whole process go much more smoothly.

Were it not for the toll stations, the Rhine journey could have been completed in a fraction of the time.[25] Tolls began to disappear during the Napoleonic era but were not abolished altogether until 1868, when navigation from Basel to the North Sea was finally declared free.

The Rhine journey could exact a physical toll as well. The longer the river passage, the more likely an emigrant was to get sick. The high water table and stagnant pools along the Upper Rhine caused outbreaks of dysentery, typhoid, cholera, and malaria; poor sanitation and close quarters spread the diseases among the boat's passengers, who then carried the pestilence downstream and infected others. When an outbreak occurred on a barge train, the sick were placed in a boat of their own. Death was not uncommon even along this first stage of the journey.[26] It would have been surprising if no one in the Schwaigern group fell ill during the nearly two months they spent drifting down the Rhine.

In late May, Conrath Gehr and the Schwaigern families arrived at Fort Schenkenschanz, an immense stone fortress built where the Rhine splits into the Nederrijn and Waal Rivers, on the Dutch border. The fort was the first customs station on Dutch soil.[27] There were only three more toll stations—about another week of travel—until they reached the city of Rotterdam. They could not simply sail on, however. Soldiers guarding the crossing hailed them to stop. A resolution passed by Dutch authorities in 1735 required German emigrants bound for America to present a valid passport before they could cross into Holland. They also had to show evidence of an existing contract with one of the shippers stationed there, or prove they had sufficient funds to pay for their ocean passage. Further, all boats to Rotterdam were assigned a military escort, to ensure that the emigrants would be shipped out of the country and not left behind. These regulations, strictly enforced, were to prevent indigent, sick, and orphaned travelers from entering the country and becoming a financial burden on its citizens.[28]

As the families presented their papers, they would have noticed many other boats at the checkpoint. The year 1738 was turning out to be an extraordinary year for emigration. Not only had Palatines begun showing up in Dutch territory earlier than usual — in April, before the ships were ready for boarding, and before some of the fleet had even returned from the previous year's trading run — they were arriving in greater numbers than anyone had anticipated.[29]

By early May, eyewitnesses reported heavy passenger traffic on the Rhine. A boatman from Heidelberg claimed to have seen nearly 3,000 emigrants — adults and children — headed for Rotterdam and Amsterdam. A resident of Geroltzheim (a town halfway between Mannheim and Worms) wrote to friends in Amsterdam about the "sad state of affairs" he had witnessed along that stretch of the river: thirty-two boats filled with travelers in misery.[30] The Schwaigern families and Conrath Gehr were almost certainly among that throng.

Historians cite increased recruiting activity in the Rhineland and in Switzerland the previous fall as the main reason for the heavy migration in 1738. Agents lured prospective emigrants with tales of how the English entertained the passengers during the voyage and granted them large amounts of land and freedom from taxes for twenty years.[31] Poor vintages in recent years, talk of changes to conscription laws, and rumors of impending war between England and Spain also may have entered into residents' decisions to leave.

On the one hand, the hordes of people at the border were a windfall for the shipping companies, who sent representatives to meet the travelers and steer those who had not yet signed contracts onto their ships.[32] On the other hand, the shippers were unprepared for the sheer volume of people seeking passage to America. There weren't enough vessels to meet the demand, and the shippers had to scramble to charter more from England.[33] They also had to find someplace for the travelers to wait, as Dutch officials would not allow them to roam the city. This was devastating news for the emigrants: after weeks of camping along the banks of the Rhine, many were sick and short on food and money. How long would it take before the ships were ready, they wondered, and where would they go in the meantime?

For many of the Palatines who set out for America that spring, the timing of their arrival in Rotterdam would determine whether they lived or died at sea.

CHAPTER THREE

Port of Departure

When the Schwaigerners reached Fort Schenkenschanz at the end of May, they'd been in transit for at least six weeks, with more than eighty miles of winding river travel to go. Yet it was clear they were nearing the sea. The Rhine was at its widest here — nearly a half mile between banks — and noticeably affected by the tides. The craft on the river were larger too, built to handle coastal wind and chop. Every spring, the Rhine and Waal Rivers spilled their banks, flooding the land surrounding the fort. With the border checkpoint now an island, the Palatines must have felt the sea had traveled inland to greet them.[1]

At Fort Schenkenschanz the Rhine begins to branch off into the large and small distributaries that make up the Rhine delta.[2] The emigrants would continue west on either the Waal or Nederrijn Rivers, which change names and branch off further before reuniting at Rotterdam as the Maas. Most Palatines left from Rotterdam because it was easy to get to from the Rhineland and there were a number of British merchants in that city who had business contacts in Pennsylvania. By 1738, sixty Palatine vessels had already sailed from there, almost all landing in Philadelphia.[3]

The shipping firms that transported the Palatines to America were operated primarily by British merchants residing in Rotterdam and engaged in the Anglo-Dutch trade. The short and easy voyage between London and Rotterdam had fostered trade between the two maritime nations as far back as the 1500s. By the early 1700s there were so many British expatriates living in Rotterdam that the city was nicknamed "Little London."

Among their diverse business ventures was the colonial staple trade, which, due to the Navigation Acts, could only be conducted on British-owned and -manned ships. Each year these firms sent merchant vessels on trading voyages to America. They carried manufactured goods and luxury items from Britain and Continental Europe — wool, linen, silk, and cotton cloth; iron, copper, brass, lead, and pewter wares; cutlery, leather goods, and books — as well as wine, medicines, and "groceries" (coffee, tea, spices, dried fruit, and chocolate). The ships returned to England with staples such as rice, flour, sugar, tobacco, and indigo. They also brought timber (ship's masts, planks, shingles, and barrel staves), tropical hardwoods, naval stores (pitch, tar, and turpentine), and animal skins. Some of these goods were then re-exported to the Continent.[4] Each trading voyage took approximately a year to complete, with the timing of the ship's departure from Rotterdam — in June and July — dictated by the growing seasons in North America.

Unlike the commodities brought back to Europe, which filled the ship but were of low value relative to their bulk, the manufactured goods delivered to the colonies took up relatively little space on board. So why not fill the unused space with paying passengers — *human freight?* That is how the transport of German-speaking emigrants aboard British merchant ships from Holland began: as a way for ship owners and shipping firms to make more money on the westward leg of their transatlantic trading voyages.[5]

In the early years of the Palatine trade, travelers were required to pay most or all of the fare up front, but shippers soon realized they could attract more passengers by extending credit. One way an emigrant could finance his passage was through indentured servitude. In exchange for passage, the emigrant signed a contract, or indenture, before the ship departed Rotterdam, agreeing to work for a master for a set number of years (usually four to seven). Upon the ship's arrival, the captain sold the indenture to the highest bidder. This arrangement could be risky for both emigrant and shipper, however: the emigrant had no say in who his master would be, and families could be split up. Likewise, if the emigrant died at sea or was very ill upon arrival, the shipper lost his investment.

Beginning in the 1720s, a new way developed to finance the voyage: redemptioner servitude. A variation of the indenture system, the emigrant signed a contract promising to pay the fare within a certain period of time after arrival, usually several weeks to a month after landing. This system proved more satisfactory to both parties. The emigrant had flexibility in how he repaid the fare debt. He could sell his labor to a master or employer of his own choosing, or he could arrange to have family or friends "redeem" him at the port of arrival. Sebastian Dieter's uncle, Peter Lohrman, provided this service to Schwaigern emigrants, riding from his farm in Germantown to the docks in Philadelphia to pay off their travel debts and release them from the ship. Some travelers paid their debts with the sale of smuggled goods, while others were allowed to simply post bond, leaving their luggage on board as security. The redemptioner system was less risky for shippers in that if the emigrant arrived ill, the amount of debt he owed remained the same. And if the emigrant died at sea, family members usually were contractually bound to cover his fare.[6]

In sum, the transport of Palatines was a mutually beneficial business arrangement in which shippers maximized the profit on their cargo space while emigrants received a way to get to America even when they couldn't pay the fare up front. What began as an afterthought evolved, by the middle of the eighteenth century, into a successful commercial enterprise that served as the model for the transport of millions of Europeans to America in the centuries that followed.[7]

Two of the most successful shippers in the Palatine trade were the
Stedmans and the Hopes, both merchant families of Scottish de-
scent. The three Stedman brothers — John, Charles, and Alexander
— began transporting Palatines from Rotterdam to Philadelphia
in 1731. John, stationed in the Dutch port, commanded five Palatine
voyages between 1731 and 1737.[8] By 1738, he was considered a vet-
eran of the trade, as only he and one other captain had made more
than two Palatine runs.[9] He was well regarded by the Germans,
who praised him for keeping to his contract and for the humanity he showed his passengers, particularly during rough crossings.
Charles, also a mariner, and Alexander, a lawyer, lived in Philadelphia. Charles commanded his first Palatine voyage in 1737: he carried the Lohrman family and a large group of Amish to Philadelphia aboard the *Charming Nancy*.

The Stedmans owned shares in several ships in addition to the
ones they commanded.[10] They also operated a merchandise store on
Water Street in Philadelphia, where, according to an ad in a local
newspaper, they sold dozens of types of "fine and coarse" fabric, furniture, housewares, spices, "sundry sorts of Druggs," sewing notions,
and "a great many other Goods too tedious to be here mentioned."[11]
In the spring of 1738, both John and Charles were preparing to make
runs from Rotterdam to Philadelphia (aboard the *St. Andrew* and
the *Charming Nancy*, respectively), as well as outfitting two other
ships they partially owned.[12]

Archibald Hope, Sr., was the patriarch of a family of merchant
bankers with offices in both Rotterdam and Amsterdam. Six of his
eight sons ran the business with him. Archibald, Jr., and Thomas
were Amsterdam bankers. After the younger Archibald's death in
1733, Thomas was joined by brother Adrian. These two became ac-
tive in the slave trade. Henry was a merchant in Boston, and Isaac
and Zachary were Rotterdam traders. It was the elder Archibald,
along with Isaac and Zachary, who were involved in the transport
of Palatines to America.

The Hope firm sent their first Palatine ship to Philadelphia in 1719 but did not become a regular participant in the trade until the mid-thirties. Even then, shipping Palatines was only a very small part of the Hope firm's business. During the mid-1750s, the peak years of German migration, the shipping of emigrants made up less than 2.5 percent of the firm's annual revenue.[13] They were, however, responsible for developing the redemptioner system in the 1720s and provided financing to other merchants engaged in the trade.

In the 1730s, the Hope firm was accused of having a monopoly over the trade, even though the Stedmans loaded more than twice as many ships and carried more than three times as many Palatines to America between 1730 and 1763.[14] The firm may have gotten that reputation because emigrants who showed up at the border without any means to pay for the ocean voyage would automatically be sent by the Dutch authorities to the Hopes, who would ship the travelers as redemptioners or indentured servants. In 1735, for example, a group of Swiss emigrants hoping to settle in South Carolina arrived destitute at the Dutch border. The Hope firm agreed to transport them to Pennsylvania as indentured servants after having the travelers sign a contract stipulating that the fares of those who died at sea would be covered by the surviving passengers.[15]

According to the extensive research of historian Marianne Wokeck, there were dozens of other shippers involved in the Palatine trade, but most took part in just one voyage. The Hopes and Stedmans were regular participants and dominated the market during the middle decades of the century. Wokeck estimates that together these two firms transported more than 40 percent of all Palatines to North America before such immigration came to a halt at the start of the Revolution.[16]

In 1738, the two firms found themselves in a difficult situation. Swarms of emigrants had appeared at the Dutch border earlier and in larger numbers than expected. While the Rotterdam shippers waited anxiously for the arrival of additional ships from London, agents for the Stedmans and the Hopes worked the crowd at Fort Schenkenschanz, competing for the signatures of the healthiest and wealthiest among the weary travelers, and finalizing the contracts of those with preliminary agreements.

The Dutch government had recently enacted regulations to prevent indigent foreigners from becoming stranded in its territory. Now shippers had to obtain permission from both the States General and the provincial governments to transport emigrants from the Dutch border to Rotterdam or Amsterdam. They were required to pay for the military escort assigned to each barge. They also had to pay a fee and post bond as a guarantee that the emigrants would be loaded onto ocean vessels and shipped out quickly. The firms would be held liable if they didn't comply.[17]

It's not known when the Schwaigern families and Conrath Gehr first contracted for passage, but by the time they had completed the customs inspection at Fort Schenkenschanz, they were signed on with the Hopes for passage aboard one of the eight vessels the firm would send to America that year. But if the travelers thought they would be taken straight to their ship, they were sorely mistaken. No ship was ready for boarding. A city ordinance, issued just the year before, directed shippers to take emigrants to a holding area in the village of Kralingen, just outside of Rotterdam, to wait for vessels to become available.

Kralingen is located in the middle of a peatland. Beginning in the tenth century, removal of large amounts of turf for use as heating and cooking fuel had caused numerous ponds and lakes to form there and left the land vulnerable to river flooding. In the thirteenth century an earthen dike was built around the area to protect it from the Maas.

The camp was located next to the dike, near the ruins of a fifteenth-century chapel dedicated to St. Ellebregt, patron saint of seafarers. The eighteen-by-seventy-two-foot stone structure had been demolished by Spanish troops in 1572, at the start of the Eighty Years' War, but the rubble continued to be used as a pilgrim-

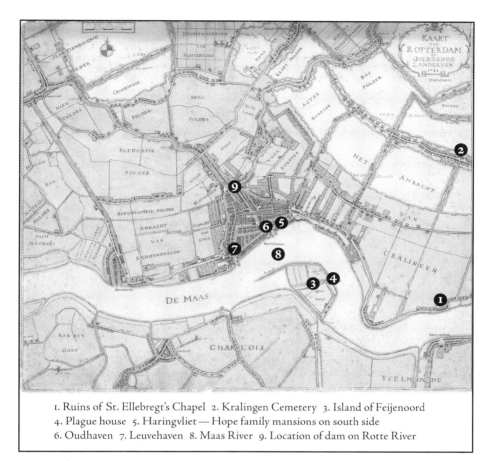

1. Ruins of St. Ellebregt's Chapel 2. Kralingen Cemetery 3. Island of Feijenoord
4. Plague house 5. Haringvliet — Hope family mansions on south side
6. Oudhaven 7. Leuvehaven 8. Maas River 9. Location of dam on Rotte River

Map of eighteenth-century Rotterdam and the surrounding area.
Engraver: Abraham Dubreuil, 1784. Image courtesy of the
City Archives of Rotterdam / Stadsarchief Rotterdam

age site for sailors and fishermen from the Rotterdam area. It was
here — in a soggy field near the crumbled remains of St. Ellebregt's
Chapel — where the transients were forced to wait.[18]

By early May there were already some 200 people in the camp,
including a large number of elderly and children. Another thousand
would arrive within days.[19] No ships would be ready to load for sev-

eral more weeks, which meant that when the Schwaigern families
and Conrath Gehr arrived at the camp in early June, the makeshift
settlement was crowded and dirty. Some travelers slept on boats
tied to the riverbank; others set up tents in the field behind the broken chapel, or lay under the open sky. The campsite was overrun
by dysentery and high fever, the suffering made worse by extreme
fluctuations in the weather. According to a report compiled from numerous eyewitness accounts, eighty infants died there within a short
time, due to the "many cold rains followed by great heat in Holland
at that time."[20] It's uncertain if the illness started in the camp or was
carried in from the Rhine.

The Kralingen cemetery was located about two miles inland
from the camp. Village records indicate that about two dozen Palatine children were buried there between 1735 and 1737, some three
to a coffin and *van de armen*, or "without payment." On June 9, 1737,
the mayor of Rotterdam decreed that the Palatines "shall no longer
bury their dead in the cemetery of Cralinge [Kralingen], where little
space remains." From then on they were to be taken across the Maas
River to the island of Feijenoord for burial on the grounds of the
city's plague house. The caretaker was to "point out the burial places
and keep note of the corpses that are buried."[21] No records of such
burials can be found.

The Schwaigerners and the courier Gehr were released from
confinement no later than mid-June and assigned to the *Princess
Augusta*. The vessel had left London in late May and, after crossing the North Sea, arrived on May 30 at Hellevoetsluis, a fortified
naval port at the entrance of the Rhine delta.[22] From there, it took
several more days to reach Rotterdam, as ocean vessels had to follow
a circuitous route to avoid the sandbars clogging the delta estuaries. Once anchored at the city, the Hope firm had to reconfigure
the cargo ship to accommodate passengers, then load food, casks of
water, copper kettles, and fuel for cooking. All of this involved hiring carpenters and purchasing provisions from local merchants — a
process that normally took up to ten weeks to complete.[23] That June
it was done in about two to three weeks.[24]

We'll never know just how many Palatines passed through Kralingen that spring, how long they were forced to stay in the camp, and how many died there. It's entirely possible that some of the Schwaigern children were among the dozens of dead. Jerg and Elisabetha Gebert's son, Daniel, was sixteen months old. The oldest of the seven children in the group was eleven. What we do know is that the timing of our travelers' arrival in Rotterdam forced them to wait in a disease-ridden holding camp, then placed them on board a ship that had been hastily prepared to carry them. Although they couldn't have realized it at the time, the odds were beginning to stack up against them.

Rotterdam began in the 1260s as a tiny settlement of herring fishermen located where the Rotte River drains into the Maas (at that time called the Merwe). To control flooding and reclaim land from the surrounding peat bogs, the inhabitants built a low earthen dike along the north bank of the Maas and a dam across the Rotte. By the eighteenth century, nearly 50,000 people lived in the city, among them a large number of British merchants. Rotterdam's *havens* (inner harbors) could accommodate vessels of 200 to 300 tons, allowing the entrance of more than a thousand ocean-going vessels each year.

From Kralingen our group was taken by barge to the city. They passed the island of Feijenoord, where so many of their fellow Palatines — and perhaps family members — had been buried. They may have been dropped off at one of three deep inner harbors: the Oudehaven, the Leuvehaven, or the Haringvliet, the latter named for the place where the herring fishermen once delivered their catch. The havens of eighteenth-century Rotterdam were lined with elm trees and stately five- and six-storey townhouses. Many of these brick and stone residences were occupied by merchants of trade, who kept a warehouse or office on the first floor of the structure and lived in the elegantly appointed rooms above. To keep an eye on their ships, the owners could simply glance out their front windows. The Hopes owned several row-house mansions on the south side of

View of the city of Rotterdam from the Maas River, 1748.
Engraver: J. June. Image courtesy of the City Archives
of Rotterdam / Stadsarchief Rotterdam

the Haringvliet, a street that came to be referred to as the *Rijkelui Haringvliet,* or "Rich People's Haringvliet."[25]

Most likely the *Princess Augusta* and other Palatine ships had been brought into Oudehaven (Old Harbor) and tied to the quay. That would have been easier than transferring passengers and their bulky chests from a longboat to a ship anchored in the Maas River. Once loaded, though, the ship would have moved to the river until it was time to leave. This is where the ship lay in June 1736, according to a minister who delivered a farewell sermon aboard the vessel, just before it set out on its first Palatine voyage.[26]

From the river, the city of Rotterdam would have been an astonishing sight, its skyline a forest of chimneys, ship's masts, and church steeples. What the emigrants also may have found surprising was the size of their ship. It appeared to be only a few feet longer than the largest samoreus on the Lower Rhine, yet it was expected to carry well over 300 people across the vast Atlantic.

The *Princess Augusta* was named for the teenage daughter of the Duke of Saxe-Gotha-Altenburg. In 1736, she had married Frederick, Prince of Wales, the son of King George II (George himself was of German stock). The arranged marriage was reported to be a happy one, even though the bride spoke no English and the wedding took place just days after the couple met. By 1738, Augusta had given birth to the couple's first son, George III, who would someday rule the British Empire. Had the Palatines known this they might have taken it as an auspicious sign: traveling on a ship named for the German-born mother of the future king of England, and chartered by a firm called Hope.

PART II

The Voyage

CHAPTER FOUR

The *Princess Augusta*

T he *Princess Augusta* was a 200-ton, full-rigged ship, meaning she had three masts, each rigged with square sails, and
a carrying capacity equal to 200 "tun" casks of wine.[1] It
may have come as a surprise to those about to board her, but at a
little over 100 feet long and 25 feet wide (an estimate based on merchant ships of similar tonnage), she was one of the larger ships in the
Palatine fleet. She was British-built in 1720, almost certainly under
a different name, in all likelihood sold in 1736 and renamed after
the newest member of the royal family. At a time when the average
lifespan of a merchant vessel was between fourteen and seventeen
years, the *Princess Augusta* was well past her prime.[2]

The three principal owners lived in Ramsgate, England, a seafaring community on the southeastern coast, at the entrance to the English Channel. Nathaniel Austen was a sixty-two-year-old banker
and a forebear of novelist Jane Austen. John Redwood, age thirty-
five, had been married to Catherine Austen, the banker's daughter,
until her death in 1737. George Long was the third owner, and also
the ship's captain. There were probably smaller shareholders as well.

Long was just twenty years old in the spring of 1738, married, and
the father of a two-year-old son. Even by eighteenth-century stan-

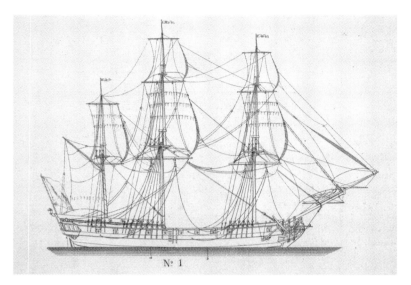

A full-rigged ship similar to the *Princess Augusta*. Frederik Henrik
af Chapman, *Architectura navalis mercatoria, navium varii generis
mercatoriarum . . .*, plate 62, no. 1 (Stockholm: Holmiæ, 1768).
Image courtesy of the Statens Maritima Museer /
Swedish National Maritime Museums

dards, Long was young to be part owner and captain of such a large
vessel. But he had spent much of his childhood on a ship, learning
the ropes from his father, William Long, a master mariner.

Long had commanded the *Princess Augusta* the previous year on
a voyage to Arkhangel'sk (Archangel), a Russian city on the White
Sea.[3] Ramsgate vessels frequently visited ports on the Baltic and
White Seas, bringing back naval stores that England so desperately
needed for its shipbuilding industry. Before setting out, the young
captain wrote his will, leaving to his wife, son, and any children "to
be begotten" all his real estate and personal property, including his
"utinsills of household Sea Adventure."[4] With a crew of just eleven
men, he embarked on a nearly 5,000-mile journey that took him
around the Scandinavian Peninsula and inside the Arctic Circle,
where from mid-May to early August the sun never sets. His safe

return in October helped earn him command of the ship the following year.

The 1738 voyage would be George Long's first Palatine run, but the *Princess Augusta* had been to Pennsylvania at least once before.[5] In 1736, the Hope firm chartered the ship to carry Palatines to Pennsylvania, then sail to South Carolina to pick up staple products to bring back to England. Under the command of Samuel Marchant, the ship delivered 330 Palatines to Philadelphia, but the voyage was not without incident. The ocean crossing itself was timely and uneventful. The trouble began in Delaware Bay, about a hundred miles downriver from Philadelphia. According to an account by Swiss passenger Durs Thommen,

> [A]s we saw land a new pilot came to us and we thought all was well and won. All evening we got good wind from behind so that the ship moved vigorously. The new pilot, however made cast anchor because it was not far (from there) dangerous; in the morning when the anchor was lifted again and we had barely gone 30 feet the boat ran into a rock, and it crashed that one thought it would break in the middle. The anxious crying began, and one could see where there was faith or not. Then the captain had a warning shot fired and had a flag of distress hoisted, but we drove far out to the sea so that we saw no land anymore for days and even thought we would never see it again.[6]

When the *Princess Augusta* finally anchored at Philadelphia on September 16, customs officials impounded the ship and everything in it, on suspicion the passengers were smuggling. Then, days later, the lifeless body of one of the crew was found floating in the Delaware River. According to a local newspaper, he "had been missing almost a Week. It's suppos'd that he fell over board in the Night."[7]

Two months later, after considerable legal wrangling and some ship repairs, the *Princess Augusta* cleared out for South Carolina with 136 barrels of flour, bread, and butter, arriving in Charleston on December 3. She returned to England early the next year with tobacco and barrel staves. Marchant had salvaged the troubled voyage.

He was not available for the *Princess Augusta*'s 1738 Palatine run, however, having died in 1737 in the Bay of Honduras. With Marchant's death, and the success of Long's voyage to Russia, perhaps it was not surprising that Long had been given command of the ship for its next trading run to America.

Long's crew for the 1738 voyage numbered sixteen men, which was about average for a merchant ship that size.[8] The Navigation Acts required that at least three-fourths of a ship's crew be British, and so the *Princess Augusta* would set out that year with twelve British and four foreign sailors.[9] Long's first mate was Andrew Brook, a thirty-six-year-old seasoned sailor from a prominent merchant marine family in nearby Margate. As second in command, Brook would oversee the day-to-day functioning of the ship. Given their age difference, Brook was probably hired as a mentor to Long. The two men were related through marriage (Brook's mother-in-law was a Long), so he could be trusted to support the young captain.

In addition to a captain, first mate, and likely a second mate, the *Princess Augusta* would have carried a quartermaster to steer the ship, a carpenter to keep it seaworthy, a boatswain to summon the crew to work, maintain the rigging and the sails, and keep track of the ship's stores, and a gunner to oversee the ship's eight cannon. There was probably a cook on board as well. The rest of the crew would have been common seamen. George Brooks and Robert Hughson, presumably British, were among the crew. The names of the others are not known.

The *Princess Augusta*'s owners had used London shipbroker Abraham Coleman to hire the ship out to freight.[10] Presumably, Coleman had been contacted by the Hope firm to charter the ship for a transatlantic voyage that would begin in Rotterdam in June 1738 and end in England the following spring. The *Princess Augusta* was one of eight Palatine ships the Hopes were sending to America that year. Some they owned and others they chartered. Given the timing of the ship's arrival in Rotterdam and the speed with which it was readied for passengers, the *Princess Augusta* was probably not part of Hope's initial convoy but hired after it became clear at Fort Schenkenschanz that more vessels were needed.

The Palatine trade formed a triangle of sorts. As in 1736, the Hope firm planned to send the *Princess Augusta* on a three-part voyage. On the first leg of the journey, Captain Long would take several hundred Palatines on board at Rotterdam and transport them to Philadelphia. If all went well, the firm's consignment agent in that city, a Quaker merchant named Benjamin Shoemaker, would handle the details of the passengers' arrival and prepare the ship for the second leg.

From Philadelphia, the ship would carry provisions to the West Indies.[11] These might include wheat and other grains, flour, bread, livestock, meat, and dairy products, and perhaps timber as well.[12] The Pennsylvania Germans were highly productive farmers. Although there was no market in England for their agricultural surplus, there was a need on the slave plantations of the British West Indies, which supplied England with its most valuable import: 50,000 to 100,000 hogsheads of sugar annually.[13]

Palatine ships typically stopped at the main sugar islands of Barbados and Jamaica, but also might call at St. Christopher, Nevis, and Antigua.[14] These islands depended on food supplies from the mainland because almost all of their agricultural land was being used to grow sugar cane. In the tropics, Captain Long would load his ship with sugar and molasses, and might also take on dyewoods, such as logwood, fustic, and braziletto, or hardwoods such as mahogany and lignum vitae (the latter was used in ship fittings because of its extreme hardness and natural oils).[15] The ship would carry the goods back to England for use there or for re-export to the Continent. In all, eight Palatine ships — from a fleet of twenty-two — would travel to the West Indies in 1738.

Six of the others would head to South Carolina after dropping off their passengers in Philadelphia. These would deliver foodstuffs, then pick up rice grown in the inland swamplands or naval stores extracted from the longleaf pines that grew along the sandy coastal plain. They might carry some tropical dye- or hardwoods as well, which had been previously imported to Charleston from the West Indies. Whether Palatine ships eventually headed to the southern colonies or to the Caribbean, however, the timing of their voyages would be critical to their chances of success. Captains needed to leave Europe in early summer, both to avoid peak hurricane season and to arrive in port in time to get a share of the fall harvest, before it was loaded onto other ships. They then needed to return promptly to England, before the market was flooded with goods and prices fell. A delay at any point during the three-part journey could jeopardize the profitability of the entire run.

The *Princess Augusta* departed from London shortly after May 25 and arrived at Rotterdam in the first week of June. There Captain Long met with the Hopes to sign a charterparty, drawn up by the merchant house, granting the use of his vessel. The contract would have spelled out the terms of the first leg of the voyage. Each subsequent leg would have a separate charterparty signed by Long and one of Hope's "correspondents" at the port of departure.

Although the charterparty for the *Princess Augusta* has not been found, those of other Palatine ships chartered by Hope in 1738 still exist in the Rotterdam City Archives, and their language is nearly identical. Long would have agreed to let out the *Princess Augusta* to transport a load of Palatines from Rotterdam to Cowes on the Isle of Wight (for a customs inspection), and then to Philadelphia. Long was to "gett his Ship ready with all Possible Speed" to take on passengers, and make sure the ship was "well manned with proper Officers and Marriners, victualled with Sufficient Provision, and found of all things necessary for such a Ship and voyage."[16]

As "freighter," the Hope firm would determine how many passengers to place on board the ship; they also would supply the provisions to feed them and pay for and build the bunks to house them. None of this was guesswork: from their experience carrying troops, felons, slaves, and English indentured servants, shippers knew how to transport large groups of people across the Atlantic.

The charterparty allowed Long about forty days to discharge the passengers in Philadelphia and begin reloading for the West Indies. The Hope firm would pay him 330 British pounds sterling for the successful completion of this first leg. Some of this sum would be used to pay the crew. Long would be given a separate stipend to have the bunks removed and the vessel returned to its original form as a cargo ship. He was to return to Shoemaker "all the Provisions, Water Casks, Wood Planks, Spars &c. as shall be found on board the said Ship, of what the said Fraighters put on board her." The contract was signed by the Hopes, Long, and a notary public. Pressed for time, the parties got right to work.

As a first step, Long's men broke down the bulkheads that separated the living quarters of the crew from the rest of the 'tween deck (the storage area between the top deck and the hold). This opened up additional space to lodge more passengers, with the crew relocating to a temporary shelter built on the top deck.

Next, carpenters constructed bunks to fill the available space. The wooden platforms were built in rows along both sides of the vessel and stacked two or in some places three levels high (before 1765 there were no regulations regarding the minimum height between bunks).[17] The rows were set perpendicular to a center aisle, so that passengers could get into and out of bed without having to climb over other bunks.

To house the crew, the carpenters built a roundhouse on the top deck, framed in oak to withstand wind and waves. They also constructed two privies, one on each side of the ship, and a brick-lined sandbox for a cooking hearth.

While the ship was being refitted, the firm purchased and loaded enough food and water to last fourteen weeks, which was reckoned more than enough for an average Palatine voyage. The "victuals" provided by Hope included salted beef, bacon, peas, rice, bread (a rock-hard, tasteless, unleavened biscuit), aged cheese, butter, syrup, and flour. Hope also may have provided beans, oatmeal, barley, and salted fish. The meat, peas, beans, and grains would be boiled in a ninety-gallon copper cauldron over a coal fireplace on deck, with the firm providing both cauldron and coal.

Drinking water was the most important provision on board the ship. In order to remain pure on the long journey, it had to be taken from an unpolluted source and stored in clean casks that had been used for nothing but water. When merchants cut corners and used wine or beer barrels instead, the water invariably turned foul, sickening those who drank it.[18] Unfortunately for the passengers on the *Princess Augusta*, some of the water casks had previously held wine. Whether this was a deliberate act or not, no one knows. To be fair, the Hope firm had just a few weeks to prepare for a transatlantic voyage; they probably relied on a supplier — who might not have revealed the history of the barrels. Had there been more time, proper casks might have been found.

With provisions loaded, Captain Long was ready to take on board, "as many Passengers, as the said Fraighters Shall Judge he can Conveniently carry under the Decke, and in her hold so many of goods and Bagage as She above her Materials and Provision safely will Stow and carry."[19] While this clause was part of a typical contract, it leaves no doubt about who was responsible for the crowded conditions on board Palatine ships operated by the Hopes.

Long might not have realized that the contract he signed contained a clause not found in the charterparties of other Palatine shippers: "And lastly in case the said Ship in the said voyage should be cast away in so farr that the said Passengers should loose their passage to Pensilvania the said agreed fraight is to be void."

In other words, if the ship wrecked and failed to land the passengers in Philadelphia, Long would not be paid and, by extension, neither would his crew.

This was a shrewd move on the part of the Hopes, who knew full well that two of their vessels — the *Princess Augusta* and the *Oliver* — were nearing the end of their seafaring lives.

The hundreds of passengers assigned to the *Princess Augusta* — including the Schwaigern families and Conrath Gehr — were finally allowed to board in mid-June. While the stevedores used block and tackle to hoist their crates and larger chests onto the ship, the emigrants climbed the gangway, carrying bundles of bedding and small chests packed with the items they would need during the voyage: clothing, cooking pots and utensils, medicines, bibles and hymn books, and — most critically — extra food and drink to supplement the ship's rations. It was important that these personal supplies not end up buried in the hold, where the travelers would not have access to them during the voyage.

Among the crowd were two women who shared the same first name — believed to be Catharina or some variation of it. We don't know where they were from or if they were traveling together, but these women would outlive most of their fellow passengers and find themselves, a year later, the last of the survivors on Block Island.

Also on the scene were Michael Schneider, his wife Anna, and their two young sons, Georg and Johann.[20] Unrelated to the Schneider family from Schwaigern, these Schneiders may or may not have contracted with the Hope firm. When they tried to board the *Princess Augusta*, they were turned away because they could not pay at least half the fare up front. Worse yet, their luggage had already been loaded onto the ship, and the crew were unwilling or unable to retrieve it. Panic stricken, the family now had to find passage on another ship and pray that their property arrived safely in Philadelphia without them. Only months later would they realize how lucky they had been.[21]

As the crew lashed the cargo in the hold, the emigrants were directed to the hatchway that led to their living quarters. Even with the hatches open and the window boards removed, it was dark and dank inside. With less than five feet of headroom and narrow bunks lining both walls, the space must have seemed more like a catacomb than a passenger compartment to the adults.[22] But perhaps five-year-old Christian Dieter and four-year-old Christoph Schneider found the arrangement fascinating — assuming they were still alive and well.

The first newspaper article to report the wreck stated that the *Princess Augusta* had carried 340 passengers.[23] In the immigrant trade, however, only individuals over the age of fourteen were counted as "whole freight" and charged full fare. Children ages four to fourteen were counted as "half freight" and paid half fare, while children under four were not counted at all. By this arithmetic, a ship's cargo of 340 "freights" could easily have consisted of 400 souls or more.[24] In fact, the same newspaper later stated that there had been 400 Palatines on board.[25]

Eighteenth-century passenger agreements are scarce, but judging from the ones that have been found, historians have concluded they did not change much over the course of the century. Based on the language in a Hope contract dated 1756, the passenger agreement that the Schwaigerners and Conrath Gehr signed would have promised them a "good, comfortable, and well-sailing ship" to transport them to Philadelphia. Each whole freight would be allotted a "firm bunk" six feet long and one-and-a-half feet wide. The crew would distribute "good and proper provisions" according to a weekly menu. Each whole freight would receive on Sundays and Thursdays one pound of beef cooked with rice, and on Wednesdays one pound of bacon with peas. Over the course of the other four days, each full freight would receive another pound of bacon, two pounds of flour, one pound each of butter and cheese, and six pounds of bread (the bread given all at once). Each whole freight was also promised a daily ration of "good fresh water"—usually two quarts, some of which was needed for cooking—and a quart of beer "as long as it remains good." In addition, the contract allowed passengers access to the cooking fire during daylight hours in good weather.[26]

All of this might sound adequate until we remember how passengers were counted. Assuming they all were still alive, Sebastian Dieter's family of five counted as just 2½ freights. By contract, they would have been allotted 2½ bed spaces and 2½ rations of food and drink at mealtime. The five members in Marcell Schneider's family counted as 3 full freights, while Jerg Gebert and his wife and child were reckoned at 2 freights. As a result, the fourteen emigrants from Schwaigern totaled just 9 whole freights. Stophel Schaber, who was destitute, would have enjoyed more bed space and provisions than his wealthier friends only because he was traveling without children.

Even if the passengers had been satisfied with the contract, however, the Hopes didn't always hold up their end of the bargain. In 1737, a group of 270 Palatines had contracted with the firm for passage to Philadelphia on board the *Three Sisters*. During the crossing from Rotterdam to England, they found the water and beer to be undrinkable and the rice inedible, and not all passengers received their share of meat. Upon reaching Cowes, the passengers left the ship and refused to return, convinced they would be starved at sea. One resident of Cowes was not surprised, telling the Palatines, "Hope had destroyed many poor souls in that manner."[27] He advised them to take their case to King George.

Several passengers did just that, filing a petition stating that on their voyage from Rotterdam, "they suffered very much from hunger on board of the said Ship, which had taken on little or no Provisions in Holland." While stopped in Cowes, they were "spending the rest of their substance, nor does it appear that the ship is to be victualed." The king sent a representative to investigate. He found that the water taken on at Rotterdam was "stinking" because it had been stored in wine casks. In addition, ten of the twenty barrels of beer on board were bad, and the rice was of poor quality — no worms, but "very dusty." The Hope firm's representative in Cowes agreed to add more provisions and, after a five-week layover, the *Three Sisters* resumed the voyage.

When the *Princess Augusta* arrived at Rotterdam in early June, a smaller ship named the *Oliver* was already there, heavily laden with Swiss emigrants bound for Virginia. The vessel was owned by the Hope firm and had been chartered by a group of Swiss entrepreneurs who had recently purchased 30,000 acres from a wealthy Virginia planter and land speculator, William Byrd II. The emigrants had left home in March and arrived in Rotterdam at the end of May.[28] Less than two weeks later, they were ready to sail.

The *Oliver* was a bilander, a two-masted merchant ship designed for coastal trade and used occasionally in the North and Mediterranean Seas. Not surprisingly, it was the smallest vessel in the

Palatine fleet. At 100 tons burden, it measured less than sixty feet in length and was only four-and-a-half feet high between decks. Built in 1720, it was also one of the oldest ships in the fleet.[29] Within the past several years the *Oliver* had made two voyages to America. In 1735, it carried 200 Palatines to South Carolina; in 1736, it brought 170 more. In 1738, Captain William Walker and his crew of four-teen British sailors planned to take the vessel to the James River in Virginia. Despite the ship's small size and advanced age, the *Oliver* was packed with nearly 300 passengers — almost twice as many passengers per ton as the *Princess Augusta*.[30]

The *Oliver* departed Rotterdam for Cowes during the first week in June, in the company of four other Palatine ships, all operated by the Hope firm.[31] The *Princess Augusta* was still being readied for passengers at that time and would remain in port for another two to three weeks. In the meantime, additional ships operated by other firms began arriving in Rotterdam. The thousand or more emigrants that had been at the Kralingen camp since early May were finally allowed to move, as "the people were parceled out to the different ships, over two hundred in some, in others over three hundred, in others four hundred or more." According to a report based on the eyewitness accounts of emigrants who had passed through Rotterdam, "they were packed in so tightly and crowded into each other that throughout at least one third too many were lodged on the ships. Everywhere the bedsteads were double-deckers, in some indeed they were triple-decked above each other. The crates of many were either smashed, and the people had to store their goods as well as they could (because the captains and the Newlanders had themselves so many crates and goods . . .) or were left behind and sent along on other ships."[32]

In late June, the *Princess Augusta* finally departed Rotterdam, bound for Cowes. Before leaving, Captain Long probably brought a pilot aboard to guide them through the winding estuaries to the North Sea. The most direct route was down the Maas River, past the fortified seaport of Brielle, a distance of twenty-two miles. In recent years, however, the Brielle Passage had become a tortuous maze of sandbars, at the end of which was a massive, shifting bank of sand that blocked the path of larger ships.[33] Now deep-water vessels had to follow a circuitous route that was three times longer and took them past the port of Hellevoetsluis. (See inset of map in chapter 2.)

Yet even this route was not free of shoals. A grounded ship could sometimes be dislodged by having passengers run from one side of the vessel to the other. In some cases, a ship could be towed free by sailors in a longboat. In other cases the passengers and some of the cargo would need to be removed in order to reduce the ship's draft. Even with a pilot it could take a week, sometimes longer, to reach the North Sea. The combination of distance, obstructions, unpredictable wind, changing tides, and the inability to sail at night could make these first few miles of ship travel surprisingly tedious.

Historians don't know what kind of sendoff the *Princess Augusta* received, whether she left alone or in the company of other ships. Her passengers were following in the tradition of a small group of English religious exiles, who had set out from Holland more than a century before to build a new life in America. But unlike the Pilgrims aboard the *Mayflower*, whose delays in the English Channel caused them to arrive in the New World later in the season than they had planned, landing hundreds of miles from their intended destination on a barrier beach one of their party described as a "hideous and desolate wilderness," the Palatines on board the *Princess Augusta* hoped to arrive in pleasant weather at a large city populated with fellow Germans ready to welcome them with open arms. That was the plan, at any rate, as they headed out to sea.

CHAPTER FIVE

Crossing the English Channel

Just past Hellevoetsluis, the *Princess Augusta* moved into the open waters of the North Sea. Before long the passengers were vomiting their most recent meals and taking to their narrow beds. This would have been the first experience with seasickness for most Palatines, though many letters from America warned about the condition. "I cannot describe how sick you get if you are sick at sea," wrote one German settler, reflecting on his own voyage to Pennsylvania. For those passengers who were already ill when they boarded in Rotterdam, the ship's rocking would have only added to their misery.

Mercifully, it took Palatine ships just a couple of days to cross the North Sea to England, where all ships headed to America paused for a customs inspection. Parliament had passed a series of trade laws in the second half of the seventeenth century designed to exclude foreign countries from trade with England's colonies. The Navigation Acts required that all European goods bound for the colonies be carried in British ships manned by majority British crews. Each vessel had to stop first at an English port, where its cargo was to be unloaded, inspected, and registered, and duties paid on goods that were not British-made. For Conrath Gehr, who was carrying chests filled with merchandise that his employers would have preferred not to declare, this may have been the most dreaded part of the voyage.

Captain Long's charterparty with the Hope firm directed him to take the *Princess Augusta* to the port of Cowes on the Isle of Wight.[1] The Isle of Wight is located about midway along the English Channel, a 350-mile-long stretch of notoriously rough water and contrary winds separating England and France. Most ships bound for America cleared customs at a Channel port because these were much less crowded than London and offered a straight shot to the Atlantic. Cowes was the port favored by most Palatine shippers. In 1738 about half of the twenty-two vessels in the fleet would stop there, with the rest divided among Deal, Dover, and Plymouth.[2]

To reach Cowes, Long sailed southwest toward the Strait of Dover, which marks the boundary between the Channel and the North Sea. As he neared the strait, Long passed his hometown of Ramsgate, navigating around the treacherous Goodwin Sands. Described by Shakespeare as the "shyppe swallower," this ten-mile-long bank of shifting sand, located six miles off the coast of Deal, is believed to have destroyed more than 2,000 vessels over the centuries. At low tide part of the shoal is exposed and the sand is firm. But as the tide returns, the bank turns to quicksand, engulfing stranded ships and preventing them from floating off. Their graves are marked by the masts sticking out of the water. Yet this same navigational hazard created the Downs, an area of safe anchorage between the sandbank and the English coast. Here, within sight of the chalk cliffs of Dover, merchant and navy vessels — sometimes hundreds at a time — sought refuge from storms, gathered to form convoys, and waited for the favorable winds that would permit entrance to the Channel.

The prevailing winds at this latitude blow from west to east. This makes entering the Channel from the eastern end quite challenging for ships under sail. Vessels could remain stuck in the Downs for days or even weeks, making it all the more remarkable that Long was able to take his ship from Rotterdam to Cowes so quickly. The winds and currents must have been in his favor, as the ship arrived in early July after just one week at sea.[3]

The *Princess Augusta* and the *Oliver* arrived at Cowes at about the same time, even though the *Oliver* had left Rotterdam about two weeks before her. The tiny ship had passed by the island of Goeree on June 12, but after several days on the North Sea, a storm forced Captain Walker to return to Hellevoetsluis.[4] Upon arrival in port, Walker quit his command, considering the vessel dangerously overloaded.[5]

Six Italian-Swiss passengers also fled the *Oliver*, claiming in a deposition that "they hadn't been satisfied at all with the services as provided."[6] The men sought refuge in the basement of a house along the waterfront, but on June 27, agents for the Hope firm tracked them down and warned that if they didn't return to the ship immediately, they would be left behind. Furthermore, the men wouldn't "be able to claim any refund for their passage, and no one whosoever could raise any complaint or legal action against us."[7]

The runaways refused to go back to the ship. They demanded the Hope firm reimburse their fare or "they would sue for damages and interest, as was their legal right." The men explained that the shipper "had not given sustenance to them." Each person received only about a week's worth of bread, cheese, and butter during the four weeks they had been on board. In addition, they complained that they "didn't have enough room to be comfortable, that water had been refused to two sick children who had died; and that they also would have died if they had continued this journey."[8]

The Hope firm gave them "assurance of everything one could assure them of in such a situation," but the men were adamant about not returning — even though they still had relatives on the ship.[9] In the meantime, Walker was replaced by Captain William Wright; on July 2, the *Oliver* left Hellevoetsluis for Cowes without the runaways.

The *Oliver* made the crossing in two days, arriving on July 4 at Cowes Roadstead. This was a sheltered anchorage just outside the harbor, where ships waited their turn for inspection and to receive orders from their shipper's agents. The *Princess Augusta* and the *Oliver* would spend the next two weeks at Cowes together, "partly to have our ship inspected and found solid and seaworthy," a passenger on the *Oliver* later explained, and "partly to unload and load anew."[10] Several other Palatine ships were there as well, including the Stedman brothers' *St. Andrew* and *Charming Nancy.*

The port of Cowes is located at the mouth of the Medina River, which flows north from the center of the island and divides the town in two. In West Cowes was the Watch House, from whose balcony a lookout scanned the Channel for approaching ships.[11] The Customs House was across the river in East Cowes, near the wharves and warehouses of the waterfront. The staff at the two offices communicated by signal flags.

When a ship arrived in port, officials called tidesmen rowed out to the vessel and stood guard to make sure no goods were smuggled on or off the ship. The captain was then taken to shore, where he presented his paperwork to officers in the "Long Room" of the Customs House. The Collector of Customs reviewed the documents — bills of lading, the ship's manifest, and a list of the crew — to make sure they were in order. The ship was then docked and the cargo unloaded, inspected, and registered. Once duties were paid on foreign trade goods, the ship was reloaded and cleared for departure.[12]

The stopover in Cowes normally took about two weeks but could take longer if the ship needed repairs. East Cowes had a large shipyard and a community of tradesmen — ropemakers, sailmakers, blockmakers, blacksmiths, and anchorsmiths — to support it. Along the northern shore of East Cowes was an area called Shrape Mud, where captains could careen their ships. What a sight that must have been for the Palatines, to see ships just like theirs lying on their sides on the tidal flat, while workmen scraped the shaggy carpet of seaweed and barnacles off their hulls.[13]

A ship also could be delayed at Cowes if smuggled goods were discovered aboard. Only British subjects were allowed to participate in transatlantic trade with the colonies, but foreign emigrants were allowed to carry newly purchased goods from the Continent as

long as the items were for personal use and not for resale. Such emigrants were required to tell the captain of the nature of the wares
they were carrying, so he could declare them and the owners could
pay any necessary duties. It was illegal to hide items from inspectors, to pass off merchandise as household goods, or to represent
new wares as old ones (by rubbing new pots with charcoal, for example). If any passengers were caught in violation of these laws, the
contraband would be seized and sold off. In extreme cases, the ship
itself could be impounded.

Early on in the Palatine trade, inspectors often turned a blind
eye to smuggled goods, figuring that the sale of such items would
be a one-time occurrence that helped a family get established in the
New World. Some inspectors could be bribed as well. This might
explain how the *Princess Augusta* passed through Cowes in July
1736, on a previous Palatine run, carrying an enormous quantity of
new household utensils, tools, fabric, clothing, and luxury items on
which no duties had been paid. (Many of these items were of the
kind that colonial merchants routinely imported from Europe for
sale in their shops, which suggests that some passengers were paid
to carry them.) Two months later, when the ship arrived in Philadelphia, customs officials there accused the passengers of smuggling.
They searched the ship and confiscated the Palatines' property,
both new and used, and took legal custody of the ship as well.[14]
The resulting court case took nine months to resolve, with Captain
Marchant arguing for the return of the passengers' property. The
Palatines' used household goods were eventually returned to them
the following summer, but the new items were ordered sold off and
the proceeds forwarded to the Crown — minus one-third given as a
reward to the customs inspectors.

We don't know whether the ship's history meant that the *Princess
Augusta* came under greater scrutiny on its 1738 voyage, but customs
officials certainly would have been interested in the merchandise
Conrath Gehr was delivering to Caspar Wistar. As a naturalized
citizen, Wistar was allowed to import European merchandise —
as long as duties were paid on the goods in England. But the mer-

chant's instructions to his business partner in Neckargemünd suggest that he wanted to avoid the tax. So did Gehr manage to smug-
gle the goods through Cowes, and if so, how did he do it?

He might have split up the shipment among a number of passengers, and paid them to pass off the items as used household goods.
He might have asked Captain Long to claim some of the items as
his own, as captains were allowed to carry a certain amount of merchandise duty-free. He might even have hidden some of the items
where inspectors would not look. The Cowes office had a staff of
fewer than fifteen men, making inspection of every nook and cranny
on every ship in the busy port virtually impossible.

Or, he might have paid off the searchers. The Collector of Customs at Cowes in 1738 was a man named Newland Reynolds, a merchant on the Isle of Wight. He had purchased the position in 1723
from the previous collector for the enormous sum of 500 pounds.
The Crown had measures in place to help prevent bribery: the collector paid a surety when he took over the job, which he would lose
if fired for cause, and his account book was subject to review by an
independent official. Perhaps an auditor did find some irregularities
in Reynolds's accounts, for in November 1738, three months after
the *Princess Augusta*'s departure, he was dismissed for "Mal practices" and forfeited his surety.[15]

While a ship was detained for inspection, the passengers were
allowed to disembark. They would be rowed ashore in a ship's longboat or by the local fishermen who provided ferry service to ships
at anchor. The Schwaigern emigrants were probably taken to West
Cowes, as it was the larger of the two villages, with a population
of about 1,300 people, and had several shops and taverns. Many
of its houses were built of ship's timbers and cow dung, but even
the meanest among them had lovely gardens, a feature that visitors
often commented upon.

Once on land, the Schwaigern families would have taken the opportunity to wash clothes, bathe themselves and their children, and
refill their water jugs. It was said that the island's springs were so
pure that casks of water taken to the West Indies were "brought

back again perfectly sweet." If they had money to spare, the families could purchase more food and drink to augment the ship's rations, and maybe a few trinkets as souvenirs. Along the shore, the Palatines could have fished, caught crabs, speared lobsters, and harvested oysters. The Dieter and Schneider children might have gathered periwinkles at low tide, while their parents cooked a meal over a campfire fueled with scavenged driftwood and dry brush.

We don't know what the islanders thought of their many German-speaking visitors (thousands passed through during the eighteenth century), but in numerous journal accounts the Palatines described their stay at Cowes as a pleasant one and the island as a place of great natural beauty. In July and August, the fields were filled with white butterflies — *Pieris brassicae,* or "summer snowflakes," as the residents called them — that migrated from the Continent in fluttering clouds. Naturalist Peter Kalm, who passed by the Isle of Wight on his journey to Philadelphia in 1748, wrote how they "never settled, and by their venturing at so great a distance from land they caused us real astonishment."[16] So attractive was the diverse landscape with its "alternation of marine and land views," the "mild and salubrious" climate, and the "extremely wholesome" air, according to early travel guides, that by the end of the eighteenth century the island had become a popular vacation destination.[17] In 1845, it became the summer retreat of Queen Victoria and Prince Albert.

While the passengers wandered about on land, Captain Long and his crew would have made final preparations for the Atlantic crossing. East Cowes had a thriving "victualing trade," so any provisions that hadn't been loaded in Rotterdam would be purchased there and taken aboard. All empty water casks would be refilled, and any necessary repairs made. Finally, with the customs inspection complete and the cargo, crew, and passengers back on board, Long would wait for the tide and an east wind to take them back into the Channel.

On July 17, with local pilots on board, the *Princess Augusta,* the *Oliver,* and four other Palatine ships left Cowes to a salute of cannon fire and reentered the Channel. The convoy didn't get far. According to London's *Daily Gazetteer*, the *Princess Augusta*, the *Oliver*, and two of the other vessels were "put back" at Cowes on July 22, probably due to a storm or a hard west wind.[18] The ships remained stuck in port for several more weeks.

By mid-August, the *Princess Augusta* and the *Oliver* had each set out again, but after sailing for several days through "contrary weather and a storm," according to a passenger on the *Oliver*, the ships sought shelter at Plymouth, a large naval port at the western end of the Channel. Both vessels would remain there for at least a month.[19]

Most Palatines skipped over the Channel crossing when recounting their journey to America, probably because it was less physically demanding than the trip down the Rhine, and less terrifying than the voyage across the furious Atlantic. In 1738, however, storms and adverse winds along the Channel caused significant delays. A large number of emigrants were already sick when they boarded the ships in Rotterdam, and many deaths that might have occurred on the Atlantic happened along the English coast instead.

In Philadelphia later that fall, newly arrived immigrants reported that the "harbingers of suffering could be seen on several ships even on this short voyage," and "some had already been buried at sea [the North Sea] and at Corves [Cowes], the place of customs."[20] Samuel Suther, a teenage passenger on the *Oliver*, lost his father and two sisters in the Channel. According to an 1843 biographical account of Suther, they "found their graves on the shores of England, where the ship was detained several months, in order to repair damages sustained in encountering a severe gale."[21] Considering that the two ships were traveling under the same conditions, it's likely that the Channel crossing claimed some lives on the *Princess Augusta* as well. Would it have been any consolation to know that these dead would be spared the horrors to come?

CHAPTER SIX

Life and Death on the North Atlantic

In mid-September the *Princess Augusta* lay at anchor in Plymouth Harbor, an ancient Channel port on the southwest coast of England — the same port from which a small band of English Separatists had sailed a century earlier in a tired old wine-trading vessel called the *Mayflower*. There were more ships here than anywhere else along the Channel. The size of Plymouth Sound and its proximity to the Channel's entrance made the port a shipping station, a place where fleets would gather before sailing out into the Atlantic.[1] The Channel was wide here, giving ships sea room to tack across the wind. It was said that if you could make it to Plymouth, then you could get out of the Channel, although it might take more than one try.

At Plymouth, Captain Long had one last opportunity to replenish the ship's food and freshwater supplies, depleted since the ship left Cowes four weeks ago. He could have taken on additional passengers and cargo if there was room, although this seems unlikely. Long also would have tried to arrange to sail in convoy with other ships. The *Princess Augusta* and the *Oliver* were still in company, but it would have been safer to travel with several merchantmen and a naval escort, if possible.

Long was anxious to get under way. It had been three months since the *Princess Augusta* departed Rotterdam, nearly all of it spent bottled up in the English Channel. Four of the ships in that season's Palatine fleet were already in Philadelphia; four more would appear on the Delaware River within the next ten days. That meant a third of the fleet would be in port (and most of the rest well under way) before the *Princess Augusta* had left England.

The delays cost Long and the ship's other owners money, starting with wages owed the crew. Additionally, the longer the *Princess Augusta* sat in the Channel, the more provisions would be consumed. These would need to be replaced or there would not be enough to sustain the passengers and crew during the Atlantic crossing. The delays also interfered with Long's plan to sail to the West Indies after dropping the Germans off in Philadelphia. Timing was everything in the transatlantic trade. Long needed to get to the Caribbean before the goods he planned to carry back to England were loaded onto other ships.

Perhaps most worrisome of all, the *Princess Augusta* would be leaving at the height of the hurricane season. The ship would be taking the southern route and riding the trade winds, the same prevailing wind system that pushed half a dozen of these monstrous storms across the Atlantic each summer and fall.

Sometime in the latter half of September, the *Princess Augusta* left Plymouth Sound and reentered the Channel. (Researchers believe the *Oliver* left with her.) A day or two later, the ship reached the Lizard, a rocky peninsula marking the southernmost point of the British mainland. This was the last of Europe most emigrants would ever see. No one could have predicted the stopover in England would last so long. What should have taken no more than about six weeks, including travel time from Rotterdam and the customs inspection at Cowes, took the *Princess Augusta* at least twelve. But the ship was finally on the Atlantic, and the young captain was faced with 20 million square miles of ocean to navigate. He must have been grateful to have First Mate Andrew Brook at his side.

Long set his vessel on a southwest course, to meet up with the

trade winds that would carry them across the ocean.[2] To reach the
trade winds, the *Princess Augusta* would have to sail past England's
two naval rivals — France and Spain — and the Bay of Biscay that
lies between them. The same winds that made it difficult for ships
to exit the English Channel could blow a ship into the bay, which
was known for its sudden and fierce storms and enormous swells.
Beyond the bay was the island of Madeira, several hundred miles
off the coast of Morocco. Merchant and naval vessels often stopped
there to take on more water and provisions. Journal accounts show
some Palatine ships did too, giving the Germans their first glimpse
of orange, lemon, and palm trees and fields of sugar cane and rice.
South of Madeira were the Canary Islands, where the prevailing
winds began their westward bend across the Atlantic.

As the *Princess Augusta* turned her back on the coast of England,
the color of the water changed from sapphire to midnight blue. Two
hundred miles out, the gently sloping sea floor abruptly fell away,
and the water, its depth now unfathomable, turned black.

Life on the *Princess Augusta*, as on all Palatine ships, consisted of
long stretches of boredom overlaid with seasickness and second
thoughts, punctuated by episodes of sheer terror. Because the passengers outnumbered the crew by twenty-five to one, it was impera-
tive that Captain Long maintain calm and order. The best way to do
that was to replicate at sea the daily routines of life on land.

Meal preparation was the central activity of each day, prepared
at the "firebox," a brick-lined sandbox located on the top deck.[3] The
ship's cook, with the help of some of the passengers, served one hot
meal at midday, boiled in a 90-gallon copper cauldron suspended by
an iron crane over the fire.[4] The Hope firm stipulated in its contract
that the passengers had access to the fireplace from 6:00 a.m. to
6:00 p.m., weather permitting. Except during mealtime, the families took turns at the fire, fixing themselves simple dishes.[5] The
Schneiders' eleven-year-old daughter, Catharina, might have helped
her mother make coffee, tea, or soup to serve their group. Cooking

at sea could be hazardous, however, as hot food often got spilled on a rocking ship. The crew kept a watchful eye on the firebox, as an open flame and hot coals could set the vessel ablaze if not tended properly.[6]

The food served aboard ship was a trinity of awfulness: unhealthy, unappetizing, and sometimes inedible. The meat was tough and salty, and months if not years old; the bread, a flat, flavorless, tooth-shattering biscuit called hardtack, was often infested with weevils and maggots.[7] The passengers softened these "flour tiles" by dunking them in hot tea or soup. Some travel accounts mention how the Palatines occasionally got a few bites of fish, dolphin, or shark that the crew had speared or caught with a hook and line. The fresh food was a rare but welcome change.[8]

The drinking water on board a Palatine ship (or any eighteenth-century transport ship, for that matter) was often worse than the food. Typically, each adult passenger was given two quarts of water per day, but some of that had to be used for cooking.[9] Travelers at the time described it as "putrid," "foul-smelling," "vile," and "stinking." Fortunately, the water rations were supplemented by a daily quart of beer, and often a small amount of brandy.[10]

Emigrants usually regretted that they had not brought more food and drink from home, as they seldom suspected that the journey would last so long and the ship's food be so unpalatable. Joggi Thommen, a Swiss emigrant who traveled aboard the *Princess Augusta* in 1736 (under the command of Samuel Marchant), wrote home that "eating and drinking is not enjoyable. And the ship's complement [crew] does not keep their promises. One had to provide oneself with bread, wine, flour, dried stuff, and sugar."[11]

It's not known whether Thommen and his fellow passengers had misunderstood the travel contract or been deliberately short-changed by the crew or the Hope firm, or if rationing had become necessary near the end of their twelve-week crossing. Rationing was common on prolonged voyages, since running out of food and especially water could be fatal.[12] The Palatines on the Philadelphia-bound *Love and Unity*, which made an unscheduled stop at Martha's Vineyard in 1731, suffered that fate. During their twenty-four-week crossing, around a hundred passengers died of starvation. The fifty survivors were forced to eat mice and rats.[13]

Like regular meals, bathing and laundering also could contribute to the health and well-being of the passengers. Because ships were so crowded and fresh water was reserved for cooking and drinking, the air below decks was thick with the stench of body odor. Whenever possible, rainwater was collected and one day each week set aside as wash day.[14] Sometimes passengers brought their items up on deck and simply laid them out in the sunshine and fresh air. Despite their best efforts at keeping their bodies and belongings clean, lice were a problem for both passengers and crew.[15] Delousing became part of one's daily routine.

On most ships, the captain ordered the passengers to scrub below decks once or twice a week with vinegar, which was supposed to result in a "sweeter-smelling ship." To keep down the mouse and rat population, they were told not to leave food and refuse lying around.[16] Still, rodents infested every ship.[17]

In between meals, chores, bouts of seasickness, and storms, the Palatines passed the time singing, telling stories, playing games, mending clothes, and knitting stockings and caps. They read scripture daily and held religious services once or twice a week — more often if they were traveling as a congregation with their own minister. But the chronic deprivation and confinement at sea sometimes led to bad behavior, from stealing and drunkenness, to arguments, fistfights, and all-out brawls (by some accounts, involving both men and women). "The journey is so troublesome for people who are not able to patiently submit to everything," wrote one Swiss emigrant in 1733.[18]

The daily life of the crew was arguably worse than that of the passengers. Their job was dangerous, physically demanding, and never-ending, but the greatest burden fell to the captain. As commander of the *Princess Augusta,* Long was responsible not only for the safety of the ship — worth £20,000 sterling (about $4.7 million today), according to Boston newspapers[19] — but for the lives of hundreds of men, women, and children. He had to navigate the ocean with the crudest of instruments, unable to determine with precision how far west he had traveled.[20] He had to be able to predict the weather based on subtle changes in sky, wind, and sea. A captain's insistence on order could make him seem heartless; at the same time, he would be blamed for everything that went wrong on the ship, from bad food and water to rationing to crowded conditions to the fee structure — even though all of these were the responsibility of the merchant house who had hired the ship.[21]

Most captains who took part in the Palatine trade made one voyage and then quit. It was so much easier to carry dry goods than human cargo. John Stedman, who made a half-dozen runs, was shocked at the quarrelsome behavior of his German passengers aboard the *Pennsylvania Merchant* in 1733. According to a witness on board, "the Captain often said he had taken many people over to this country already but had in all his days never yet seen any thing like this. He thought they must have been possessed by demons."[22]

Despite the aggravation of transporting this delicate and demanding cargo, many captains remained concerned for the well-being of their passengers. Stedman, for example, was singled out in numerous accounts for his humanity. He was known to distribute extra food and water when possible and to break into his own provisions and medicine supplies to give to the sick.

In addition to chronicling the sufferings of shipboard life, many Palatines wrote of a natural world they had never seen before: winged fish that left the water to escape the "sea hogs" that chased them, and enormous creatures that spouted water high in the air "as if it came out of pipes." They wrote of the "sea dogs" that swam alongside the ship in groups of a hundred or more, and the menacing "sea wolves" that followed behind, eating garbage and human waste. One passenger on a 1728 voyage was startled at the sight of a "so-called Devil fish which was very large and hideous."[23] Peter Kalm noted in his 1749 travel journal the round, purple-colored "blubbers," some of which have a "nettling and burning quality" when touched. He was also amazed by the luminescent sea life:

In the Channel and on the Ocean we saw at night-time sparks of
fire, as if floating on the water, especially where it was agitated,
sometimes one single spark swam for the space of more than one
minute on the ocean before it vanished. The sailors observed that
they appeared commonly during and after a storm from the north,
and that often the sea was as if full of fire, and that some such shin-
ing sparks would likewise stick to the masts and sails.[24]

Regardless of the marvels of nature seen at sea, after months on
board a creaky, crowded, stinking ship, with one's fate in the hands
of an inexperienced captain and a temperamental sea, the Palatines
on board the *Princess Augusta* would never look at life in the same
way again.

In early October, about two weeks after losing sight of the Lizard,
the *Princess Augusta* met another ship at sea. They were now about
750 miles southwest of England, and perhaps 200 miles off the
coast of Portugal. Researchers don't know how long the *Princess
Augusta* and the *Oliver* remained together after leaving Plymouth,
but it's likely that they had lost sight of each other by then. Captain
Long knew that sooner or later they would encounter another ship.
Ships usually met at least two other vessels during a normal Atlantic crossing.[25]

When traveling alone, however, crossing paths with an unknown
ship could be an anxious event. Merchant ships were constantly on
the lookout for pirates. During wartime they had privateers and
enemy warships to worry about as well. In 1738, England was still
a year away from war with Spain, yet English shipping was already
being harassed by the Spanish. Newspapers published complaints
by British mariners and government officials about Spanish pirates
and privateers "visiting, searching, and taking our Ships in their
voyages to and from our Plantations in America."[26]

The Spanish were not the only threat. The *Princess Augusta* had
obtained a "Mediterranean pass" for protection from the pirates of

the Barbary Coast, which included what are now the North African states of Morocco, Algeria, Tunisia, and Libya. The Barbary pirates preyed on shipping in the Mediterranean and along the coast of West Africa. In exchange for safe passage, the pirates required foreign countries to pay a yearly tribute to the Barbary sultans. Without such payment, their ships could be seized and the crewmen held for ransom or sold into slavery.

When the other vessel was spotted, Captain Long would have studied its movements and tried to determine with his spyglass both its nationality and how many people it carried. Merchant ships the size of the *Princess Augusta* usually employed around fifteen men and were only lightly armed — in this case, with just eight cannon. In contrast, pirate ships of similar size might carry more than eighty men and were veritable floating arsenals.[27]

The normal course of action was to sail away from any ship that could not be identified by signal flag. If the captain found himself uncomfortably close to another ship of uncertain origin, he might order all male passengers on deck, to give the appearance of a ship well manned and capable of defending itself.[28] If fired upon, however, the passengers were to surrender immediately.

In most instances, the ships encountered at sea were other trading vessels.[29] And such was the case with the ship that the *Princess Augusta* met off the coast of Portugal: it was an English merchantman — the *Richard and Thomas* — under the command of a Captain Angwin. The cargo ship was bound from Jamaica to London, probably with a load of sugar and perhaps some coffee, tobacco, and cotton. Long and Angwin may have communicated by speaking trumpet. Or, weather permitting, the captains might have met on board one of the vessels, drank to each other's health, and exchanged provisions, letters, and news. During their encounter, Angwin surely would have told Long about the devastating hurricane that had struck the West Indies in mid-August.

When Angwin arrived home, he informed a London newspaper of his encounter with the "Prince of Asturias of Ramsgate" (names of ships and captains often were misprinted in eighteenth-century newspapers, even when there was no language barrier). On October 19, the *Daily Gazetteer* printed the following notice:

Gravesend, Oct 17:

> Capt. Angwin of the Richard and Thomas, from Jamaica, spoke with the Prince of Asturias of Ramsgate, bound for Philadelphia, in Latitude 44 Degrees 30 Minutes North: She has been 15 Days from Plymouth, and about 250 Leagues to the Westward of the Lizzard, all well.[30]

The *Princess Augusta*'s first two weeks on the Atlantic had been uneventful. There almost certainly were cases of seasickness on board, but that was to be expected in open water. And the illness some of the passengers carried onto the ship in Rotterdam seemed thus far contained. In the coming weeks, however, all that would change, as fever swept through the vessel both below decks and above.

A letter from Caspar Wistar to Georg Friedrich Hölzer in April 1739 provides a window on shipboard conditions. He wrote that disease began to spread about three to four weeks after leaving England, and that Captain Long, six sailors, and many of the passengers had died before the ship was halfway across the Atlantic. It's not clear whether the water supply gave out, was undrinkable, or if the illness itself caused excessive thirst, but, according to Wistar, the passengers "so dreadfully begged for water, and some died with an empty jug at their mouths, and others had the jug in their hand when they were found dead on their beds."[31]

Their affliction was most likely dysentery, an infection of the lower intestines transmitted by ingesting contaminated food or water.[32] In the eighteenth century, the disease was usually referred to as the "flux," or — more graphically — the "bloody flux," because of its hallmark symptom, bloody diarrhea. The victims suffered high fever, headache, nausea, and excruciating abdominal pain; their persistent sweating, vomiting, and diarrhea led to extreme dehydration. Standard treatment at that time included bloodletting, emetics (to induce vomiting), purgatives (to evacuate the bowels), and glisters (enemas). Not surprisingly, these did more harm than good, as recovery depended largely on restoring the body's fluids, not draining them.

Newspaper accounts later would blame the outbreak on the "badness of their Water taken in at Rotterdam in Cask[s] that had before contain'd white and red Wines."[33] Wistar told Hölzer "they had filled their water into vine [wine] barrels in Holland, and the water turned so bad that everyone fell ill." But dysentery is caused by a pathogen, and such pathogens are spread through contact with human feces, not wine sediment.[34] If the passengers did indeed contract dysentery from the ship's water, the source of contamination probably was not the barrels but the river, canal, or well from which the water was taken, or the poor hygiene of the men who filled the barrels or distributed water rations on the ship. In a confined setting, lacking the basics of hygiene, the illness would then have spread quickly from one passenger to the next.

It is also possible that the disease had nothing to do with the ship's water, but instead was picked up on shore. Disease was rampant in the rain-soaked Kralingen camp, where many of the Palatines had been forced to stay before boarding their ships, and most of the Palatine fleet suffered outbreaks of dysentery that year. Indeed, witnesses said some of the passengers were already sick when they boarded the *Princess Augusta*. Even those who appeared well upon boarding may have already been infected, however, as dysentery has a highly variable incubation period.[35] Some researchers have even suggested that the illness actually began along the Rhine River, as one of the ships hardest hit by dysentery — the *Davy* — originated from Amsterdam, not Rotterdam.[36]

Approximately 240 of the passengers aboard the *Princess Augusta* died at sea. Most perished on the Atlantic in the span of about ten weeks.[37] In the beginning of the epidemic, the dead would have received a proper burial: the body wrapped in a blanket, weighted with stones or a cannonball, and slid off a plank face-up and feet-first into the sea (a position believed to prevent the soul of the deceased from

Burial at sea. Wood engraving 1887, after a drawing by Carl Schildt.
Image: INTERFOTO / Alamy

returning to haunt the ship). Small children who died might have been placed in a weighted sack and lowered into the water.[38] But as the pace of death quickened and the number of able-bodied adults diminished, the corpses were probably just heaved over the side. That is what had occurred on the *Love and Unity* seven years earlier, when two-thirds of the passengers died of starvation during the six-month crossing. According to survivors, their bodies were thrown overboard naked and without anything to weigh them down.[39]

Conrath Gehr, the courier hired to transport rifles to Caspar Wistar in Philadelphia, somehow survived the epidemic. We know that Jerg Gebert's wife, Elisabetha, did too, but we don't know who else among the Schwaigern party was still alive at this point in the voyage. Thirteen of the fourteen people in the group would eventually perish before reaching shore.

The same illness also killed half of the crew, leaving only about seven or eight men to handle the ship. Captain Long, who had just turned twenty-one, left behind his young wife, Mary, his two-and-a-half-year-old son, George, and a daughter, Catherine, who had been born while Long was at sea. Andrew Brook took over as commander, and George Brooks was promoted to first mate. Short-handed, Brook would have enlisted help from the remaining able-bodied male passengers. Though untrained, they could at least help haul lines and pump water out of the hold. The crew needed all the help they could get battling one of the worst storm seasons the Atlantic had seen in years.

The epidemic that swept through the *Princess Augusta* was likely aggravated by the series of storms that the ship encountered on the North Atlantic. In an average year, more than a hundred disturbances form with hurricane potential, fueled by warm water and steered by the prevailing winds. Of these disturbances, nearly a dozen become tropical storms, and half of those become full-blown hurricanes. While only a few hurricanes strike land each year, those that remain at sea can wreak havoc on shipping.[40]

Hurricanes are monstrous weather systems, averaging 300 miles in diameter, with outer bands of torrential rain, thunder and lightning, and gale-force winds extending hundreds of miles farther. Some hurricanes barrel across open water before dissipating, while others meander or even stall and pick up strength. They can last from a week to a month over water, and at the height of the season there is usually more than one in the Atlantic.[41] During the eighteenth century, sailors had no way of knowing where such storms were. They could sail right into them or be overtaken by them.

Atlantic hurricanes could delay or extend a voyage for weeks or months; they could blow a ship off course, landing passengers far from their intended destination. Worse yet, they could damage or even destroy a fragile wooden vessel. On the open ocean, hurricanes can generate waves up to fifty feet high. Following such a storm, the water's surface would be littered with floating debris.

The immigration season of 1738 was marked by unusually violent weather at sea, believed by some researchers to have been caused by the start of a new La Niña cycle.[42] Two hurricanes had already struck the Leeward Islands in the West Indies before the *Princess Augusta* lost sight of England. The first was witnessed by Captain Angwin in mid-August; one newspaper referred to it as "the most furious Hurricane that ever was known in these Parts."[43] A second storm struck one month later. Newspaper accounts on both sides of the Atlantic described the destruction: ships adrift without sails and masts, with decks so torn up that nothing but the floor timbers could be seen. Vessels were spotted at sea with no men aboard; others found "Bottom upwards." Fifty ships were reported lost in the two storms, though the toll was likely much higher.[44]

There are no known diaries from passengers aboard the *Princess Augusta*, but passengers on other Palatine vessels mention the terrifying ordeal of storms at sea: the rolling and pitching that flung wailing people out of their beds, and the violent slam of the hull, like hammer to anvil, in the trough between waves.[45] "The sea rose up so high," wrote a Swiss traveler to South Carolina in 1737, "that when one looked into it, it was just as if one were sailing among high mountains all covered with snow."[46] In 1735, another traveler wrote how twice they "saw the ocean not far from us, drawn up like smoke, so that the water reached up to the clouds, and the ship would have been in great danger if it had struck us."[47] Passengers compared the sound of the waves hitting their ship to the roar of a cannon. Even with the hatches and portholes closed, it was impossible to keep the water out.[48]

For their own safety, passengers were forced below decks, often with the hatches locked. They would remain sealed up in the pitch-black, airless quarters during storms that could sometimes last for days. "The 16th and 17th of January we had a great storm, day and night," wrote a Swiss emigrant in 1737, "so we were nailed into the hold in order to keep the water out. Since we were 212 souls and the space was very small, we thought we would surely die."[49] Little wonder, then, that sailors sometimes referred to their ships as "floating coffins."

While the disease-stricken passengers huddled in the suffocating darkness below decks, Brook and his men aboard the *Princess Augusta* would have worked nearly to death, trying to manage the ship in the howling wind and roiling sea. Some would have lashed the tiller and made sure the ship was shut tight, while others scampered up the rigging and climbed out on the yards to furl the sails and lash them down — all without any sort of safety lines. In particularly rough seas, they would have tied themselves to the rig to keep from being washed overboard. In dire circumstances, only one sailor would have been left on deck to watch the tiller, while the others took turns pumping water from the hold.

Caspar Wistar's letter makes no mention of the weather, but the *Princess Augusta* is believed to have passed through the same storms as the *Oliver*.[50] A deposition given after the voyage by Italian-Swiss passenger Carlo Toriano states that, after leaving Plymouth, the *Oliver* sailed on the open sea with favorable winds for six weeks. But then the weather changed. "We were tormented during more than 10 consecutive weeks by very furious storms and contrary winds which not only threatened us to perish at any moment but we also lost the mast of the ship and at the same time our poor captain died of a blood flux."[51] An account based on the memoirs of Samuel Suther, a teenage passenger on the *Oliver*, described how the ship was "tossed upon the mountains of waves, by the angry winds of thirteen successive storms, upwards of four months."[52]

As the *Princess Augusta* passed through these storms, the suffering among the sick and dying passengers must have been unbearable. Nailed into the hold of the leaking and battered ship, even those still relatively healthy would have experienced each new tempest as a reminder of their mortality. "One sees always death present in a Storm," wrote a traveler on his voyage to Georgia in 1734.[53] After two days of frightful weather at sea, when the wind finally abated, he was even "more sensibly convinced of this Truth, that there may be but a moment between Life and Death."

Throughout the fall of 1738, ships carrying weary Palatines appeared singly and in pairs on the Delaware River. The first three to arrive — the *Winter Galley,* then the *Glasgow* and *Two Sisters* — landed their passengers in early September and in relatively good condition. The first signs of trouble appeared with the fourth ship: the *Robert and Alice.* The captain reported many of the 300 passengers had been sick and 18 had died at sea. Four more ships arrived between September 16 and September 20: the *Queen Elizabeth,* the *Thistle,* the *Friendship,* and the *Nancy.* They had 425 deaths among them. The next ship, the *Fox,* didn't arrive until October 12, and it too had suffered casualties — as many as half of the 153 passengers on board.[54]

And things only got worse from there. Four more ships arrived near the end of October: the *Davy* (after the captain, first mate, and second mate died at sea, the ship's carpenter took command and brought the ship up the Delaware),[55] John Stedman's *St. Andrew,* the *Bilander Thistle,* and the *Elizabeth.* On November 9, the *Charming Nancy,* commanded by John Stedman's brother, Charles, limped into port. As the ships anchored near the city, passengers continued to die. At night, the sailors pitched their bodies into the river.[56] By now, nearly all of the Philadelphia-bound Palatine ships had arrived in port, but the number of sick and dead among them was staggering.

On November 28, a group of fourteen concerned Philadelphians, all native Germans, sent an open letter to the homeland, informing them of the tragic circumstances of the 1738 immigration season. They wrote: "This year the sea has reaped quite a different harvest. By moderate reckoning, of fourteen ships which have so far arrived, . . . more than eighteen hundred have died at sea and here in Philadelphia."[57]

They were particularly concerned about two ships that had left the Dutch port in June, one bound for Virginia and the other for

Pennsylvania —"of which one has reason to believe that hardly any-one will survive inasmuch as they have been at sea for over twenty-four weeks."[58]

Those two missing ships were the *Oliver* and the *Princess Augusta*.

By early December, the *Princess Augusta* was approaching the southeastern coast of North America. Andrew Brook was in com-mand, assisted by George Brooks, Robert Hughson, and the other surviving crewmen, and likely a small number of adult male passen-gers. Only about a third of the original number of passengers were still alive. Some were children, which is surprising given that the average mortality rate for children on a "healthy" ship was around 9 percent.[59]

What happened between this point and the day that the ship arrived at Delaware Bay is one of the great mysteries of the story. Brook must have known when he sighted land that he was hundreds of miles south of "Cape James" (the early name for Cape Henlopen, at the mouth of the bay). The passengers probably knew this, too. They had been told that it would be cold in Pennsylvania this time of year, and yet the air was as mild as a spring day. But did that even matter now? After what they had endured on board this ship of death, the sound of the lookout shouting "Land! Land!" must have filled them with relief and utter joy. Their trial by water, it seemed, was nearly over. They had lived to see America.

CHAPTER SEVEN

An Unscheduled Stop

To call the *Princess Augusta* an immigrant ship is to misrepresent the main purpose of the voyage, which was to pick up raw materials and staple goods from the British colonies in North America and transport them back to England. The passengers on board the merchant ship were incidental cargo, and the ship's departure from Rotterdam had been carefully timed not for the comfort and convenience of the passengers, but to coincide with the availability of the cargo the ship had been sent to get. Any delays along the way jeopardized the profitability of the trading voyage. This could explain why, with just a week or so of travel left before arriving in Philadelphia, Captain Brook chose to make an unscheduled stop in Charleston, South Carolina.

"Charles Towne" had been established in 1670 by eight English noblemen who were granted the Carolina territory by King Charles II as a reward for helping restore him to the throne.[1] The proprietors intended for the settlement to become "a great port towne," and by 1738 the population had grown to around 6,000, making it the fourth-largest city in North America, behind only Boston, Philadelphia, and New York. Visitors in the early eighteenth century described it as a "neat pretty place," with "regular and fair Streets" and large, beautiful brick buildings. Its inhabitants were said to be a "genteel Sort of People . . . well acquainted with Trade."[2]

Blessed with a deep, protected harbor two miles wide, Charleston was the only major port in the southern colonies. By the late 1730s, nearly two hundred ships cleared from there each year, laden with thousands of deerskins, tens of thousands of barrels of pitch, tar, and turpentine, and hundreds of thousands of board feet of pine, cedar, and cypress. Much of the city's prosperity, however, came from the export of "white gold": rice grown on large plantations in the cypress swamps of South Carolina's Low Country. More than 30,000 barrels — 20 million pounds — of the staple crop were shipped yearly, some to the West Indies but most of it to England and the Continent.[3]

Because rice cultivation was so labor-intensive, the enormous wealth it generated for planters and merchants would not have been possible without the forced labor of tens of thousands of captive Africans who passed through Charleston's slave markets in the early 1700s. In 1740, South Carolina's total population numbered about 60,000 — two-thirds of them slaves. When Swiss immigrant Samuel Dyssli arrived in Charleston in 1737, he found half of the city's residents were enslaved blacks. "Carolina looks more like a negro country than like a country settled by white people," he wrote to his brother.[4]

The most likely reason Brook stopped in Charleston was to try and salvage the trading voyage, the success of which had been threatened by the *Princess Augusta*'s delays in the English Channel and that summer's damaging weather in the West Indies. The *American Weekly Mercury* in Philadelphia reported that in July, the island of Antigua had received "such excessive Rains, that their Crops were greatly Damaged thereby, so that few Vessels were like to get Freights."[5] The wet weather in July had been followed by hurricanes in August and September. Running behind schedule and likely aware of the small chance of securing freight in the tropics, Brook must have decided there was no point in going there.

The Hope firm had sent the *Princess Augusta* to Charleston two years earlier. Moreover, the ship now had room for cargo after the death of so many passengers. In South Carolina, Brook could pick up animal skins, naval stores, timber, and especially rice — one of England's most valuable imports. Rice was harvested in early September but had to be threshed, husked, winnowed, ground, and sifted before it could be packed in barrels. This was a laborious process assigned mainly to female slaves and took weeks to complete. The first barrels usually were not ready to ship until early November, just before the Palatine ships began to arrive from Philadelphia. This year, five ships were headed to Charleston. Brook had no idea where those ships were (in fact, two had entered port in late November; the other three would not arrive until the third week of December). It was a gamble, but if he acted now, in early December, the *Princess Augusta* might be able to take a share of the exports to make up for the loss of its trade in the West Indies.

But what Brook found when he arrived at Charleston was a city still reeling from months of devastating weather and disease. Widespread drought and scorching heat had begun in late spring and persisted through the end of summer. The temperature was said to have reached 125 degrees Fahrenheit, causing people to drop dead in the streets and fields.[6] Late August brought flooding rains that would last into winter. Crops died and food shortages set in.[7]

Even worse, since May the city had been in the grips of the "speckled monster." Smallpox had arrived at Charleston Harbor on a slave ship and quickly spread to the city's residents. By October half of Charleston's population — both whites and blacks — had been infected, and 310 had died. The epidemic would last eight months, during which time farmers and planters from the countryside refused to bring their produce to market, afraid of contracting the disease. Tradesmen, laborers, and merchants in the city were too ill to work. When word of the epidemic spread to other ports, ships stayed away, including those carrying needed foodstuffs from the northern colonies.[8]

Winter was the peak shipping season at the port of Charleston, and the city's eight wharves should have been crowded. But according to merchant Robert Pringle, "Since the first of May that the Small Pox broke out here, we have had Little or no Trade & for Five & Six months this Town look'd more like an Hospital then a place of Trade & till within the Two Months past, hardly any manner of Bussiness has been done."[9]

Ironically, the rice yield in 1738 was the best in years, although the rains delayed harvesting. After harvest, the planters withheld their crop, to try to raise prices. Late into December, according to Pringle, there was very little rice to ship.[10] Those Palatine vessels that had already disposed of their passengers in Pennsylvania could wait a few more weeks for the rice to come to market. The *Princess Augusta* — with more than a hundred sick passengers still on board — could not.

There may have been additional reasons for Brook's diversion to Charleston, of course, foremost among them the health and safety of the passengers and crew and the seaworthiness of the ship. Brook could have stopped to take on more food and water, plug leaks, and repair shredded sails and tattered rigging. He could have recruited sailors to replace the seven or eight men he had lost at sea. It's also possible that, after more than five months aboard ship, the passengers had been clamoring to get off, intending to finish the journey to Pennsylvania on foot. Most immigrants had no concept of distance in North America, believing they could walk from one colony to another just as they had walked between towns in Europe.

Brook might have encouraged his passengers to end their journey there and take advantage of a settlement fund established in 1735 by South Carolina's General Assembly. This was essentially a cash bounty to be used for "purchasing tools, provisions and other necessarys for poor Protestants lately arrived in this Province." The funds were raised by charging a duty on the importation of African slaves. Priority was given to those Palatines who built their homesteads in townships "most exposed," that is, closest to Indian or Spanish territory.[11] Brook would have benefited from the settlement fund too, as a portion of the bounty went to the merchants or ship captains who imported the settlers.[12] The statute was intended to remain in effect for three years. Unfortunately, the funds had begun to dry up by the end of 1737. It's not known whether Brook was aware of this fact before crossing the Atlantic.

Although the Hope firm preferred sending Palatine ships to Philadelphia, the stopover in Charleston also could have been part of a preplanned scheme to take the passengers to a different destination without their knowledge or consent. Later emigrants were warned about this. According to Gottlieb Mittelberger, who traveled to Pennsylvania in 1750 and returned home four years later, "It often happens that the merchants in Holland make a secret contract with their captains and the Newlanders, to the effect that the latter must take the ships with their human freight to another place in America, and not to Pennsylvania where these people want to go, if they think they can elsewhere find a better market for them." The passengers, he wrote, are forced to "submit to the captain's will, because they cannot know at sea where the ship is steered to."[13]

It's also possible that by the time land was sighted, Brook simply wanted to be rid of his cargo and sailed for the nearest port. Unscrupulous captains sometimes dumped their passengers in this way. To guard against this occurrence on the ships they owned, the Stedmans included a clause in their charterparties that forbade the captains in their employ from taking passengers to any port other than the one named in the contact.[14]

Customs house records for the port of Charleston no longer exist, and the *South-Carolina Gazette* does not mention the *Princess Augusta*'s arrival or departure. Evidence of the stopover comes from two other sources: a brief and terse statement in a letter Sebastian Dieter's uncle, Peter Lohrman, wrote home in October 1739 ("The ship's captain, that rogue, brought them to Karlin,"[15] he told friends and family in Schwaigern) and the presence of a particular cargo at the time of the wreck. According to nineteenth-century historian Samuel T. Livermore, when the ship came ashore on Block Island, it was carrying rough logs of lignum vitae.[16] A hardwood grown in the West Indies, lignum vitae was an extremely valuable trade commodity, exported in large quantities from Charleston. So dense that it sinks in seawater, the wood is very resinous and resists rot and insects. These qualities make it well-suited for components of the ship's rigging such as blocks, belaying pins, and deadeyes, as well as for mortars and pestles, mallet heads, and tool handles — any purpose requiring strength and durability.

In the end, it was probably a combination of reasons that brought the *Princess Augusta* to "Karlin." There is no evidence that any passengers were forced off the ship. In fact, Charleston officials would hardly have allowed sick immigrants to land in their stricken city. But the tone of the Lohrman letter suggests that the passengers did not benefit from the stopover. Most likely, Brook was simply doing his job: protecting the business interests of the ship's owners and the chartering firm. It was a shrewd move on his part, but one that ultimately sealed the ship's fate.

PART III

The New Land

CHAPTER EIGHT

Shipwreck!

Sometime during the second week of December 1738, the *Princess Augusta* headed back to sea, converging with the warm ocean current Ponce de León once described as "more powerful than the wind."[1] The ship rode the Gulf Stream northeast, past a string of barrier islands that protected the North Carolina coast. At Cape Hatteras, historically a brutal point to round, the crew broke free of the current and turned north, toward Virginia. They passed Cape Henry and Cape Charles, named for the sons of King James. The two headlands define the entrance to Chesapeake Bay, home of Virginia's tobacco ports and the destination of the *Oliver*. As they proceeded northward, the passengers noticed it was getting colder and colder by the day.

What's known about the movement of the ship in the final week of the voyage comes from a deposition given by two crewmen, George Brooks and Robert Hughson, to Rhode Island officials shortly after the wreck.[2] They described how the *Princess Augusta* arrived at Cape James (now called Cape Henlopen) at 6:00 p.m. on December 19, "having undergone many extream Difficulties" to get there. The ship lay twelve miles off the coast in sixty feet of water when Brook ordered the crew to drop the stream anchor (a small anchor at the stern).³ The wind was calm but there was a very strong southerly current and swells from the east.

At 11:00 p.m. Brook ordered the anchor raised, and the ship stood to the southwest until 2:00 a.m. on December 20. By then a hard northwest wind had begun to blow — typical of this time of year in Delaware Bay and precisely what William Penn had warned about in his promotional pamphlets. So the crew "wear'd" the ship to the northeast, a maneuver whereby they changed direction by swinging the stern through the wind. It was a way to turn a square rigger in strong winds and rough seas, when tacking was too difficult or dangerous.⁴

Over the next six days, the shorthanded and frostbitten crew battled high winds and heavy seas. The fierce conditions forced them to cut away their mizzen mast, pulled loose several planks two to three inches from the square of the stern, and pushed the ship hundreds of miles up the Atlantic seaboard. During that time, the ship was "Scant of Provisions," and the crew were "very weak handed by the Death of half of their Hands and the excessive Cold the Rest endured that Some were Frozen and rendered almost incapable of lending any Assistance yet notwithstanding all these and many other exceeding great Difficulties, He, the said Andrew Brook, endeavoured by his utmost Skill & Strength to gain his said Port."⁵

Below decks the Palatines lay motionless in their filthy beds. Christmas Day, which the Lutherans typically marked with hymns and a reading of the nativity story in the Gospel of Matthew, passed by in silence.

At 8:00 a.m. on December 26, the ship was about seven miles southeast of the eastern end of Long Island, "the weather still continuing Bad [with] Cold violent Winds, Snow Storms & the Like." Desperate for water, the crew searched the hold and found several casks with "scarce one gallon in them." Taking stock of the situation — the unrelenting weather, the number and dire condition of the "poor Souls on board," and especially the lack of water — Brook and his crew decided to try for Rhode Island, about twenty-five miles away.⁶

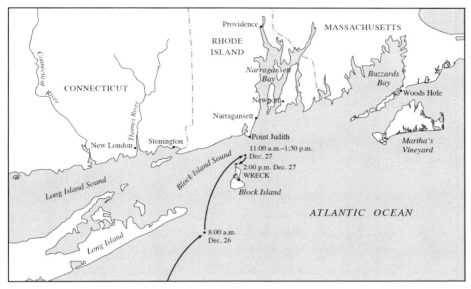

The final hours of the voyage.
Map: Patti Isaacs, 45th Parallel Maps and Infographics

The "thick Weather" continued through the night and into the morning of December 27, during which time the *Princess Augusta* entered Block Island Sound. By 11:00 a.m., however, the weather had cleared a little and Point Judith, a small fishing village along Rhode Island's southern coastline, was visible four to five miles to the northeast. Brook ordered the ship's flag hoisted to the main top-mast shrouds, signaling the ship was in distress. The *Princess Augusta* lay to under topsails for about an hour and a half, but no help came. Finally, Brook called all hands to the stern and persuaded them to try again for Philadelphia — to which they all agreed — and if the wind took them short, they would try for New York or Rhode Island again, "For they could not possibly hold on any longer."[7]

By this time the weather had turned foul again and the ship was caught in the middle of a squall. With a wind from the northeast, the *Princess Augusta* steered away to the southwest to pass between

Block Island and Long Island. But "it was so exceeding thick of Snow" that Brook could not see more than three times the length of the ship. Then, at about 2:00 p.m., Brook "saw Something loom as a cloud"— probably the 100-foot-tall clay bluffs along the northeast coast of Block Island. He ordered the helm hard to port, but it was too late. The *Princess Augusta* slammed into a submerged sandbar that extended a mile and a half from the northern end of the island. The ship remained "stuck fast" for two hours. As the tide rose, she "justl'd off" but did not travel more than a hundred yards before striking again. This time an eight-foot plank peeled from the hull and was driven into the sand; frigid seawater rushed in.[8]

That was the crew's testimony, but it may not be the whole story. Several months after the wreck, Caspar Wistar wrote a letter to Georg Friedrich Hölzer, relaying another version probably told to him by Conrath Gehr and other survivors. Wistar wrote that Brook had deliberately prolonged the voyage in order to extort money from the passengers: "After the captain's death the helmsman took charge, a rascal who tormented those poor people and afflicted them with more misery, sailing back and forth close to land, in order to suck up the last money they still had." Wistar described how, with no water to drink, Brook sold them half measures of wine and brandy for exorbitant sums. "From Plymouth," he continued, "they sailed for 14 weeks and were close to an island by the name of Roth Island, where they ran aground at a place called Black Island at 3 PM."[9]

With no water left on board, it made sense for Brook to ration wine and brandy. Perhaps he used the opportunity to try to recoup some of the revenue lost from missed trading opportunities and the death of passengers who still owed part of their fare. But it is unlikely that he purposely delayed the voyage, given the physical danger to himself, his crew, and the ship — not to mention the financial risks. By contract, he would not have been paid by the Hope firm if the ship wrecked before the passengers landed in Philadelphia. And if Brook didn't get paid, neither would his crew.

Curiously, the mariners' deposition after the wreck doesn't mention that the Delaware River had been frozen when the *Princess*

Augusta reached Delaware Bay. No ships could enter or leave the port of Philadelphia from December 18 to January 25.[10] This was not unusual, however, as Philadelphia was located 100 miles inland on a tidal river, which made it more prone to freezing than ports like Boston and New York, which were located on the coast. (During the winter of 1732–33, the port of Philadelphia was closed from late November to early March due to a fifteen-inch-thick layer of ice on the river.) Had Brook headed straight to Philadelphia instead of stopping in Charleston, he might have arrived on the Delaware River before it froze.

The real mystery, then, is not who or what caused the ship to run aground on Block Island, but what happened during the two to three weeks prior. Why did Brook stop in Charleston, and what happened there? Why didn't Wistar mention the stop in his April 6 letter? Did Brook know the Delaware was frozen, and was he "sailing back and forth close to land" hoping for a thaw? And if Brook had taken on a load of lignum vitae in Charleston, why not water too?

Without additional evidence, we can only guess at what transpired aboard the ship as it was driven up the Atlantic coast by furious winds and seas. But taken together, the crew's deposition, the Lohrman letter, and the Wistar letter prove that the ship was never lured to Block Island by a false light, or abandoned and set adrift by the crew. The ship simply struck the shore, violently and unexpectedly, and in two days' time was no more.

CHAPTER NINE

Rescue and Recovery

The shoreline where the *Princess Augusta* went aground originated some 20,000 years ago, when a glacier covering half of North America began to melt and recede. A rise in sea level turned a pile of gravel, sand, and clay into an island; coastal erosion then gave that island its distinctive pear shape. Along its broad southern coastline are towering bluffs that bear the brunt of the open Atlantic's powerful blows. Sediment knocked loose from the bluffs is carried by currents up the west side of the island, then deposited at the northern end, called Sandy Point.

Over thousands of years, this geologic process has created an underwater sandbar that extends a mile and a half into Block Island Sound. During the eighteenth century, a hummock — a low, scrub-covered mound — sat at the end of it and could be reached on foot at low tide. (Once a popular picnic site, the feature has since washed away.) This sandbar has long been a menace to shipping. Its position shifts slightly from year to year, and its depth changes frequently. What's more, the sides of the sandbar are unusually steep, which means that even if Captain Brook had taken frequent soundings, he would not have known of its presence until he was upon it.[1]

The islanders were not surprised to learn that a ship had grounded there in a snowstorm. What caught them off guard was the large number of passengers on board — around 100, it appeared — and their desperate state of health. The 300 or so residents of Block Island, hunkered down for winter with just enough food and drink to last until spring, and cut off periodically from the mainland because of rough winter seas, were not prepared to handle a humanitarian crisis of this scale.

The most detailed account of the rescue and recovery comes from a letter to the editor of the *Boston Gazette*, written by a committee of islanders led by head warden Simon Ray. The letter was penned in early March 1739, more than two months after the wreck, and was intended to counter negative reports of the islanders' behavior that had previously appeared in local papers. This account, along with Caspar Wistar's April 6 letter to Georg Friedrich Hölzer, provides a timeline of events in the hours and days immediately following the wreck.[2]

In the late afternoon of December 27, after the ship had grounded for the second time, Captain Andrew Brook went ashore to find help. There were no houses near the spot where the vessel was stranded, so Brook had to trudge through snow-covered sand dunes to find someone who could assist them.

Brook was fortunate enough to encounter Simon Ray, the island's respected leader. Though Ray's home was six miles away, he, like other residents, owned multiple parcels of land scattered about the island. Several of Ray's plots were located on Corn Neck, which is probably where Brook stumbled across him. The captain and the warden hurried back to the ship, mustering as many men and horses as they could along the way.

The ship must have come to rest fairly close to shore, where the sandbar was still exposed, for when the rescue party reached the scene, wrote the committee, they found the ship's bowsprit jutting over land. Ray believed the ship would float off on her own with the rising tide, but Brook disagreed. He told Ray that a plank from the

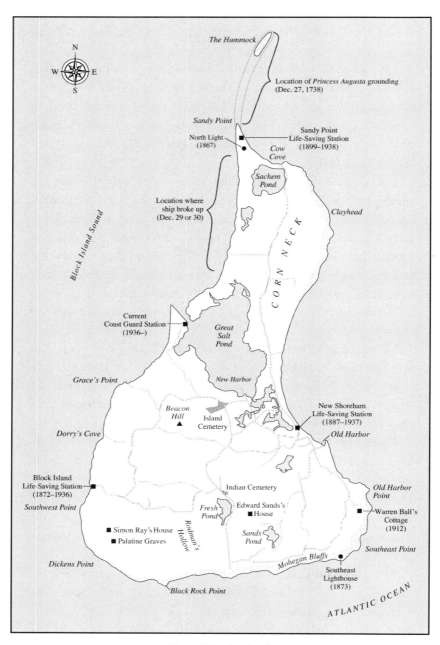

Map of Block Island.
Map: Patti Isaacs, 45th Parallel Maps and Infographics

bottom had been driven into the sand, and the ship's hold was full of water. Nevertheless, Ray advised Brook to drop the sheet anchor (the largest and heaviest on the ship), so that the *Princess Augusta* would not float off with all the passengers' belongings. After repeated appeals, Brook complied.

Considering the lives and personal property at risk, Brook was remarkably uncooperative. He refused to help Ray and his men move the passengers and their belongings to safety, instead using those precious first hours to unload his own chests and those of his sailors. What's more, he refused to break into the ship's store of bread to feed the hungry passengers, even though he admitted to having 15,000 pounds of hardtack on board.

That day, without any help from Brook or his crew, the islanders got most of the Palatines off the ship. Removing them was no easy task. The ship had grounded in an area of notoriously rough surf. During storms, waves from opposite directions collide over the sandbar, shooting water straight up in the air like a geyser. And the same longshore current that feeds the bar also produces dangerous riptides. Even today people are warned not to swim there. "But the greatest Difficulty," wrote Ray's committee, "was in transporting those Objects of Pity, carrying some in Blankets, some on Mens backs, others on Horses (the Snow being deep) to two Cottages, a Mile from the Ship, the most of those People being sick, froze and almost starved."

The cottages on Corn Neck, used by farmers and their slaves during the growing season, were probably unoccupied at the time. But at least they would provide the castaways with temporary shelter against the bitter wind. The closest inhabitants lived at least four miles from the wreck site, in the center of the island.

It was just a week past the winter solstice, so much of the rescue work on that first day took place in the dark. Temperatures plunged after sunset, and there were no trees or buildings at Sandy Point to block the wind. The islanders undoubtedly built a bonfire on the beach, fueled by the large pieces of driftwood and mounds of seaweed that frequently wash up there, and perhaps some wooden parts of the *Princess Augusta* herself, such as the bedsteads. According to Ray, two women froze to death on the beach before the islanders could carry them to safety. Wistar claimed the number was eight.[3] We don't know which figure is correct or of any reasons for the discrepancy.

The next day, the islanders returned to the beach and waited for Brook to come ashore. Once again Simon Ray and the islanders pleaded with the captain "to have Compassion on those distressed Objects" and give them bread — the Palatines hadn't eaten in two days — and to help carry their chests from the damaged ship. Brook told the islanders he could not spare the ship's longboat or any of his crew because he needed them to save the ship's tackle. Even more galling, Brook had solicited the help of some island men for this task. Ray and his companions volunteered to unload the chests themselves, but Brook dismissed their offer, leaving the passengers' belongings on board for the time being. No doubt Brook was aware that it was customary for ship captains to take over the chests of the deceased who had no survivors on board: that was how they ensured that the dead paid their debts.

It was probably on this day that the Palatines were moved from the cottages on Corn Neck to larger quarters. Some were taken to Simon Ray's house, at the other end of the island, where he lived with his wife and four daughters (ages five to twelve at the time), along with several slaves. Although Ray was one of the island's leading citizens — his father had been one of the sixteen original settlers — according to Livermore, his "dwelling was unpretentious."[4]

Other passengers recovered at the farmhouse of forty-seven-year-old Edward Sands, who hailed from another well-respected family. Sands's grandfather, James, said to have been the wealthiest man on the island, also was one of the original settlers. Edward Sands's house was located about halfway between Fresh Pond and Sands Pond, in the southeastern part of the island.[5]

That night, for reasons known only to him, Brook ordered the anchor raised, and the ship floated off with the tide, just as Ray had suspected it would.

The following morning, December 29, Ray and his men returned to the wreck site to find the *Princess Augusta* adrift in the sound, with all of the Palatines' goods and money — and reportedly two passengers — still on board.[6] At this point a group of islanders decided to take matters into their own hands. They rowed out to the ship and removed twenty chests, which were then "brought on shore and housed."

According to Wistar, some of the passengers also returned to the ship on December 29 to retrieve their belongings. "[A]fter they had done so for several hours there was a bad storm, which shattered the ship into pieces, and that large ship was smashed into small pieces within three hours. Everything sunk and was destroyed," he wrote, "not including the chests which belonged to Conrath Gehr, and several others that weren't on board." Ray reported the ship was "stove to pieces" on December 30, when a hard west wind blew it ashore on the west side of the island. The Palatines' goods were dumped into the surf, and a considerable amount washed up on the beach "much damnified."

Officials on the island tried to safeguard these goods for their rightful owners, but "many clandestine Actions were done," admitted Ray. Some islanders may have been looting, but others were staking claims. Maritime law dictated that those on land who helped salvage equipment and cargo from a shipwreck were entitled to a share — usually one-third — of what they saved. While technically legal, such behavior struck some as immoral in this case, and so a constable was appointed to seize the coveted goods. As it turned out, he too succumbed to temptation but was caught and his dereliction of duty exposed.

Appalled by the crew's neglect of the Palatines and the mishandling of property by both crew and islanders, on January 1 a witness to the scene wrote an anonymous letter to Governor John Wanton in Newport. A synopsis of the letter appeared in the January 15 issue of the *Boston Post-Boy*.[7] Curiously, the article does not identify the ship by name, though it provided many other details, such as the size and value of the vessel, its origin and destination, the identity of the deceased captain, the total number of passengers (340) along with their economic status, the death toll on the island thus far (20), and the number that survived (85). More to the point, it exposed the acting captain's callous disregard for the Palatines and the theft of their property by some islanders. According to the article,

> [Captain Brook] being often desired by some of the Gentlemen of the Island, to suffer the Passengers to take their Goods out of the Ship, he absolutely refused it; tho' many of them saved their Silver and Gold: Tho' all possible Means were used to prevent clandestine Actions, many have lost by Extortion and other ways, a great Part of the little which they saved.
>
> After the Ship broke to pieces there were abundance of Goods came ashore, but the Owners cannot have any of them, without paying a third Salvage, besides which a great Part of them are confiscated, together with great Quantities of Silver and Gold: In short, Tongue and Pen cannot relate the present Circumstances of the poor Palatines, whose Number is said to be but only 85 Persons.

The sixty-six-year-old Governor Wanton acted quickly. A stretch of clear weather and a break in the cold enabled him to send two magistrates to the island within days of receiving the letter, to "see how Matters are, that those poor People may have Justice done them."[8]

Wanton's men returned to Newport on the evening of January 16 and submitted their findings to the governor. A summary of the report appeared the following week in four of Boston's five newspapers.[9] Again the ship was not named, but the article does describe one reason the Palatines gave for leaving their homeland.

> [The ship] being chiefly owned by Persons belonging to Ramsgate in England, and Commanded by *George Long*, left Plymouth sometime in August last, bound for Philadelphia, with about four hundred Palatines on board which they took in at Rotterdam, that an exceeding bad Feavour and Flux prevail'd among them, that but about one hundred and five were landed upon Block Island, and

that since their arrival there, their illness continuing, the number is reduced to about ninety; Capt. *Long* with several of the Mariners dyed on the Passage, the chiefest reason assigned for so great a Mortality, is the badness of their Water taken in at Rotterdam in Cask[s] that had before contain'd white and red Wines; the Hull of the Ship (which had no Cargo in belonging to the Owners of her) together with the chiefest part of the Goods of the Palatines are entirely lost in the Sea, great care has been taken by the Authority that what is saved may be secured for the benefit of those Surviving distress'd People, many of whom it is said left their Country purely to enjoy there Religious Priviledges in *America*.

The Palatines' stated reason for moving to America is curious, given that most German-speaking emigrants of this time left home not because of religious persecution, but because of political oppression, economic uncertainty, and the constant threats of war and disease. The Dieters and their friends, for example, all belonged to Schwaigern's Lutheran church, which was the tallest building in the village. Characterizing themselves as religious refugees, however, would have struck a chord with Governor Wanton and Simon Ray, two men with a strong religious bent.

As a Massachusetts-born Quaker, Wanton understood what it meant to be persecuted for one's faith. His father, Edward, had witnessed the execution of Quaker Mary Dyer on Boston Common in 1660. In fact, Dyer's stoicism had inspired Edward Wanton to join the Society of Friends. In the late 1600s, his sons John and William moved to Newport, Rhode Island, a city with a large Quaker population in a colony founded by Quaker exile Roger Williams. John became a successful merchant, embarked on a long and distinguished career in government, and, like his father, developed into a gifted preacher.[10] Known for his oratorical skills, which drew large crowds and attracted converts, John Wanton traveled as a missionary throughout New England and Pennsylvania, the Quaker stronghold to which the Palatines had been headed before they wrecked.

Simon Ray was not a Quaker, but he was married to the granddaughter of Roger Williams, with whom his father had been close friends.[11] Like his father, the younger Ray was Anabaptist. Both men had served as Block Island's lay preacher, as there had been no clergyman living on the island for quite some time. According to Livermore, both men had held nondenominational services in their home "on Lord's days, to pray, sing a suitable portion of the Psalms, and read in good sermon books, and, as they found occasion, to let drop some words of exhortation in a religious manner on such as attended their meeting."[12] Further evidence of Ray's interest in the spiritual appears in his correspondence with one of Boston's leading ministers at the time, Benjamin Colman, about the state of religion on the island, particularly among the Native Americans.[13]

If citing religion as the reason for their migration was stretching the truth, it was a prudent move on the part of the Palatines. Wanton's magistrates and the island's officers came up with a prompt solution for handling the passengers' scattered property. Salvaged goods were to be used to defray the costs of housing and feeding the Palatines on the island; anything that was left over would be divided equally among the survivors. All islanders suspected of looting the passengers' possessions were to take an oath that they would return the stolen goods, and the authorities were to make sure that no castaways suffered from extortion.

There may have been another reason for Wanton's prompt attention to the Palatine matter as well. As a wealthy Quaker merchant in the fifth-largest city in America, he very likely had business and personal ties to Quaker merchants in Philadelphia, some of whom were involved in the Palatine trade.[14] Wanton may have known Benjamin Shoemaker, to whom the *Princess Augusta* was consigned; or Caspar Wistar, who had merchandise on board the ship. He may even have known Archibald Hope in Rotterdam, who had chartered the ship. All of these men were Quakers. Wanton also owned land in Pennsylvania. He had inherited it from his father, who had been close friends with Philadelphia merchant Edward Shippen, also a Quaker. Quakers had a reputation for honesty in their business dealings, and a sense of moral obligation to help the castaways on Block Island likely extended to Wanton's Quaker friends and associates in Philadelphia as well.

While the governor's men were conducting their investigation on Block Island, the crew of the *Princess Augusta* were giving their depositions. On January 11, George Brooks and Robert Hughson were deposed by Simon Ray as to the cause of the wreck. Captain Brook appeared before Ray on the following day to give his "statement of sea protest," as required by maritime law. This quaint-sounding formality, still required today, is a notarized statement made by the captain upon entering port, declaring rough weather as the cause of any damage that has occurred to the ship or its cargo. Brook swore that "Notwithstanding the great Care and Diligence used by him (which he exerted to the Utmost of his Strength & skill) to perform the Voyage aforesaid the said Ship was misfortunately by the foulness of the Wind & Weather, It being an exceedingly thick Snow Storm drove on Shore on this Island on the 27th day of this instant about 2 of the Clock P. M. On which Island notwithstanding his greatest Care and Pains She was wreck'd."[15]

The captain and crew's sworn statements would normally have been delivered to a public notary right away, but the nearest office was located in Newport, and a storm of rain and snow on January 11 and 12 prevented the men from sailing there. Ray noted that "the weather being so extream hard That it is impracticable for Boats to pass and no Likelihood for any Alteration thereof for the Better."[16]

Brook and his men finally did reach Newport at about three o'clock on January 27, one month after the wreck. They handed their signed depositions to notary James Martin, who entered them into the public record book, along with a statement declaring that: "the Boisterous Winds & Seas, the thick Snow Storms & Extremity of Cold [were] the Cause of the said Ship Princess Augusta running a Shore upon said New Shoram alias Block Island."[17] Incidentally, these depositions are the only documents that identify the ship by name. Once they had been filed away, her name was forgotten. Until the documents were unearthed 200 years later, in 1939, she would be known simply as the Palatine ship.

As it turned out, Brook and his men had made it to Newport just in time. The next day a "violent Storm of Wind and Snow" hit southern New England, during which a schooner bound from Newport to New York City struck the north end of Block Island, the passengers and crew narrowly escaping with their lives.[18]

One week after the *Princess Augusta* had grounded on Block Island, her previous traveling companion, the *Oliver*, was nearing the Virginia coast. The small and aging ship, now with about 250 survivors aboard, had spent a harrowing sixteen weeks on the Atlantic battling more than a dozen consecutive storms that cost the ship one of its masts. Captain Wright and the first mate had died of the "bloody flux" during the voyage, along with 50 to 60 passengers, most of them children. According to several ships that passed them at sea, the *Oliver* also was running low on food and water.

On January 3, with boatswain Francis Sinclair in command, the ship reached the Virginia capes at the entrance to Chesapeake Bay. The passengers, who hadn't had anything to eat or drink in days, insisted at gunpoint, according to one report,[19] that Sinclair go ashore for provisions. Sinclair dropped anchor in Lynnhaven Bay, an island-strewn inlet four miles west of Cape Henry, and fired several guns to summon a pilot. When none came, he took about twenty-five passengers with him in the ship's longboat and headed to shore, landing on what turned out to be an uninhabited island. That night was one of the coldest of the winter, as a violent northwest wind arose. Unable to return to the ship, most of the party froze to death around a campfire they had built in the woods.

The same wind caused the *Oliver* to break free of one anchor and drag the other. By morning, the ship was stranded near shore, filled with water to the upper deck. Two nearby vessels came to the *Oliver*'s assistance. Newspapers reported that the rescuers found the dead "floating in the Ship like so many Logs of Timber."[20] Of the more than 200 people still on board, 40 to 50 bedridden passengers had drowned between decks. The rescuers managed to ferry the survivors to shore, where 70 of them subsequently froze to death on the beach and in the marshes, for lack of shelter. The 90 who survived were, like the Block Island castaways, taken in by locals and, in time, nursed back to health. Newspapers reported that the ship had been the richest to come to Virginia in twenty years, but most of the *Oliver*'s considerable cargo was lost.[21]

Like the *Princess Augusta*, the *Oliver* might have met a different end had the captain, nearing the ship's final destination, continued onward instead of stopping. A report in the January 19 issue of the *Virginia Gazette* stated that "when the Ship came within the Capes, the Wind was so fair, that if they had kept under Sail, instead of anchoring at Lynnhaven-Bay, they might have been safe at Hampton in about 2 Hours; but the People being almost famish'd, having nothing to eat for several Days, insisted on the Captain's coming to Anchor there, and going ashore to get Provisions." With the cards already stacked against the voyage — overcrowding, disease, the death of the captain and mate, and horrific weather at sea — one bad decision made near the end of the journey sealed the ship's doom.[22]

By the end of January, news of the *Princess Augusta* wreck had appeared in every Boston paper, and reports of fifteen to twenty deaths among "those poor distressed People the Palatines" no doubt stirred the public's memory. In December 1731, only seven years earlier, the Palatine ship *Love and Unity* had arrived unexpectedly at Martha's Vineyard, just forty miles to the east of Block Island. According to the survivors, Captain Lobb and his crew had deliberately withheld food during their prolonged voyage, causing the deaths of two-thirds of the passengers — about a hundred people in all. Lobb was tried for breach of contract and murder in separate trials, but was acquitted on both counts. The captain then sued several Palatine men for defamation of character and for reimbursement of his court costs. Unable to post bond, the Palatines were sent to jail. Although they were soon found not guilty of slander and released, their ordeal on Martha's Vineyard took nearly a year to resolve and was covered extensively by both Boston and Philadelphia newspapers.[23]

Now German emigrants were once again in dire straits on New England's shores. Moved by the plight of the shipwrecked Palatines, the Reverend Benjamin Colman of the Brattle Street Church in Boston sent a letter to Governor Wanton, offering a generous sum of money to help support the survivors.

> Ye account our newspapers give us of ye miserable Circumstances of ye poor Palatines, cast away on Block Island, moves me to let your Honour know, that if there be not enof saved out of ye Wreck to give them a Competency for their present Subsistence, and barring disposing of themselves into some Way of Business; & it appears to your Honour that they need our Help, I have Moneys in my Hand to ye Value of one hundred pounds, which shal be paid there to your Honours Order; in the Distribution whereof I entrust your Honour to desire ye faithful advice of Mr. Raye of Block Island, who is I think a principal Gentleman there & with whom I have had some correspondence in ye matter of introducing ye Preaching of Gods Word in that Island.[24]

One wealthy Boston merchant, Peter Faneuil, went even further in his efforts to help the survivors. In 1731, some Bostonians had housed passengers from the *Love and Unity*; now Faneuil took into his care two women from the *Princess Augusta*. It's not known who these women were or how the arrangement came about, but Faneuil certainly had contacts in both Newport and Philadelphia. After inheriting his uncle's estate, the bachelor had recently become one of the richest men in America, and there would have been plenty of room in his Beacon Street mansion to put up several strangers for a time.

By early February, the Block Island incident was no longer a local story. Word of the wreck had traveled south, appearing in the *New York Gazette*, the *New York Weekly Journal*, the *Pennsylvania Ga-*

zette, and Philadelphia's *American Weekly Mercury*. The *Virginia Gazette* in Williamsburg picked up the story in March. It was then that Simon Ray and the other officials decided to let the public know of the difficulties the Block Islanders had faced during the disaster, and of the extraordinary lengths they had gone to in order to save the castaways. On March 2 they sent the lengthy letter to the *Boston Gazette* mentioned earlier in this chapter. "I pray you to insert the following Account into your next," the islanders wrote, "Those on the Spot being best capable to relate the Affair, that the World may judge whether said Officers discharged their Duty."

The men recounted the harrowing events of the first four days: how the islanders begged Captain Brook to help get the passengers off the ship and to feed them from the ship's stores (which he refused to do), and how Brook "had more regard to the saving said Tackling &c. than in saving the Palatines Goods." They admitted that some islanders had taken part in "clandestine Actions" and "Insolences," but added that the island's officers had "made it their chief Business, to see the distressed provided for, and that no Injustice or Extortion be done to them."[25]

There were a total of eleven newspapers published in the American colonies at the time, and all but the *South-Carolina Gazette* reported on the wreck. Only two — the *Boston Gazette* and the *New York Gazette* — carried the committee's letter, however, which meant that most Americans did not hear the islanders' side of the story.

The *Princess Augusta* disaster received more press coverage than almost any other maritime disaster of its time. Most of the reporting appears to have been based on information supplied by participants in the voyage, rescue, or recovery, and yet many discrepancies remain. For example, evidence shows the ship left Plymouth in the latter half of September, yet Boston newspapers reported it had left in August. Also in question was the actual number of passengers on board. The anonymous letter sent to Governor Wanton stated that the ship had left Europe with 340 Palatines on board. The governor's magistrates reported there had been 400 in all. While eighteenth-century newspapers were notoriously inaccurate, it is possible that both numbers are correct: the former figure may represent the number of *full freights* listed in the ship's manifest, and the latter the actual number of *people*. Caspar Wistar's count was higher still. He told his business partner that of "92 [landed] there were only 62 people alive of the *total sum of 600.*"[26] Certainly that last number is mistaken, but if the previous two are correct, then there were a third more deaths on the island than reported in the newspapers.[27]

In addition to questions of fact, there are questions of motive. Why, for example, did Captain Brook refuse to feed the Palatines when he had so much bread on board? Newspapers suggested that he was reluctant to "break bulk," which means to open a sealed container. Why was his first priority saving the ship's gear rather than unloading the passengers and their belongings? And why did he let the ship drift off with all of the Palatines' chests still on board?

Perhaps the best explanation for Brook's behavior is that he was trying to mitigate the catastrophic financial loss of the voyage. The Hope firm's charterparty with George Long stipulated that if the ship wrecked and failed to land the passengers in Philadelphia, the captain would not be paid. Brook may have hoped to sell the bread, the ship's tackle, and anything else not nailed down, in order to pay his crew. He may have held on to the passengers' chests as collateral against unpaid fares and other outstanding shipboard expenses — a perfectly legal and standard practice in the Palatine trade.

In the months after the wreck, Brook needed to salvage his reputation as well. By February, reports of the wreck had appeared in London newspapers; a notice appeared in early May in Brook's hometown paper, the *Kentish Post*.[28] After such a disaster, how would he ever be given command of another ship? By today's moral standards, Brook's behavior appears to border on criminal negligence, but he had a lot of people to answer to back in Europe: the Hope firm, shipowners Austen and Redwood, and George Long's widow.

Questions also surround the islanders' conduct. How widespread was the looting? Who wrote the anonymous letter to Governor Wanton, and what did the author mean when he or she said many Palatines had lost property through "Extortion and other ways"?

And finally, what did the Palatines think of how the authorities disposed of their property, having already lost much of it through shipwreck and theft? Did they consider "Justice done"?

These questions may never be answered, but at least two key elements of the wreck's legend can now be laid to rest. Although it's probably true that the Palatines lost property by the "clandestine Actions" of some islanders, there is no evidence that the castaways were physically harmed or left to die. On the contrary, the survivors were taken in by Block Island's small community of farmers and fishermen, who did their best under the worst of circumstances — and at their own peril — to nurse them back to health. We also know that the ship was not destroyed by fire. Bed boards, furniture, and wooden crates may have been taken from the grounded vessel and used to build a bonfire during the rescue, and no doubt some timbers were salvaged after the ship broke apart. But the fact of the matter is that the *Princess Augusta* met her end not by flame but by wind, water, and earth.

Most of the Palatine deaths on Block Island occurred within the first few days after the grounding. The cold front that had moved into southern New England on the afternoon of the wreck would last for almost ten days. By January 8, however, the weather had turned "fair & Warm for the Season," melting the snow cover and allowing for the ground to be broken.[29]

Simon Ray owned a large tract in the southwest corner of the island, overlooking the sea. The dead were buried in a mass grave at the edge of Ray's farm, about 400 yards southeast of his house.[30] (Tradition states that there were actually two gravesites, one long since destroyed by the plow.) In 1947, a granite monument was commissioned to mark the final resting place; it reads, simply, "Palatine Graves." Located on private property at the end of a maze of dirt

The monument that marks the location of the Palatine
graves on Block Island. Photograph: Jill Farinelli

roads, it is almost impossible to find without a guide. The names of
the dead, like so much other knowledge, have been lost to history.
In fact, nobody knows precisely how many bodies lie beneath the
grass-covered mound, but Wistar's figure of thirty dead could be
the most accurate.

In the March 19, 1739, issue of the *Boston Post-Boy*, the following item appeared in the (Newport) Rhode Island Customs House
news: "Last Wednesday arrived here between Fifty and Sixty Palatines from Block Island, viz. Men, Women and Children, who sail
for Philadelphia with the first fair Wind."[31]

CHAPTER TEN

On to Pennsylvania

ost of the survivors left Block Island on the evening of March 14, just hours before "a very great Storm of Wind and Rain" swept across southern New England. This latest gale — the fifth that winter — produced heavy seas and caused extensive damage to the wharves in Boston.[1] During the two-and-a-half months the castaways had spent recovering from their ordeal, two more vessels had wrecked on the island. The second occurred just a week earlier in March, when a sloop from the West Indies, laden with rum and molasses, was cast away in a snowstorm and lost most of her cargo.[2]

Conrath Gehr and Elisabetha Gebert were among the sixty or so Palatines who were ferried across Block Island Sound to Newport, where arrangements had been made for two sloops to transport them to Philadelphia. Ships were passing freely on the Delaware again after a winter so brutally cold that the river had been frozen on and off for seven weeks, shutting down traffic throughout most of December and January.[3] Coastal trade between Newport and Philadelphia had since resumed, with one- and two-masted cargo vessels shuttling freight, mail, and passengers between the two cities.

The Palatines spent about a week in Newport, a community of around 6,000 people, located at the entrance to Narragansett Bay. On the evening of March 20, thirty of the survivors left for Philadelphia. Around thirty more left on a cold and rainy evening two days later. Boston newspapers reported their departure, but not the names of the ships they traveled on.[4] In its March 29 issue, however, the *Pennsylvania Gazette* announced the arrival that week of two sloops from Rhode Island: the *King's Fisher*, under the command of Joseph Worth, and the *Martha*, under Captain Edward Barker. These may have been the vessels that finally delivered the Palatines to their original destination.

It would have taken the sloops several days to reach Cape James (now Henlopen) and Cape May, the two capes that mark the entrance to Delaware Bay. Fifty miles inland, the bay narrows to less than three miles wide, a point that mariners consider to be the mouth of the Delaware River. The sloops had to travel another fifty miles upstream to reach the port of Philadelphia.

For the large Palatine ships that arrived each fall, this last part of the journey could be hazardous. The bay is strewn with dozens of sandbanks, some more than ten miles long, and river travel is impeded by shoals, shallows, and islands. There was no accurate chart of the waterway until the mid-1700s, so the heavily laden immigrant ships had to rely on a local pilot to navigate the hazards.[5] Even with a pilot, it sometimes took deep-ocean vessels eight to ten days to complete this final leg. The sloops carrying the Block Island Palatines, however, would have crossed the bay and sailed upriver to Philadelphia in just a couple of days, and probably without a pilot. Like the Rhine River craft, such sloops were easier to navigate in shallow water, and Captains Worth and Barker were familiar with the route from their repeated voyages between Rhode Island and Pennsylvania.

The survivors arrived in Philadelphia to a crowded, chaotic waterfront lined with shipyards, private wharves, warehouses, and wholesale stores. By 1739, the "greene Country Towne" envisioned by Penn in 1682 had become the third-largest city in the American

colonies, and one of the largest in the British Empire. Its growth
and prosperity were a direct result of its location on a major waterway. The Delaware River was narrow but deep at this spot, perfect
for anchoring large ships close to shore. With more than 200 vessels clearing port every year for coastal and international destinations, many of the city's 10,000 residents worked in the shipbuilding
trades or were engaged in maritime commerce.

Penn had laid out his town in a neat grid, with generously sized
house lots and space set aside for public parks. A wide avenue
named High Street (today's Market Street) ran west from the riverbank through the center of town. This was where the courthouse
and the market stalls were located, and where prominent residents
like Casper Wistar, Benjamin Shoemaker, and Benjamin Franklin lived. While many of the private residences were constructed
of brick or stone in the elegant Georgian style, the city as a whole
was becoming increasingly crowded and dirty, especially along the
waterfront.

The landing experience of the Block Island Palatines was nothing
like that of the Palatines who arrived in the fall, with the rest of
the fleet. There was none of the fanfare that normally attended the
entrance of a large and crowded immigrant ship in port. No one
would have rowed out to meet them with apples, peaches, beer, and
fresh bread. There was no cannon fire announcing their arrival, and
no crowd at the docks looking to buy servants, rent rooms, or sell
food, drink, and wares to the newcomers.

However, the stragglers from Rhode Island also were likely to
have escaped the tedious administrative procedures that Palatines
were normally subject to. There was probably no customs inspection of their meager belongings, no quarantine by health inspectors
a mile outside of the city, and no march to the courthouse to take
the oath of allegiance.[6] (From a historian's perspective, that last
omission is indeed unfortunate, because an oath of allegiance list
can be used to partly reconstruct a ship's passenger list.)

Had the *Princess Augusta* actually made it to Philadelphia, the
ship would have been met by Benjamin Shoemaker, the consign-

ment agent hired by the Hope firm to receive the ship in port and "dispose" of its cargo. His most important task would have been to settle passengers' accounts — that is, to collect unpaid fares and sell into indentured servitude those passengers who could not pay their debts.[7] It's not clear what Shoemaker's role would have been in 1739, with the *Princess Augusta* destroyed and most of her passengers dead. (The whereabouts of Captain Brook and his men at this point is not known.)

The merchant may have wanted to wash his hands of the entire deal. In fact, he was still trying to collect unpaid fares from voyages dating as far back as 1735, and some of the passengers from the 1736 voyage of the *Princess Augusta* still owed him money. It was very difficult to collect debts once passengers had left the ship, and debtors could scarcely be kept on board forever. At some point, sick and unsold passengers needed to be cleared so cargo could be loaded for the next voyage.

Peter Lohrman, the former Schwaigern resident, was at the waterfront when the sloops arrived. He had ridden from his farm in Germantown when he heard the vessels were coming up the river. In early February, Lohrman and his wife had read with horror about the wreck in the *Pennsylvania Gazette* — about the great loss of life at sea and the disturbing events that had taken place on the island. If the Lohrmans weren't already aware of the fates of their friends and family on board the *Princess Augusta*, they were about to find out. Of the group of fourteen from Schwaigern, only Jerg Gebert's wife, Elisabetha, had survived. The Lohrmans' nephew, Sebastian Dieter, his wife, and three children had all perished.

Lohrman would see to it that his nephew's estate — or what was left of it — was properly settled. There was no will to probate, though it's unlikely Dieter had left home without one, given his wealth and marital status, and the fact that immigrants were urged to write wills before embarking on their journey to America. The document probably went down with the ship.

On April 3, 1739, the Register-General of Pennsylvania granted a joint "letters of administration" to Lohrman's son-in-law, Martin

Schwartz, and three other trustworthy men. This document gave them legal authority to administer Dieter's estate in the absence of a will. The four men were required to post bond in the amount of £100 as a guarantee they would make an honest and thorough inventory of what remained of Dieter's assets. Sadly, there wasn't much: one chest, three kettles, an iron pot and pan, one bed (probably the coarse linen feather mattress listed in his estate inventory in Schwaigern), two hats, and some "trumperies" (knickknacks of little value). His personal effects were appraised at just over 4 pounds, or about 28 florins.[8] Before leaving Germany, his estate had been valued at 500 florins, after taxes.

The surviving items — cookware and bedding — were the kinds of household objects emigrants kept at their bunks for use during the voyage. Perhaps they survived because they were accessible and easy to carry off after the ship's grounding. The rest of the family's property, which had been stored in the ship's hold, either sank during the wreck, was damaged beyond use, was confiscated by Block Island authorities to pay for the Palatines' keep, or was spirited away by some of the islanders.

In October of that year, Lohrman wrote a letter to friends and family in Schwaigern, relating the fate of the town's former residents who had traveled on board the doomed ship: "First about the Bastian Diethers, they left in an unlucky year, barely a third of the shipload remained alive. Bastian, his wife and children, Marcell Schneider with wife and children, Stophel Schaber, Jerg Gebert — of all those only Jerg Gebert's wife is still living."[9]

Lohrman wrote that the captain, "that rogue," brought the ship to "Karlin" and then to "RotEÿland." He noted that the ship sank two days after the wreck and everything on it was lost, and that the castaways arrived in Philadelphia the following year.[10]

So what would become of Elisabetha Gebert, now that her husband, their little boy, and their friends and traveling companions were all dead? Perhaps she stayed for a time in Germantown, either with the Lohrmans or with some other Schwaigern transplants. After that, she might have moved to Virginia, where her husband's brothers lived. Or she might have settled permanently in the Philadelphia area and bound herself out to a local family. She likely remarried and raised another family, perhaps finding some peace after such a horrifying ordeal. If she started life over under a new name, however, this all but ensures that historians will never trace her.

Conrath Gehr not only survived the voyage, he managed to save the chests he had been hired to deliver to Caspar Wistar in Philadelphia. While he and the other castaways recovered on Block Island, news of the shipwreck spread quickly via newspapers and word of mouth. Information about the ship's fate — and the high death toll on other Palatine ships that season — also made its way back to Europe via the returning fleet.

On March 21, 1739, Hölzer wrote to Wistar, telling him that those in the homeland had heard of the illness and death that had devastated the previous year's Palatine fleet. People were so frightened by the news that few would be traveling to America this year. "I'm deeply saddened by the fact that so many people lost their lives in such a miserable way," he wrote to his friend in Philadelphia.[11] He had been told about the wreck of the *Princess Augusta* by a local Neckar boatman, who had heard of it from a returning newlander. According to Hölzer, "the ship Conrath Geer was on, with Captain Lang at the helm, was involved in the Accident, and that it was located not far from Rood Island, at a distance of 150 [?] from Philadelphia, and broke up on a sand bar. And although several people were saved, all of the wares sank."

At this point Hölzer was under the impression that all of their merchandise had been destroyed in the wreck. In his letter to Wistar, he lamented the financial losses that the two men had just suffered, which totaled 497 gulden (florins). He explained that his wares had been packaged together with Wistar's guns, and that some additional items for Wistar's brother-in-law, Georg Hüttner, had been included as well. "I wouldn't have thought things would turn out so badly for Captain Lang," he added. "Well, the Lord has given, the Lord has taken, his name be praised."

The reality of the situation, as revealed in a series of letters Höl-zer and Wistar exchanged in 1739 and 1740, was more complicated. Because transatlantic mail delivery could take up to two months (even longer in wartime), their letters to each other crossed in the mail, and it was more than a year before both men fully understood what had happened to their goods.

Wistar did not receive Hölzer's March 21 letter until July. By then the Philadelphia merchant had already spoken to Gehr, who had arrived in the city in late March with the rest of the Block Island survivors. To Wistar's surprise and delight, he carried with him all of the chests, including the one containing the precious guns. Gehr told Wistar not everything could be saved, however. Some of the goods had been lost in the wreck.

After meeting with Gehr and taking possession of the chests, Wistar wrote a letter to Hölzer, dated April 6. He told his business partner: "As far as Conrath Gerr's journey is concerned, the account on how miserably they fared is appalling." According to Gehr, some of the passengers were already ill when they boarded in Rotterdam, and it took the ship almost three months just to reach the Atlantic. Several weeks out, other passengers began to sicken and die from drinking water that had been stored in wine barrels. Among the dead were Captain "Lang" and six sailors. Gehr said that the helms-man (Brook) then took charge and extorted money from the thirsty passengers by deliberately prolonging the voyage and selling them wine and brandy for exorbitant sums. When the ship grounded on that desolate island, only 92 of 600 were still alive. "These people also experienced a very bad sojourn at that place," wrote Wistar, "as it is a bad place with only few residents, and food and drink are very limited." The number of survivors eventually dwindled to 62, Wistar noted. "It is piteous to listen to those events from beginning to end."[12]

Hölzer responded to this letter almost a year later, on Febru-ary 9, 1740: "I have read in detail about Captain Lange's total ship-wreck, the arrival of Conrath Geer with the guns, and of the loss of the remaining goods, as well as the misery and pitiful condition of our poor countrymen on this ship, and on the other 14 ships.

May God the Lord have mercy on the poor people who remained, and move kind souls to have pity on them."[13] But Hölzer had not yet learned the full truth about Gehr: at some time during the intervening months, the courier had been discovered in Philadelphia with the goods he initially claimed had been lost in the wreck.

By late spring of 1740, Hölzer was in possession of the remaining details of the story. He had received a letter Wistar had written on November 12, 1739, informing him that Gehr had some of Hüttner's property in his possession.[14] Hölzer responded to the news with disgust. On May 21, 1740, he wrote the following to Wistar:

> I was astonished to read how unfairly Conrath Geer is using, and dealing with, the left-over wares. I had expected him to be a better person, compared to what I'm hearing now about him from different people from the New Country. He appears to be a Christian in word only, and an arch-rogue. This wanton man gave your brother-in-law Hüttner some of the wares I had given him to take along, but not the rest. If some of it was lost, the other part should also have been lost, no matter what happened, since everything had been packed in one chest. Of course I'm more than willing to help bear my share of the loss, and in the end this fraudster does not stand to gain much from this.[15]

None of the merchants' subsequent letters mention Gehr or the recovery of the stolen goods, which is surprising given that Gehr remained in the area and did not attempt to keep a low profile. He is believed to have married in 1740 and settled in nearby Germantown, where he operated a public house. Around the same time, Gehr became a follower of the Newborn faith, considered by mainstream Protestant sects to be a cult. On Sundays he turned his tavern into an "assembly of worship" and charged attendees 3 pence each to listen to lectures on "*physic* and natural science." The anti-religious sermons were followed by a round of drinks paid for out of the admission fee.[16]

Gehr's irreverence caught the attention of Henry Melchior Muhlenberg, a prominent traveling Lutheran minister. Reverend Muhlenberg was so taken aback by Gehr's behavior that he wrote about the "poor blasphemer" in his journal. He said overnight lodgers had complained about how Gehr harangued them with talk of a godless, random universe and his view that preachers were paid to lead the masses around by the nose. Perhaps it did not occur to Muhlenberg that Gehr's contempt for religion might have stemmed from his traumatic journey to America — from the scale of human suffering and the futility of prayer that he witnessed at sea. The minister described Gehr as one of those "poor, sinful worms [who] start out in this free land with hot heads and boldness; then they develop quickly in their corruption; and finally they fall into the pit of their own making just so much more the quickly."[17]

And, unfortunately, that seems to be precisely what happened to Gehr. Not long after his tavern lectures were shut down, he became involved in a money-making scheme, was arrested for fraud, and thrown in jail. It's not known how long he was incarcerated, but by then he had several children to support and his mother-in-law had to move in to help out the family. As the story goes, Gehr took to reading the Bible again while in prison.[18] Maybe that was just a cynical ploy, or maybe there was hope for him yet.

And what of the remaining emigrants known to have been connected with the *Princess Augusta?*

The two women taken in by Peter Faneuil in Boston also eventually made it to Philadelphia, after he arranged passage for them on a ship captained by a friend. On April 24, 1740, Faneuil wrote the following letter to Peter Baynton, one of his commercial correspondents in Philadelphia: "This accompanies Capt. Burgess Hall, who carries with him to your parts two unfortunate Palatine women, that were some time ago shipwrecked, in their voyage from Europe to your place, who, being objects of charity, which the providence of God has thrown in our way, I take leave to recommend to you, as such, not doubting you will so far commiserate their condition, as to direct them the nearest way, to get among their friends, with such other relief as you may think necessary."[19]

Michael and Anna Schneider and their two sons — the family

that had become separated from their luggage when they tried to board the *Princess Augusta* in Rotterdam — found passage on another ship that the Hope firm had chartered, the *Adventure Galley.* Originally scheduled to take a load of Palatines to Philadelphia, the ship instead dropped them in London, where they were transferred to the Georgia-bound *Two Brothers.* They arrived on the Savannah River on October 7 and were redeemed by the Salzburger community of Ebenezer, located about twenty-five miles inland. They were not in Pennsylvania, but at least they were alive.

In 1739, the community's pastor, Martin Boltzius, sent a letter to the Schneiders' relatives in Philadelphia, inquiring about their luggage. A reply came on December 30, 1740, which said that the ship — and all the Schneiders' belongings — were lost. That day, Reverend Boltzius recorded in his journal that "most of the German people on the ship had died and that the ship itself, when it came into the vicinity of Rhode Island, went aground, the helmsman and everyone else left aboard had fled, and therefore his trunk had been lost. This Schneider and his wife and children had wanted to go to Pennsylvania on the abovementioned ship; but, because he could not pay even half the passage, they did not accept him. Rather he was finally brought with other German people to this colony by Captain Thomson, and was taken on at his repeated request as cowherd in our congregation."[20]

Although the identities of other *Princess Augusta* survivors remain unknown, their numbers are counted among the estimated 3,410 Palatines who passed through Philadelphia as part of the 1738 migration.[21] Some of these stayed in the region only briefly before moving on to German settlements in other colonies. Others set down roots in the ring of counties surrounding Philadelphia. These German-speaking families — no doubt a few courageous and resilient castaways among them — are the ancestors of today's Pennsylvania Dutch community.

That leaves only the two women, both named Catharina, who stayed behind on Block Island after their fellow emigrants left for Philadelphia. Their story is told in the next chapter.

PART IV

The Legend

CHAPTER ELEVEN

The Witch and the Slave

Two young women made the extraordinary decision to stay behind on Block Island while the other survivors resumed their journey to Philadelphia. They are known to us only as Short Kate and Long Kate, nicknames given by the islanders to distinguish between the two, who were presumably both named Catharina or some variant.[1] We don't know their ages, whether they were related, or with whom they had traveled. All we know of the women derives from Block Island tradition and from stories handed down through descendants of Long Kate.

According to a brief history of the island written by William P. Sheffield in 1876, both women were left destitute by the wreck, but Short Kate appeared to be "well bred." She never married, had no children, and worked as a domestic servant to various families on the island. Her date of death is unknown, but according to Sheffield she is buried in the corner of a private burial ground off Corn Neck Road, a site known today as Sheffield Cemetery.[2] Several graves appear to be marked with fieldstones in one corner of the site, but there is no tombstone bearing her name (or any other German name).

Unlike Short Kate, who lived and died in relative obscurity, Long Kate had a more colorful life on Block Island. Described as exceedingly tall with very light skin, Long Kate married an African slave named Newport (or New Port), who was owned by the Sands family.[3] Long Kate became a notorious figure in the community. Nineteenth-century accounts describe her as a "seeress" who supported herself by fortunetelling. She has been blamed for starting some of the rumors surrounding the ship's destruction.

What made these two women choose to live out their lives on a sparsely inhabited island off the New England coast? Short Kate's reasons for staying are not known. But Long Kate, according to island folklore, cried out after the *Princess Augusta* ran aground that she would marry the first man who rescued her, and New Port came to her aid.[4] As romantic as that sounds, it is more likely that the people she was traveling with died at sea, leaving her no reason (or no money) to continue on to Pennsylvania. She also may have been too ill to travel or too frightened to set foot on another ship. Gloria Hazard Miller, sixth-great-granddaughter of Long Kate and New Port, says that she was told the following story: before Long Kate left her homeland, she visited a fortuneteller, who predicted that she would someday marry a very dark-skinned man. Perhaps Long Kate decided that New Port was the man foretold to her. Or perhaps in New Port — a man brought to the island against his will and alienated from English society — she had found her soul mate.

Not much more is known about New Port than about his German-born wife. We don't know if he was brought to Rhode Island straight from Africa, or if he first spent time in the West Indies, as was often the case. He may not even have been born in Africa. Miller, an avid genealogist, believes he may have been born on the island of Eleuthera in the Bahamas to a member of a different branch of the Sands family (whose ancestors settled the island in the 1640s) and one of the family's slaves. Presumably New Port was named for the colonial capital of Rhode Island, perhaps because that's where he had been sold to the Block Island Sands family.

In 1738, when the *Princess Augusta* wrecked, New Port was owned by John Sands II, and possibly Nathaniel Littlefield as well.[5] As was the custom, New Port used the surname of his master and was known as New Port (or Newport) Sands. (If Miller is correct about the Bahamas connection, it may have been his actual surname.) Over the years, claim to the enslaved African was passed down through the Sands family, first to John's son Edward (believed to be the nephew of the Edward Sands who took in the shipwreck survivors), and then to Edward's son (also named Edward) in 1778.[6] Slavery was not abolished in Rhode Island until 1842, and so New Port would not have tasted freedom unless it was granted to him by the Sands family.

According to a 1730 census, there were 250 whites, 20 "Negroes" (both enslaved and free), and 20 "Indians" (probably indentured servants) on Block Island.[7] While the Sands and Littlefield families owned the largest number of slaves, they were not the only slaveholders. A number of other families, including Simon Ray, owned slaves and passed the claims to them on to their heirs.

According to her great-granddaughter, Mrs. Violet Hazard, Long Kate initially went to live among the slaves on a farm belonging to the Sands family; not long after, she married New Port.[8] There was no law in Rhode Island at the time forbidding marriage between whites and blacks. Still, historians and descendants believe that the union was one of cohabitation, or a common-law marriage. In 1798, the Rhode Island legislature passed a statute declaring that "no person . . . shall join in marriage any white person with any Negro, Indian, or mulatto." That statute remained on the books until 1881, nearly forty years after slavery was abolished in the state.

The union of Long Kate and New Port produced three children, whom they named Jenny (or Jane), Cradle (probably an anglicization of "Gretel," a likely nickname for Margaretha), and Mary. The question is whether they were born free or enslaved. According to slave codes in colonial America, children inherited the status of their mother. (This arrangement ensured that the biracial offspring of slave masters and their female slaves also would be held in bond-age.) Long Kate had certainly arrived on the island as a free woman, but what was her current status?

Some researchers and descendants believe that the couple's children were enslaved, but several facts suggest otherwise. First, unlike their father, the children were not listed as heritable property in the wills of John Sands and Nathaniel Littlefield. Second, it appears that the children did not take the Sands surname, using Port instead. Third, a number of Long Kate and New Port's grandchildren bought and sold property — something slaves were not allowed to do. It's possible that Long Kate and her three children were indentured servants for a period of time, falling somewhere on the spectrum between free and enslaved.

Of the three children, only Mary has descendants living today. Like her mother, Mary became the wife of a slave in the Sands family, and she and her husband had five children. One son, named Benjamin Port, was described in the 1903 obituary of his daughter as having had Colonel Ned (Edward) Sands as his "master," although that term was also used to describe the employer of an indentured servant.[9] If Long Kate's descendants were, in fact, enslaved, it would be one more in a string of tragedies that make up the Palatine story.

Long Kate and New Port's life together on Block Island was not easy. By all accounts, Long Kate had a strained relationship with the island's white residents. As the wife of a slave and the mother of three "mulatto" children, she no doubt had very little social standing in the community. Even more troubling to the islanders, though, was her behavior. She was reportedly given to trances, visions, and out-of-body experiences, and spun wild tales about her supernatural visits back to the homeland. According to an island resident whose parents had known Long Kate, she would sometimes hide behind a wall or under a clump of bushes, remaining unresponsive for hours. After returning home exhausted, she'd explain that she had just flown across the sea to visit with loved ones, and describe the condi-

There are more than 300 miles of stone walls on Block Island,
largely built with slave labor. (Image from a 1906 postcard published
by A. C. Bosselman & Co., New York.)

tion in which she had found them.[10] Not surprisingly, the islanders
were afraid of her, believing she was a witch. With the benefit of
hindsight, we might guess that she suffered from seizures or from
some form of mental illness.

And yet, the islanders allowed her to remain among them; some
were even said to have engaged her fortunetelling services. She was
shunned, perhaps, but not banished, disdained but not persecuted.
Unlike the women hung as witches in Salem or burned at the stake
in Schwaigern, Long Kate was allowed not only to live on the island
but to make a life there. This suggests a certain level of tolerance on
the part of Block Islanders.

We don't know when Long Kate or New Port died. An 1810
New Shoreham census listed a Newport Sands with seventeen in
his family, which would have accounted for his wife, children, and
grandchildren, plus two more.[11] Nor do we know where they or
their children are interred. At that time, African Americans and
Native Americans were not allowed to be buried in the town cemetery, which the first settlers had established in the middle of the
island, on a hill overlooking Great Salt Pond. The family may have
been buried in the Indian Cemetery, as it is called today, just north

of Fresh Pond. This was the final resting place of many of the island's Native Americans, free and enslaved blacks, and their descendants. Sadly, most of the estimated 150 graves are marked only by fieldstones, rendering the individuals and their contributions to life on the island invisible.

CHAPTER TWELVE

Ghost Ship in the Sound

One evening in late December 1739, the British trading vessel *Somerset* was passing through Block Island Sound when the crew spied a tall ship on fire. As they headed toward the burning vessel, it suddenly sank into the sea. The captain recorded the disturbing incident in his log: "I was so distressed by the sight that we followed the burning ship to her watery grave, but failed to find any survivors or flotsam."[1] This is perhaps the first eyewitness account of what has come to be known as the Palatine Light.

This apparent flaming ghost ship has haunted the waters around Block Island on and off for centuries. Because its first appearance coincided with the one-year anniversary of the *Princess Augusta* wreck, it has been connected to the disaster ever since. Like many ghost ships, it is said to be a manifestation of the souls on board, who died under traumatic circumstances and are now trapped in their journey between this life and the next. Some see the specter as a simple reminder of the tragedy; others believe it is a warning of impending doom or a threat of revenge. No doubt its continued reappearances have been the main reason the Palatine legend has survived for so long.

The Palatine Light, from an illustration in the *Providence Evening Bulletin*,
September 12, 1933. Image courtesy of the Boston Public Library

The light has been seen by hundreds of people over the years —
islanders, mainlanders, and mariners alike. The most recent known
sighting occurred in 1963, with the report of a burning vessel in
Block Island Sound that neither Coast Guard ships nor Navy air-
craft could locate.[2] In the beginning, the ghost ship appeared each
year on the anniversary of the wreck. Later on, the sightings occurred sporadically, sometimes decades apart. Many observers recalled that it materialized just before a fierce ocean storm.

In 1811, Block Island physician Aaron Willey submitted a lengthy
description of the Palatine Light to the *Medical Repository*, which
published his account in 1813. Willey spoke to a number of residents
who had seen the apparition. They described it as a pyramid-shaped
mass of fire that continuously mutated in size and brightness. Witnesses were uncertain whether the light touched the water or hov-

ered above the surface, because "none of the boatmen have courage enough to approach it." The light might be seen blazing six or seven miles out to sea or within half a mile of shore. Added Willey, "A gentleman, whose house is situated near the sea, informs me, that he has known it to illuminate considerably the walls of his room through the windows."[3]

Willey first saw it with his own eyes at twilight one evening in February 1810: "It was large, and gently lambent; very bright, broad at the base, and terminated acutely upward. From each side seemed to issue rays of faint light, similar to those perceptible in any blaze placed in the open air, and viewed in the night. It continued about fifteen minutes from the time I first observed it, and then slowly became smaller and more dim till it was entirely extinguished."[4]

He saw it again that same year on the evening of December 20. At first he thought it might be the light on board a vessel, but its "alternate motion and rest," and its unsteady "magnitude and lustre" soon convinced him otherwise. In his account, Willey explained that the light was named for the ship *Palatine*, which had been deliberately cast away on Block Island in the early 1700s in order to conceal the "murder and inhuman treatment of the unfortunate passengers."[5]

The doctor's story was reprinted in several publications in the late 1820s and 1830s, but by 1832, the sightings had apparently stopped.[6] Some said the light no longer appeared because all the people connected with the wreck were dead. Whatever the reason, there were no new reports of the phantom for almost fifty years.

During its absence, a new religious movement arose that would turn skeptics of such phenomena into believers. The Spiritualist movement was founded on the belief that the soul survives bodily death, and that it is possible to communicate with the dead through the assistance of a medium, an individual sensitive to the vibrations of the spirit world. The movement began in 1848 in Hydesville, New York, when the teenage sisters Maggie and Katy Fox convinced their parents and community that the knocking sounds heard in the Fox home were caused by a ghost. So convincing was the ruse (the girls themselves produced the knocks using apples on strings and by snapping their toes) that the sisters soon found themselves demonstrating spirit communication on stage in large cities. Within months, they became nationally known celebrities.

As the Fox sisters' notoriety grew, other so-called mediums, mostly women, claimed to have the ability to converse with the dead. They conducted public and private séances, the primary means of contacting spirits, during which they performed displays of telepathy and clairvoyance. A number of mediums went on tour and became quite famous in their own right. They would place ads in local newspapers, announcing their arrival, where they were staying, how long they would be in town, and the kinds of services they provided — usually business, medical, and romantic advice.

The central appeal of the Spiritualist movement was its hopeful message: that individuals survived the death of their bodies by ascending to the spirit realm. Particularly after the carnage of the Civil War, mediums granted a measure of solace to grieving families. But there was also, of course, the entertainment value of the séance and the methods the medium employed: trances, speaking in tongues, teleportation, levitation, table tipping, and sealed-letter reading, among others. The wealthy hired mediums for private parties in their Victorian parlors, while upscale hotels booked itinerant clairvoyants to perform for their guests.

The first hotel on Block Island was built in 1842, just a few years before the Fox sisters began their "spirit rappings." By the 1870s, Block Island had become a popular summer resort. To accommodate the increasing number of visitors, more hotels sprang up: six were built between 1873 and 1878 alone, including the grand Ocean View Hotel, where Long Kate and New Port's great-great-grandson Jack worked as a handyman. On a summer evening in 1879, the hotel had a lineup of performances which included "magic, vocal and instrumental music, and Heller's Second Sight Mystery and Spiritual Handwriting."[7] All around the island — in private homes, summer cottages, and boarding houses — residents and their curious visitors conducted séances in hope of conjuring up the fire ship. What had earned Long Kate the scorn of her community in the mid-eighteenth century was now, 150 years later, a popular amusement.

Spiritualism certainly had its critics, especially among the clergy and the scientific community, but by the late 1870s and 1880s, the movement had up to 2 million followers in the United States alone. It was during this "golden age" of Spiritualism — which coincided with a tourist boom on Block Island and along the Rhode Island coast — that the Palatine Light reappeared.

On the night of May 27, 1878, Joseph T. Northup of Wakefield, Rhode Island, was on his way home when, from the top of a hill, he saw a large ship on fire in Block Island Sound. He later told the *Narragansett Times*, "I stood and watched her some twenty minutes as she moved eastward by the island, when the flames gradually vanished away like a vessel sinking, and I never saw her again. I shall say . . . that it was the grandest sight I ever saw."[8]

On February 9, 1880, Block Island resident Matilda Rose was on her veranda at twilight when she noticed the reflection of a great bonfire in her cottage windows. Turning toward the source, she saw a large ship on the ocean with sails set, gliding past Clayhead toward Newport. The vessel moved swiftly, despite a dead calm. Even more astonishing, she told the *New York Times*, the ship appeared to be completely engulfed in fire, yet the flames had no effect on the ship or the sails. The vision lasted about fifteen minutes before dissolving into a gray mist. According to Rose, there were more than fifty witnesses scattered around the island — almost all of them, like her, descendants of the island's early wreckers.[9]

Several months later, on a clear summer night, the phantom appeared before Joseph P. Hazard, a wealthy textile manufacturer in Narragansett. He told the *Narragansett Times* that the light first came into view some two miles off the coast. He thought it was an ordinary ship until it turned and raced toward the shore. As the light expanded, it became less bright, and pitched and plunged as if riding the crests of mighty storm-tossed waves, even though the ocean that night was smooth as a lake. A devoted spiritualist and the owner of the railroad that brought tourists to the seaside resort at Narragansett Pier, Hazard continued, "It is quite probable there may be a new era of the lost spectacle, and that the 'Palatine' [may] reappear . . . in the full glory of three masts and cloud of sail that was her wont."[10]

Mrs. George S. Rathbone saw something that summer too. She told the *Narragansett Historical Register* that it looked like a burning ship low on the horizon, but she figured it was a light on board a steamship and wouldn't have thought any different had she not seen Hazard's description in print. She said the sighting was followed by a southeast gale.[11]

In 1882 the poet J. W. De Forest believed he witnessed the Palatine Light while visiting a friend on Block Island. He included an account of the sighting in the preface to a poem he wrote about the phantom ship, published as part of a collection in 1883.

> To me (not being a seafaring man), the Light did not look like a vessel, whether bark-rigged or otherwise. It rather resembled a wheatsheaf, made of silvery aurora borealis, about half a mile high and ten miles away, drifting rapidly seaward along the wide channel between Block Island and Newport. Every few minutes it toppled forward, went completely under the water-line, and then reappeared miles further east, with a preliminary glow like that of the moon rising from a marine horizon. . . . I watched the Light for thirty minutes or more, in company with a dozen other seasiders, all fascinated and puzzled.[12]

The next reported sighting was on August 12, 1885. Eric Montgomery of Philadelphia told the *New York Times* he had been standing on the veranda of a friend's house on Clayhead, watching an approaching storm, when at about eleven that night, an eerie blaze appeared. He said it resembled a whitish flame, shaped like a pyramid, and was about the size of a tall ship under sail. The flame shot out of the water at the southeast end of the island, then moved north, toward Sandy Point, where it faded from view. During the light's most brilliant phase, it was possible to read a newspaper by it. The phenomenon lasted fifteen minutes and was seen by about twenty people.[13]

In 1888, three years after Montgomery's sighting, the Spiritualist movement was dealt a blow when the Fox sisters publicly admitted their hoax. A number of other mediums were exposed as frauds around the same time, and some were charged with larceny. Many of Spiritualism's followers refused to accept that they had been duped, and momentum carried the movement into the next century. But the belief in spirit communication would never again have such widespread, mainstream appeal. And though tourists continued to flock to Block Island in ever-increasing numbers — some no doubt hoping for a glimpse of the ghost ship — there would be no more reports for another quarter century.

Then, just after nightfall on December 27, 1912, island resident Warren Ball spotted what appeared to be a three-masted schooner engulfed in flames, at some distance off the southeastern end of the island. Blizzard conditions and massive waves that evening prevented the New Shoreham Life-Saving crew from launching the longboat. Instead, two steel-hulled revenue cutters were dispatched from the mainland. As the first cutter approached the scene, the burning ship sank beneath the roiling surface. The rescue vessels, with a combined crew of around 110 men, scoured the sea all night and into the next day but found no trace of the sinking: no splinter of wood or scrap of sail, no lifeboats, no bodies.

Noting the date, the absence of wreckage, and the eerie similarity to previous sightings, some began to wonder if the ghost ship had returned. New London's *The Day* pointed out the "peculiar coincidence" that the burning vessel had been seen in almost the same spot as earlier apparitions, "and as time goes on the thought gains headway that the famous Palatine light has been seen again."[14]

And so began a new century of sightings. In the 1920s, a burning vessel was reported off Block Island, provoking the Coast Guard into an unsuccessful search. In 1933 a burning ship was seen in the waters between Newport and Block Island, but neither Navy nor Coast Guard ships could locate it. Two pilots reported a ship burning off Newport in 1958; again, a Coast Guard search turned up nothing. And in 1963, the Coast Guard received word from the Block Island airport that a ship was burning about a mile southeast of the island. Two Coast Guard vessels and a helicopter, as well as two planes from a nearby naval air station, were dispatched to the scene, but no wreckage was found. Within twenty-four hours of this last sighting, a storm moved in with gale-force winds and torrential rain.[15]

What seems most impressive about the Palatine Light is its persistence over more than two centuries, despite the debunking of the most violent aspects of the shipwreck legend. In 1923, Howard M. Chapin, librarian at the Rhode Island Historical Society, stumbled upon the original Boston newspaper reports of the incident from 1739, which describe the circumstances of the wreck and the heroic rescue efforts of the islanders in the aftermath of the ship's grounding. In 1939, the crew's depositions were discovered by Mary T. Quinn, archivist at the Rhode Island State Archives.[16] Their testimony revealed the name of the ship and its movements in the week prior to the wreck. Together, these documents demonstrated that the wreck of the *Princess Augusta* was an unfortunate accident, not part of a dastardly scheme. Furthermore, they proved that the ship *never burned* — neither accidentally nor on purpose — making the reappearance of a flaming ghost ship to mark the disaster more than a little incongruous. And yet, whatever it is, the sight continues to haunt the waters of Block Island Sound. Either the Palatine Light cares nothing for facts, or Rhode Islanders are unwilling to give up their ghost.

Many people believe that the Palatine Light is a real phenomenon: that a luminous spectacle resembling a burning ship has appeared intermittently in Block Island Sound since the wreck of the *Princess Augusta*. However, there's little agreement on the cause or meaning of the light. Numerous scientific theories have been offered as to its origins, but none as yet seems plausible. To nineteenth-century historian Henry T. Beckwith, this was proof enough that the phantom vessel was real. "[I]t must, like some other things, be believed if it cannot be explained," he wrote. His contemporary, historian

Samuel Greene Arnold, disagreed, declaring that "the superstition connected with it is of course rejected," but also lamenting that "science has failed thus far in giving to it a satisfactory explanation."[17]

Aaron Willey was among the earliest skeptics, which is not surprising given his scientific training. "By the ignorant and superstitious it is thought to be supernatural," he wrote in his 1811 letter to the *Medical Repository*. But he nevertheless considered that the phenomenon deserved further investigation, wondering if it involved perhaps "a peculiar modification of electron" or an "inflammation of phlogistous (hydrogenous) gas." He ended by noting, "I have stated facts, but feel reluctance to hazard any speculations. These I leave to you and other erudite researchers of created matter."[18]

Samuel Livermore also addressed the issue of the Palatine Light in his 1877 history of Block Island. He did not dispute that a strange light had appeared at different times in Block Island Sound, but thought it unrelated to the eighteenth-century wreck. The *Palatine Light* in reality had no more relation to the ship Palatine than it had to Bunker Hill Monument," he wrote. Not only that, those who believed that the light was a ghost ship were "persons more competent to believe in the marvelous than to read and write."[19]

The historian and minister believed that the light became linked with the shipwreck by Long Kate — that she co-opted the phenomenon, "whatever it may be," and used it to express her anger and helplessness over the situation in which she found herself. Long Kate "had her revenge on the ship that put her ashore by imagining it on fire, and telling others, probably, that the light on the sound was the wicked ship Palatine, cursed for leaving her on Block Island." Livermore suggested that the eerie illumination could have been produced when a flammable gas bubbled up from the ocean floor and burned at the surface, as happens sometimes over marshes, when methane released from decomposed organic matter spontaneously combusts.[20]

Nearly 140 years after Livermore's *ignis fatuus* theory, we still can't explain the phenomenon. One theory proposes that the light is reflected from a large fire on land, such as the conflagration that

consumed a cotton factory in Providence around the time of Willey's second sighting. Another popular explanation involves bioluminescent sea life. For example, some oceanic dinoflagellates (a type
of plankton) can emit a brief flash of light when disturbed. Such
illumination can sometimes be seen at night in the pounding surf
or in the wake behind a boat. An 1885 article in the *Meriden Daily
Republic* suggested that this phenomenon "may occur at the meeting of adverse tides and thus cause the waters to throw up a phosphorescent light." As we already know, two currents clash at Block
Island's Sandy Point, sometimes producing a geyser effect. While
such a marvel is admittedly unlikely, imagine what this would look
like if aglow.

On a September evening in the mid-1880s, Welcome A. Greene
was accompanying some fishermen aboard the steamer *Leona*. It
was a moonless night, clear but with patches of fog. The steamer was
cruising northwest of Block Island when Greene saw the "pyramidal
figure of a burning ship." It appeared to be a square-rigger on fire,
the flames working their way up from the hull to the mast and con-
suming the sails, then sinking back down to a "smouldering light."
This pattern was repeated several times. The fishermen steered toward it, but as they neared, the light got thinner, fainter, and more
dispersed. When they reached the site, they saw "lambent flashes of
transparent light" shooting upward in the air around them, across
many acres of the ocean's surface.

Greene was surprised at what happened next: the fishermen
dropped their nets and made one of the largest hauls of menhaden
that season. The captain told Greene that "when in large schools,
and in certain states of the air and water [the fish] give out a great
deal of phosphorescent light which, in a clear air, would not be noticed at a little distance." Although it's more likely that the menhaden disturbed a bloom of bioluminescent plankton rather than
discharging a light of their own, Greene understood that the display
had a natural cause and was disappointed that the Palatine Light
had lost its "ghostly credentials." As he noted in the *Narragansett*

Historical Register, "All I can say is that after we took in that school of menhaden we saw no more of the Palatine light on that night."[21]

Over the years, other observers have suggested that the ghost ship is a reflection of the moon as it rises in the fog, or that the appearance of flames is caused by an electrical discharge around the masts and yardarms of a distant ship — a phenomenon called St. Elmo's fire. Christopher Columbus experienced it on his second voyage to the New World, describing in his journal a "ghostly flame which danced among our sails and later stayed like candlelights to burn brightly from the mast."

Not every occurrence of the Palatine Light may be attributable to the same cause, of course. Perhaps the aurora borealis triggered a few reports. John Comer, a Baptist minister in Newport, witnessed the northern lights on October 3, 1728 (a decade before the *Princess Augusta* wreck). He wrote in his diary that, at the horizon, "there appeared a thick vapour, and above it a redness like unto fire, and in ye middle a hundred or more spears pointing upwards, extending towards the zenith." The light moved slowly toward the east, "not at all times of ye same brightness, but constantly made a very awful show." Comer saw the aurora a total of nine times between 1728 and 1731, and said the townspeople were terrified of it.[22]

Finally, there may be a psychological explanation for at least some of the sightings. Apophenia is the human tendency to see patterns or connections in otherwise unrelated data. Perceiving the face of Jesus on a burnt piece of toast is one example of this tendency. An individual might then take the perception a step further, and interpret the image as a sign from heaven. In a maritime community such as Block Island, where all residents would have been well aware of the dangers of the sea, it might have been easy to misinterpret a distant triangle-shaped light as a tall ship on fire. Later, knowing that their ancestors had been accused of destroying ships, that same community might have feared the return of a ghost ship seeking revenge. While apophenia is part of human nature, researchers have found that people with very strong religious beliefs — or who believe in the supernatural — are particularly prone to the phenomenon.

In the end, it doesn't matter whether the Palatine Light is a phantom, a figment, or a floating mass of dinoflagellates. Because the light has become an integral part of the legend, its reappearance has served as a continual reminder of the tale. Without it, the *Princess Augusta*, and its many passengers lost to the sea, would be lost to history as well.

CHAPTER THIRTEEN

The Dancing Mortar

The logs of lignum vitae that the *Princess Augusta* left on Block Island were too valuable to discard. The resin of this small tropical evergreen, believed to have medicinal properties, had been sought after by Europeans since the 1500s for the treatment of syphilis and arthritis, while the wood itself was prized for its remarkable durability. It is the hardest and densest wood on earth. What's more, the oily resin that infuses its fibers makes it not only self-lubricating, but insect-, disease-, and water-resistant. Compared to other woods, it's practically indestructible, earning it the nickname "ironwood."

The lignum vitae had been removed from the ship before it broke apart and stacked in a loose pile on the beach. Less than ten feet long and no bigger around than a large oak branch, the logs had been shipped from the West Indies in the rough.[1] It would have been obvious to even a casual observer that the wood had not come from a local forest. Unlike the massive oak and pine trees of New England, with their pale yellow heartwood and rough, gray bark, the tropical wood was a dark, olive-brown color, with smooth, gray-and-beige mottled bark that peeled off in random patches.

Some of the logs may have been sold to shipbuilders in Newport, who used the tough wood for belaying pins, deadeyes, and pulley blocks, the sort of ship fittings that took a lot of abuse. Some of the wood simply may have been burned that winter for fuel. By the early 1700s, Block Island's forests were nearly depleted, and residents had begun burning peat in their fireplaces instead of wood. Lignum vitae was difficult to cut, but the same properties that make the wood so durable produce a hot and long-lasting fire. And unlike a peat fire, which produces a thick smoke that permeates clothing (something Block Islanders came to be known for on the mainland), lignum vitae gives off a pleasant, spicy-sweet scent as the fire warms the resin in the wood.

Not all of the lignum vitae was sold or used for fuel, however. Some logs were fashioned into mortars for grinding corn — a chore that had been done by hand ever since the town "maniac" had burned down the island's only mill. To make a mortar, a short log was hollowed out by drilling many small holes into one end with an augur, then placing a red-hot cannon ball over the holes. The charred wood could then be chipped out with a chisel and mallet (the mallet itself likely made of ironwood).[2]

One of the mortars ended up in the household of Simon Ray, who had taken in a number of the shipwreck victims and on whose land dozens had been buried. This mortar was fourteen inches tall and ten inches in diameter, and had a capacity of four quarts. It was said to have weighed nearly as much as a boulder of the same size.[3]

The mortar served the Rays well and remained in the house even after the property passed out of the family. That seems to be when the "trouble" began. The new owner claimed the Ray house was haunted. "Sights and sounds were there witnessed," wrote the Reverend Livermore in his history of the island, "which our nerves protest against repeating." The historian interviewed half a dozen of the island's oldest and most trustworthy residents, who would have been children when the hauntings occurred. He claimed that their stories, by comparison, made the "modern fabrications of spiritualism, and the tricks of ventriloquists" seem silly.[4]

One of the ways in which the spirits of the old house manifested their presence was by making the mortar "dance." Without warning, the heavy wooden vessel would leap off the kitchen shelf and land on the plank floor with a *thud*. Then it would tip over on its side and roll around the room. When it tired of rolling, it would right itself and begin rocking side to side. For a grand finale, it would hop up and down on the floor, higher and higher, until it bumped into the rafters. Following the performance it would remain dormant on the shelf for weeks or months. Its agitation sometimes preceded an evening visit by the ghost ship *Palatine*.[5]

The Ray house was dismantled in the early 1800s, and some of its boards were used to build a house about 100 yards away. The owner of the new dwelling, Raymond Dickens, inherited the ironwood mortar. Either because of its reputation, or because it was no longer needed for grinding, the object was denied a place inside the home.[6] It served for a time as a chopping block, then was eventually used to plug a hole at the base of a stone wall, where it lay, pinned on its side, for the next fifty years. That is where Livermore found it — weathered and axe-scarred, but still solid, with "rosettes of gray and yellow moss within."

Relic hunting was a fevered pastime in the late nineteenth century, and the Reverend Livermore was not immune to its charms. In 1876 he acquired the mortar from Dickens and took it home, where he was disappointed but not surprised that the object did not dance for him. In his opinion, the only dancing that the mortar actually had done was in the imagination of its former owner, who was known around the island as an "opium-eater."[7]

Around 1880, Livermore donated the storied object to Brown University in Providence, where it was displayed in the Museum of Natural History at Rhode Island Hall. Unfortunately, the museum was not the safe haven Livermore had hoped it would be. In 1906 a fire at the hall destroyed many of the museum's specimens. The museum itself was dismantled in 1915 and the remaining exhibits put in storage. Then, in 1945, ninety-two truckloads of artifacts were dumped in a landfill along the banks of the Seekonk River.

Miraculously, the mortar escaped this purge. It was reportedly seen at the university in 1959, but its whereabouts today are unknown.[8] Someone may find it in a broom closet one day, but once an artifact has been separated from the history of its origin, it's a short leap from relic to rubbish.

CHAPTER FOURTEEN

"The Wreck of a People's Character"

B y the late 1700s, the two versions of the Palatine legend mentioned in the prologue were well established locally, and the ghost ship had been witnessed by islanders and main-landers alike.[1] But the story gained national attention in the nine-teenth century, when a handful of prominent writers, most from New England, used the tale as inspiration for poems and prose, some of which appeared in the country's most popular and widely read periodicals. Romantic, terrifying, and highly moralistic, these works were written during a time of great economic change and social unrest in America.

The most famous was a poem by John Greenleaf Whittier, titled "The Palatine," published in the January 1867 edition of the *Atlantic Monthly*.[2] Referring to the island by its Native American name, "Manissees," the poem vilifies its residents for luring the ship ashore with false lights, robbing and killing her passengers, and destroying the ship by fire. One year later, the island's wreckers are visited by an apparition of the ship in flames.

Because every word and deed has been recorded "On Nature's infinite negative," the poem predicts that the phantom ship will continue to reappear:

John Greenleaf Whittier.
Image: Classic Image / Alamy

For still, on many a moonless night,
From Kingston Head and from Montauk light
The spectre kindles and burns in sight.

Now low and dim, now clear and higher,
Leaps up the terrible Ghost of Fire,
Then, slowly sinking, the flames expire.

And the wise Sound skippers, though skies be fine,
Reef their sails when they see the sign
Of the blazing wreck of the Palatine!

A resident of Amesbury, Massachusetts, Whittier had heard
about the legend from his friend Joseph P. Hazard, a textile manufacturer from a prominent Rhode Island family. The two men, both
Quakers, may have met at a religious gathering or through their ab-

olitionist activities, or Whittier may have been one of the numerous literary figures that Hazard hosted at his gothic revival mansion in Narragansett. Hazard's fascination with the legend was fueled by his devotion to the Spiritualist movement, which was on full display at his estate: one room in his home was designated for séances, and a 105-foot-tall tower had been built next door so he could more easily converse with his ancestors in the spirit world. He'd also had a guest house built on the property at the behest of some druids whom he claimed had visited him in a dream.[3]

Hazard had written to Whittier in 1865, telling him the version of the legend popular on the mainland: that the islanders were to blame for the ship's destruction.[4] Two years later, Whittier penned his famous poem — based on information given to him by the wealthy eccentric, a man who believed he could contact the dead through his gold pocket watch.

While perhaps the best-known poet to take on the legend, Whittier was not the first. That honor belongs to Richard Henry Dana, Sr., who published *The Buccaneer, and Other Poems* in 1827. The central figure in "The Buccaneer" is Matthew Lee, a mariner from an island that "lies nine leagues away" (the approximate distance from Block Island to Newport, where Dana once lived). On a return voyage from Spain, Lee murders a wealthy female passenger and her servants in order to steal her money and jewels. He tosses her beloved white horse overboard, then abandons and burns the ship as they near the home shore. One year later, a phantom fire ship appears to Lee:

> Not bigger than a star it seems.
> And now 'tis like the bloody moon,
> And now it shoots in hairy streams!
> It moves! — 'Twill reach us soon?
> A ship! And all on fire! — hull, yard, and mast!
> Her sails are sheets of flame! — she's nearing fast!

The ghost ship is accompanied by a spectral horse, which carries Lee to a bluff overlooking the burning ship and its victims. After this incident, the islanders shun Lee; he spends his time alone, consumed by guilt. The apparition appears twice more on the anniversary of the ship's destruction. On the third visitation, Lee rides the horse into the sea, circles the burning ship, and disappears beneath the waves.

Although some historians have debated this poem's connection to the Palatine legend, Dana alludes to the source in a preface to the first edition of his *Poems and Prose Writings*, admitting that he changed some details for "poetical effect." "I shall not name the island off our New England coast upon which these events happened, and these strange appearances were seen," he wrote, "for islanders are the most sensitive creatures in the world in all that relates to their places of abode."[5] Dana's poem was reprinted in *Harper's New Monthly* magazine in October 1872, five years after Whittier's poem appeared in the *Atlantic*.

Several more works based on the legend appeared later in the 1800s. "The Phantom Ship," by Reverend Albert G. Palmer of Stonington, Connecticut, was published in the *Narragansett Times* in 1880.[6] Described by one critic as "an effusion of stupefying length," Palmer's poem was an admitted knockoff of Whittier's. It blames the islanders for wrecking the ship and murdering the passengers, and warns that the phantom ship's yearly visits will occur as long as any of the wreckers remain alive.

After witnessing the phantom ship himself in 1882, J. W. De Forest wrote a poem he described as "a faithful, coldblooded, scientific description of its appearance and behavior." Also titled "The Phantom Ship," it was published in *Harper's New Monthly* in 1883. "At that time Whittier's fine poem about it was to me completely unknown," he noted later. "I had heard of the Palatine, however, and promptly divined her in the sight before me. My own verses were written the next day at Block Island."[7] De Forest's poem assigns no blame for the wreck, though it observes that the ghost ship "prophesied storm and woe."

Two more literary figures from Massachusetts also took on the legend. In the final chapter of Edward Everett Hale's *Christmas in Narragansett* (1884), the Palatine Light appears to some dinner-party guests, one of whom later wonders if both the phantom ship and the evening's gathering had been figments of his imagination. Thomas Wentworth Higginson included "The Last Palatine Light" in his *Afternoon Landscape: Poems and Translations* (1889). In Higginson's poem, written while he was living in Newport, the phantom ship appears before a Block Island fisherman, who is tempted to return to his former pirating days until recalled by the presence of his young son at his side.

One other work, published thirty-five years before Whittier's classic, has been generally overlooked by historians and literary scholars. "The Palatine," a gothic short story, appeared anonymously in the November 1832 issue of *The Lady's Book*, a popular women's magazine published in Philadelphia by Louis A. Godey.[8]

In this approximately 7,500-word tale, the narrator decides to visit Block Island and encounters the Palatine Light during a stormy nighttime passage across the sound. The morning after his arrival, he learns the "true" story of the *Palatine's* destruction from a written confession left by islander John Dory, the last of the ship's wreckers to die.

According to Dory, the *Palatine* was an immigrant ship en route from Hamburg, Germany, to Philadelphia. Among the passengers were the Vanderlin family: mother, father, and daughter Mary. Mary and the third mate, Reynolds (who is also the captain's nephew), were in love. During the voyage, Reynolds tried to protect her and her parents from the murderous crew, who killed the English captain and brutalized the wealthy passengers in order to steal their riches. But the voyage was deliberately prolonged and the ship ended up near Block Island in a storm. Wreckers on the island, led by John Dory, set signal fires to lure the ship ashore. Dory and several of his men rowed out to the stricken ship and steered it onto a horseshoe-shaped sandbar from which there was no escape. Dory took pity on Mary and allowed her to flee to Newport with her now-widowed mother and Reynolds. (He hoped this gesture might help atone for previous crimes.) The wreckers then locked the crew in the hold and set fire to the ship. As they rowed away from the inferno, the superstitious horror connected with this ship began to be felt. Numbers affirmed that they saw some of the poor wretches burst from the hold and run up the masts, where they hung from the yards; till literally roasted and fried, they dropped into the fires below; and that when the flames raged highest, a female form was distinctly seen from all the boats, standing on the quarter deck in the very hottest of the fire, till the whole mass suddenly went out, and the last flame curled upwards, as if the arch fiend had sunk through the sea with its prey.[9]

In the story, Mary and Reynolds wed and moved to Pennsylvania. As for the wreckers, their ill-gotten gain proved a curse. They led troubled, lonely lives, and drank heavily to "drown the horrors of conscience." They were plagued by the frequent appearance of a fiery phantom ship, which returned at the death of each wrecker until the last one — John Dory — had passed.

"The Palatine" is interesting not only because it appears to be the origin of the Mary Vanderline myth (the woman trapped on board after the ship is set on fire), but because it includes details about the *Princess Augusta*'s voyage that are known to be true.[10] These include the involvement of a Dutch merchant house in preparing for the voyage, and the ship's coming within sight of the Delaware capes, then beating up the coast for six more days.

The Godey story also reflects the prejudice many mainlanders felt at the time toward their rural island neighbors. The narrator claims the island is "inhabited by a stupid race, half cod, half waterfowl." He says they are short and stout, shaped like a rice cask, and with a voice "shrill and whistling, like the wind through a keyhole." The women are so acclimated to water they have webbed feet. Moreover, "There is one trait peculiar to these islanders, and to the Bahama wreckers, to which I hardly know how to allude. However, it is considered *peculiarly* unfortunate for a vessel to be cast away upon Block Island."[11] Dehumanizing the islanders in this way helped perpetuate the myth that they had destroyed the real Palatine ship.

As noted in chapter 12, the ghostly appearances of the Palatine Light were reported to have stopped (for a time, at least) in 1832. According to legend, this happened because all the wreckers had died by then. But this seemingly arbitrary date almost certainly originated from Godey's publication of "The Palatine" in that year.

So why has such an important text been forgotten? In 1832, Godey's *Lady's Book* had been in circulation for only two years, with a high cover price and a small readership. Although the story was reprinted in several different publications in the 1830s,[12] Godey began copyrighting each issue of his magazine in 1845 (he was the first publisher to do such a thing). After that, no other publication could legally reprint the story without permission. And it seems no one did. The fact that it was written anonymously — probably by one of the women on Godey's staff — also might have contributed to its later obscurity.

At least seven writers took on Rhode Island's Palatine legend over a span of about sixty years.[13] Nineteenth-century readers clearly had an appetite for ghost stories, thanks in large part to the Spiritualist movement. But the Palatine legend was more than just a spooky tale to the writers who embraced it.[14] All were working during a time of great social and economic change in America, brought about by industrialization, urbanization, large-scale immigration, and the bloody Civil War. Despite the technological advances and material gains made during this era, segments of the population continued to suffer from poverty, exploitation, inequality, and injustice. The authors, several of whom also were ministers, became deeply involved in the reform movements that arose to address societal ills. They joined groups committed to abolition, women's rights, temperance, the humane treatment of prisoners and the mentally ill, public education, and fair labor practices.[15] To these men, the Palatine legend was a moral tale, and the fire ship a metaphor for a guilty conscience. While the treatment of the legend differed from one writer to the next, the message was the same: be careful how you treat others, for your cruelty will come back to haunt you.

How did Block Islanders feel about their ancestors being cast as murderers and thieves in these works? In 1877, the island's Baptist minister, Samuel T. Livermore, tried to set the record straight in his *History of Block Island*. "*Poetic fiction* has given to the public a very wrong view of this occurrence," he wrote, "and thus a wrong impression of the Islanders has been obtained." Earlier, Livermore had even written to Whittier about the poet's negative portrayal of the islanders. To his credit, Whittier responded with this letter:

> 21st 10 mo. 1876
>
> Dear Friend:
>
> In regard to the poem *Palatine*, I can only say that I did not intend to misrepresent the facts of history. I wrote it after receiving a letter from Mr. Hazard, of Rhode Island, from which I certainly inferred that the ship was pillaged by the Islanders. He mentioned that one of the crew to save himself clung to the boat of the wreckers, who cut his hand off with a sword. It is very possible that my correspondent followed the current tradition on the main-land.
>
> Mr. Hazard is a gentleman of character and veracity, and I have no doubt he gave the version of the story as he had heard it.
>
> Very Truly Thy Friend,
> John G. Whittier

Unfortunately, the tradition Hazard followed included the image of Block Island as a home to wreckers and a haven for pirates. There were indeed "wreckers" on the island, but they did not wreck ships: they salvaged shipwrecks. By law, wreckers were entitled to be compensated for this dangerous work. Of the hundreds of ships that have wrecked on Block Island over the centuries, none are known to have been lured there (as a practical matter, setting "false lights" would likely warn ships away from land, not draw them near). And in fact, island residents had no need to lure ships to their shore. The island's location in a busy shipping lane, amid hazardous currents, underwater obstructions, and frequent and sudden fog banks, caused ships to run aground all on their own.

There were pirates associated with Block Island as well — but none lived there. William Kidd, James Gillam, and Joseph Bradish each stopped at the island in 1699. Kidd and Bradish were said to have buried treasure there. (All three were eventually captured in Boston, then taken to London and executed.) Paulsgrave Williams grew up on Block Island but left his wife and children there in 1716, at the age of forty, to join "Black Sam" Bellamy in the search for sunken treasure in the Caribbean. Only after coming up empty-handed did the men turn to piracy. In 1723, the British royal gun-ship *Greyhound* fought two pirate ships in the waters between Block Island and Long Island. The *Fortune*, commanded by the sadistic Edward Low, got away. The other vessel, the *Ranger*, was captured and taken to Newport, where twenty-six of the crew were hanged.[16]

On several occasions, however, pirates were held in prison on the island while awaiting transport to Newport for trial. One notorious case occurred in 1738, just three months before the *Princess Augusta* wreck. On September 17, the seventy-ton sloop *Dolphin*, en route from Haiti to Boston with a small French crew and several English passengers, ran aground on Block Island.[17] During the voyage, the first mate had killed the captain and one of the passengers, and had forced two other passengers at gunpoint to throw the captain's young nephew overboard, causing him to drown. When the Block Islanders learned what had happened, they imprisoned the crew until they could be taken to Newport. The first mate and two other crewmembers were convicted of "piracy, robbery, and felony [murder]"; on November 3, they were hanged at Bull's Point in New-port. On September 3, 1740, the Rhode Island General Assembly voted to reimburse Block Island 13 pounds, 3 shillings, "for victuals and drink to the pirates at Block Island, and their guards."[18] Per-haps references like this one caused many on the mainland to think that the Block Islanders themselves were pirates, making Whittier's poem all the easier to believe.

Livermore included Whittier's letter of apology in his history of the island. He then identified the individuals he believed were responsible for starting the rumors about the Palatine ship. The main culprit, he argued, was the "fortune-teller and witch," Long Kate. But he blamed two others as well: the opium addict who lived in the former Ray house and who was tormented by the "dancing mortar," and the island "maniac," Mark Dodge, who was suspected of having burned down the island's only mill. Livermore declared that these three "are poor authority for authenticating a legend that criminates a civil, Christianized community, and reduces them to a level with barbarians and pirates."[19] In defending Block Island, he branded Long Kate and her fellow outcasts as liars.

For better or worse, Whittier's poem helped put Block Island on the map. After the 1870 construction of Government Harbor, regular steamer service began ferrying tourists from Newport, Providence, and New London, fueling a building boom of hotels and summer cottages. (Before the harbor was built, boats tied up to poles planted in shallow water.) Articles about the island began appearing in newspapers and magazines, touting its fresh air, fishing, sailing, and bathing beaches — along with its "pet superstition" and "stock attraction," the legend of the *Palatine* and the Palatine Light. Relic hunters scoured the island, knocking on farmhouse doors and offering cash for items from historic wrecks. "The great thing was to get something off the Palatine," wrote one such scavenger in an article on the "fever for antiquities."[20]

By 1885, the tourists outnumbered the natives in summer. In 1895, construction of a second harbor on the west side cemented the island's status as a tourist destination. Block Island had transformed from a peaceful farming and fishing community to a summer resort. This transformation brought prosperity to the island, to be sure, but forever changed the island's character and the residents' way of life. That may have been Livermore's real fear all along.

Whittier included his poem in *The Writings of John Greenleaf Whittier in Seven Volumes*, published in 1888. Mindful of the anger he had aroused the first time around, he prefaced it with the following explanation:

Block Island . . . was the scene of a tragic incident a hundred years or more ago, when *The Palatine*, an emigrant ship bound for Philadelphia, driven off its course, came upon the coast at this point. A mutiny on board, followed by an inhuman desertion on the part of the crew, had brought the unhappy passengers to the verge of starvation and madness. Tradition says that wreckers on the shore, after rescuing all but one of the survivors, set fire to the vessel, which was driven out to sea before a gale which had sprung up.[21]

Of course much of this explanation was wrong as well, but at least he absolved the islanders of any blame.

Still, the sting of the poem would last into the next century, at least among the remaining descendants of the island's early families. Eighty years after Livermore attempted to set the record straight, island resident and tour guide Mary Rose, writing under the pseudonym "Maizie," referred to Whittier's work as "one of the most cruel poems ever written," noting that "it was not the wreck of a ship his readers would remember. It was the wreck of a people's character, a people's soullessness!"[22] Then Rose explained why the tale had been so difficult to stop. She likened the "little white lies" that make up the Palatine legend to the seeds of a milk pod: once carried off by the wind they are impossible to retrieve, and from each one grow many more.

More than 500 Palatine ships sailed to America in the century before the Revolution. Incredibly, only a handful of the voyages ended in shipwreck. The *Princess Augusta* had the great misfortune to be one of them. Said Peter Lohrman of the party from Schwaigern who perished aboard: "They left in an unlucky year." In fact, the year 1738 was one of the deadliest in the Palatine trade. Approximately 6,500 emigrants set out for America that spring and summer, and roughly 35 percent did not survive the journey — a mortality rate ten times the average.[1] On the *Princess Augusta*, it is believed that fewer than 65 of the estimated 340 passengers survived, a staggering death rate of about 80 percent.[2]

As noted in chapter 6, a group of fourteen prominent Philadelphians, themselves native Germans, wrote an open letter to the homeland in November of that year. With the *Princess Augusta* and the *Oliver* feared lost at sea and the death toll of the fleet climbing, these men were motivated by "some conscientious and authenticated accounts of the last and numerous but also miserable and pitiful migration of the year 1738."[3] They urged their countrymen to do some "earnest soul searching" before they undertook such an "indescribably difficult" journey. They blamed that season's many deaths not only on delays in port, overcrowding on ships, and bad weather at sea, but also on the duplicity of the newlanders and the gullibility, recklessness, and poor planning of the emigrants themselves.

It was impossible for these concerned residents to overlook the suffering of the new arrivals. "Oh, how many rich and poor alike, with few exceptions, regret it," they wrote, "what tears one sees of widows and orphans, lengthy chest illnesses and quinsy, swollen bodies, scorbutic boils, swollen lame legs — these are the least relics which accompany the ill and those who had otherwise been well."[4] A month after the *Princess Augusta* survivors arrived in Philadelphia, Caspar Wistar wrote to Georg Friedrich Hölzer that, even more distressing than listening to stories of their disastrous voyage, was hearing how "those who made it through such danger and affliction are still filled with hatred, and envy, and bitterness against the others, and even worse."[5]

The immigration season of 1738 was so costly in terms of human lives that it frightened off prospective emigrants for years to come. It would be a decade before the number of travelers exceeded even 2,000.[6] And most of the captains of the 1738 fleet never made another Palatine run, including John Stedman.[7] During its twelve-week voyage, his *St. Andrew* lost 120 of an estimated 328 passengers.[8] Among the survivors were "a great number laboring under a malignant, eruptive fever," according to two physicians appointed by authorities to inspect incoming ships. Stedman returned to Rotterdam and continued in the trade only as a shipper, not a sailor.[9]

John Stedman's brother Charles, commander of the *Charming Nancy*, lost 250 of 312 passengers, along with several crew, and he himself almost died of illness.[10] He returned to sea in 1741, but that would be his last Palatine run. After that he remained in Philadelphia with his brother Alexander and took up the business of ship insurance. The Stedmans left the Palatine trade altogether in 1754, when the start of the French and Indian War temporarily halted immigration.

The Hope firm had the dubious distinction of losing two ships in one year — the *Princess Augusta* and the *Oliver*. Unlike the Stedmans, no member of the Hope family had commanded an immigrant ship or witnessed the suffering on board the vessels they owned and chartered. While their willingness to extend credit enabled even the poorest Palatines to move to America, the firm's focus was on making money and mitigating risk. They did this by shortchanging rations or loading provisions of poor quality; by demanding that the debts of the dead be paid by surviving family members, either in cash or in additional years of indentured servitude; and by taking custody of the chests left by the dead who had no survivors on board. Their charterparties forced captains to choose between the health and safety of the passengers and their wages for the voyage. Nowhere was this dilemma more evident than in the decisions Andrew Brook made just before and after the *Princess Augusta* wrecked. Caught in a snowsquall in Block Island Sound, Brook chose to try one last time for Philadelphia instead of putting in to nearby Newport, where his passengers could have obtained fresh water and medical care. After the ship grounded, he refused to relinquish custody of the Palatines' property — that of both the living and the dead — probably because he knew that he had failed to satisfy the contract with the Hope firm.

The Hopes quit the Palatine trade in 1763, but the firm, now known as Hope & Company, remained in business. Transporting Palatines had been just one part of their operation all along. Among their other activities, the Hopes participated in the slave trade and the diamond trade, smuggled tea, paper, and European wares to Thomas Hancock in Boston, and loaned money to warring nations during the Seven Years War.[11]

By 1785, Hope & Company was the leading merchant banking house in Europe. When France invaded Holland in 1794 in the lead-up to the Napoleonic Wars, the Hopes moved back to London, giving up international trade to concentrate wholly on banking. A decade later the firm helped finance the largest land deal in history: the Louisiana Purchase. Napoleon used the proceeds from the sale to help pay for his war with England.

Fast-forward to 1993: after nearly three centuries in business, the company name disappeared in a merger with another financial insti-

tution. However, the family name lives on in the form of a precious
stone, now housed in the Smithsonian Institution. Henry Philip
Hope, great grandson of Archibald Hope, was a gem collector in
early nineteenth-century London. Sometime between 1823 and
1839 he acquired a 45.5-carat, blue-colored diamond. According to
a collection catalog, "This matchless gem combines the beautiful
colour of the sapphire with the prismatic fire and brilliancy of the
diamond, and, on account of its extraordinary colour, great size, and
other fine qualities, it certainly may be called unique." The stone was
referred to as "Hope's Diamond."[12]

The German-speaking passengers aboard the *Princess Augusta*
might not have known that *hope* was both a name and a notion — an
English word of Germanic origin meaning to have confidence in the
future, to trust that something is or will be. As the shipwreck on
Block Island showed, not all journeys end as planned, but they all
begin the same way: with hope.

NOTES

Prologue

1. The U.S. Revenue Cutter Service and the U.S. Life-Saving Service combined in 1915 to form the U.S. Coast Guard. The *Seneca* had recently been transferred from Staten Island, where eight months earlier its crew had witnessed the arrival of the *Carpathia* carrying the survivors and dead of the *Titanic* disaster. The ship would soon be dispatched to the ice fields off Newfoundland—the first ship assigned to ice patrol following the sinking of the *Titanic*.

2. Block Island had three life-saving stations at the time: New Shoreham Station, about a quarter-mile north of Old Harbor on the east side of the island; Block Island Station, on the southwest coast of the island; and Sandy Point Station, at the northern tip of the island. See map in chapter 9.

3. *New York Evening Telegram*, December 28, 1912.

4. *New York Times*, December 29, 1912.

5. *Annual Report of the United States Life-Saving Service for the Fiscal Year Ending June 30, 1912* (Washington, D.C.: Government Printing Office, 1913), 221. One of the worst accidents to occur in Block Island Sound was the wreck of the passenger steamer *Larchmont*, which collided with the schooner *Harry Knowlton* on the evening of February 11, 1907, resulting in the loss of 146 souls. Dozens of frozen, contorted bodies washed up on the beaches of Block Island, while the steamer's lifeboats were only half-filled to capacity. There were 19 survivors, 10 of them crew. The disaster has been referred to as "Rhode Island's *Titanic*."

6. Aaron C. Wiley [Willey], "Metheoric Appearance Called the Palatine Light," in *The Medical Repository of Original Essays and Intelligence Relative to Physic, Surgery, Chemistry, and Natural History*, edited by Samuel L. Mitchill, Felix Pascalis, and Samuel Akerly, vol. 1, no. 1 (1813): 408–10.

7. Robert M. Downie, *Block Island—The Sea* (Block Island: Book Nook Press, 1998), 46–53.

8. *Records of the Colony of Rhode Island and Providence Plantations in New England, Vol. IV, 1707–1740*, edited by John Russell Bartlett, 581.

9. *New York Times*, October 19, 1884.

10. The 1880 sightings are mentioned in *Lippincott's Magazine*, December 1882, p. 542, and the *Narragansett Historical Register*, 1882–83, p. 152. The 1882 sighting is noted in J. W. De Forest, *Poems: Medley and Palestina* (New Haven, CT: The Tuttle, Morehouse & Taylor Company, 1902), x–xi. (This account is in the preface.) The 1885 sighting is mentioned in the *New York Times*, August 15, 1885.

11. *Atlantic Monthly*, January 1867.

12. Maizie [Mary Rose], *Block Island Scrapbook* (New York: Pageant Press, 1957), 253.

13. Marianne Wokeck, *Trade in Strangers: The Beginnings of Mass Migration to North America* (University Park: Penn State Press, 1999), 240–276; Klaus Wust, "The Emigration Season of 1738: Year of the Destroying Angels," *The Report* [of the Society for the History of the Germans in Maryland], vol. 40 (1986): 49.

14. The Lohrman letter is discussed in Aaron Spencer Fogleman, *Hopeful Journeys: German Immigration, Settlement, and Political Culture in Colonial America, 1717–1775* (Philadelphia: University of Pennsylvania Press, 1996), 75; and Wust, "The Emigration Season of 1738," 42. Wust claims the families named in the Lohrman letter were on the *St. Andrew*. While there were emigrants from Schwaigern on board that ship (a total of thirty-one left the town that year), the families Lohrman refers to were on the *Princess Augusta*.

15. Fogleman says they all survived; Wust says all but one died.

16. I found this clue in Rosalind Beiler, *Immigrant and Entrepreneur: The Atlantic World of Caspar Wistar, 1650–1750* (University Park: Penn State University Press, 2008), 144.

1. Leaving the Homeland

1. Fogleman, *Hopeful Journeys*, 56; Marianne Wokeck, "A Tide of Alien Tongues," PhD diss., Temple University, 1982, p. 47.

2. Wokeck, *Trade in Strangers*, 13.

3. According to church records, one entire branch of the Dieter family — Bechtold Dieter and his five children — died in January and February of 1630.

4. Dorothee Oehler, "Hexen und Hexenverfolgung im Zabergäu und Umgebung," *Zeitschrift des Zabergäuvereins*, no. 4 (2000): 57–78.

5. The deputy mayor in 1713 was Michael Dieter (1671–1734). He and Sebastian's father, Matthäus, were distant cousins.

6. This "witch" burning is believed to have been the last to occur in southwest Germany.

7. Fogleman, *Hopeful Journeys*, 56.

8. City Archive Schwaigern, District of Heilbronn, Inventories and Settlements, B537, pp. 201–2. Fifteen acres is a rough estimate based on the local units of measurement used at the time (1 Simri = 4 quarters; 1 quarter = 0.43 acres). No house was listed as part of his estate, suggesting he likely lived with his widowed father.

9. Wokeck, "A Tide of Alien Tongues," 4, 8.

10. In all, thirty-one Schwaigern residents (seven families and four single persons) left for Pennsylvania in the spring of 1738. In addition to Dieter's group, they included Christian and Anna Elisabetha Heinrich (siblings); Hanns Georg Behringer (town administrator's son); Barbara (Kober) and Elias Behringer (no relation to above) and their infant son; Jacob and Anna Maria Kern and their four children; Anna Maria Kern's sister, Catharina Meÿer, and Meÿer's two children; and Ulrich Jacob and Barbara Beurer. The thirty-one may have left town as one big group or in several smaller groups. They ended up on three different ships in Rotterdam, with the Dieters, Schneiders, Geberts, and Schaber sailing together on the *Princess Augusta*.

11. Wokeck, *Trade in Strangers*, 45.

12. Germany became a nation in 1871.

13. Schwaigern is located in what is now the German state of Baden-Württemberg.

14. For in-depth discussions of the reasons for emigration from southwest Germany during the eighteenth century, see Wokeck, "A Tide of Alien Tongues," 25, 44–45; Wokeck, *Trade in Strangers*, 1–18; and Fogleman, *Hopeful Journeys*, 23–28, 59.

15. Teva J. Scheer, *Our Daily Bread: German Village Life, 1500–1850* (North Saanich, BC, Canada: Adventis Press, 2010), 32.

16. Ibid.

17. The reasons Dieter and others left Schwaigern are summed up in the letter Peter Lohrman wrote home in October 1739. Lohrman said he had heard from a current resident that "things are rather bad in Schwaigern in regards to forced labor, guard duty, the authorities, having to pay duties and taxes, and disease. However, here where we are, things are much better. I only labor for one day and pay 18 pence, that is 30 Kreuzer. I don't pay any tithes, and there are no penalties. . . . Whatever I build and plant belongs to me." He goes on to say, "If the reports people tell when they arrive are true, I wouldn't

want to live there with you anymore. I can imagine that the poor are doing quite badly, and I feel for them from the bottom of my heart. I wish they'd be able to live like I do, then they wouldn't suffer any lack." Letter from Peter Lohrman, Germantown, Pennsylvania, dated October 1739, City Archive of Schwaigern, A1246.

18. Less than 15 percent of the 900,000 Germans who left the Rhineland during the eighteenth century went west; Fogleman, *Hopeful Journeys*, 31.

19. The land tract given to Penn was 45,000 square miles in size.

20. William Penn, *Some Account of the Province of Pennsilvania in America* (London: Printed, and sold by Benjamin Clark, 1681). Reprinted in Albert Cook Myers, ed., *Narratives of Early Pennsylvania, West New Jersey and Delaware, 1630–1707* (New York: C. Scribner's Sons, 1912), 202–15. Online at https://archive.org/stream/narrativesofearlo3myer#page/196/mode/2up.

21. Adolph B. Benson, ed., *Peter Kalm's Travels in North America. The English Version of 1770.* Vol. 1 (New York: Dover Publications, 1987), 33.

22. Fogleman, *Hopeful Journeys*, 193 n28.

23. For more information on the court case, see Dorothee Oehler, "Hexen und Hexenverfolgung im Zabergäu und Umgebung," in *Zeitschrift des Zabergäuvereins*, no. 4 (2000): 57–78.

24. In December 1683, Margaret Mattson, a Swede living in Philadelphia, was charged with witchcraft. She was tried and found guilty — not of being a witch but of *having the reputation* of being one. William Penn, who presided over the trial, reportedly asked her, "Art thou a witch? Hast thou ridden through the air on a broomstick?" Confused and exhausted, the elderly woman answered yes. Penn then stated that he knew of no law against riding broomsticks, and she was set free.

25. The Gebert brothers sailed on the *Pennsylvania Merchant* (Captain John Stedman) in 1731. Sebastian's brother Georg traveled aboard the *Allen* (Captain James Craiges) in 1729. Sebastian's cousin Georg sailed on the *Molly* (Captain John Hodgeson) in 1727. The Lohrmans and Eberle sailed on the *Charming Nancy* (Captain Charles Stedman) in 1737. By 1738, some of these families had followed the Great Wagon Road south and were living in northern Virginia. Sebastian's brother Georg moved to Opequon, in what is now Frederick County. Michel and Friedrich Gebert settled in what is now Shenandoah County. There were also a large number of Schwaigerners living in the Robinson River Valley (now part of Madison County), among them Sebastian's cousin Georg. See also Fogleman, *Hopeful Journeys*, 62.

26. The town administrator would have been especially interested in

Dieter's reasons for going, as his own son, Georg (Jerg) Böhringer/Behringer, age twenty-seven, also was planning to leave. He ended up sailing on the *St. Andrew* (Captain John Stedman).

27. The German term *Neuländer* was originally used for emigrants who had been to the New Land and returned home to collect an inheritance or fetch family members. In return for passenger referrals, they were given free passage back to the colonies. Increasingly, shippers hired professional recruiters — essentially bounty hunters — to steer emigrants to their firms. Many of these recruiters had never been to America and were so dishonest they came to be known as "soul sellers." Without their efforts, there would have been far fewer Palatines moving west instead of east.

28. In Lohrman's letter to Schwaigern, he advised those who wanted to move to America to "make sure to get a good escort, don't follow any New Country folks, as they are rascals." Letter from Peter Lohrman, Germantown, dated October 1739, City Archive of Schwaigern, A1246.

29. High Street is now called Market Street.

30. Wokeck (*Trade in Strangers*, 241) states that 249 passengers arrived in Philadelphia aboard the *Charming Nancy* in 1737. A passenger diary (see footnote 32) states that 25 on this voyage died at sea. Based on these two sources, the total number of passengers leaving Rotterdam would have been 274. There was a large contingent of Amish on board.

31. *Minutes of the Provincial Council of Pennsylvania, from the Organization to the Termination of the Proprietary Government*, vol. 3 (September 14, 1727): 282. The 1727 statute established an oath of allegiance. The statute was amended in 1729 to include an oath of abjuration. See also Ralph B. Strassburger, *Pennsylvania German Pioneers: A Publication of the Original Lists of Arrivals in the Port of Philadelphia from 1727 to 1808* (Baltimore: Genealogical Publishing, 1980), vol. 1, xvii–xxiv.

32. The death toll is taken from the diary of passenger Hans Jacob Kauffman, as excerpted in John A. Hostetler, *Amish Society* (Baltimore: Johns Hopkins University Press, 1993), 60.

33. *Minutes of the Provincial Council of Pennsylvania*, vol. 3 (September 21, 1727): 283.

34. Historians have used these three lists to reconstruct the passenger manifests of more than three hundred Palatine ships that arrived in Philadelphia between 1727 and 1775.

35. Fogleman (*Hopeful Journeys*, 76) says the Lohrmans left with 1,300 *guilders* (the British form of *gulden*). *Gulden* and *florin* refer to the same gold

coin then in use in parts of the Holy Roman Empire; I have used *florin* here for consistency. In the early 1700s, 7 florins were valued at approximately 1 British pound.

36. According to Fogleman (*Hopeful Journeys*, 75–76, 195–96 n16), the Lohrmans served as the financial center and communications hub for the Schwaigern transplants. On page 75, Fogleman writes that Lohrman rode to the docks to meet "Sebastian Marcel" and Jerg Gebert when the immigrants arrived in Philadelphia. This is an error in translation. Lohrman intended to meet Sebastian (Dieter) and Marcell (Schneider), who traveled with Gebert on the *Princess Augusta*. Lohrman never got to help the men because none of them survived the voyage. Wust, in "The Emigration Season of 1738," says Lohrman rode to the docks to meet the Dieter family, but the family had not survived the journey (42). Wust also says the Dieters traveled on the *St. Andrew*. This is incorrect. Other families from Schwaigern were on the *St. Andrew* in 1738, but the Dieters, Schneiders, Geberts, and Schaber were on the *Princess Augusta*. These discrepancies illustrate just how difficult the Lohrman letter is to interpret.

37. Wokeck, *Trade in Strangers*, 86.

38. City Archive of Schwaigern, District of Heilbronn, Inventories and Settlements B537, pp. 200–211. The actual entry is dated March 28. This date is according to the Gregorian (New Style, NS) calendar used in Continental Europe at that time. The corresponding date in the Julian (Old Style, OS) calendar used in Great Britain and the British colonies until 1752 — and used throughout this book — is March 17, a difference of eleven days. I have used the designations OS and NS whenever it seemed useful for clarity.

39. William Penn, *A Further Account of the Province of Pennsylvania* (London, 1685). Reprinted in Albert Cook Myers, ed., *Narratives of Early Pennsylvania, West New Jersey and Delaware, 1630–1707* (New York: C. Scribner's Sons, 1912), 259–78. Online at https://archive.org/stream/narrativesof earlo3myer#page/196/mode/2up.

2. Down to the Sea

1. For a detailed explanation of this leg of the journey, see Wokeck, *Trade in Strangers*, 117–23. While a small number of Palatine ships left from Amsterdam every year, most set out from Rotterdam.

2. Their estimated departure date is based on the dates of their inventory settlements.

3. Wokeck, *Trade in Strangers*, 118–19; Wokeck, "A Tide of Alien Tongues," 194 n43; Abbot Emerson Smith, "Some New Facts About Eighteenth-Century German Immigration," *Pennsylvania History*, vol. 10, no. 2 (1943): 105; Don Yoder, ed., *Pennsylvania German Immigrants, 1709–1786* (Baltimore: Genealogical Publishing, 1980), 178–79; Wokeck, "Promoters and Passengers," in *The World of William Penn*, edited by Richard S. Dunn and Mary Maples Dunn (Philadelphia: University of Pennsylvania Press, 1986), 267. Rhine boat fare ranged from 1 to 3 British pounds sterling (about 7 to 21 florins), depending on the age of the traveler, the distance to be traveled, the amount of baggage, and whether one made his own arrangements or used the services of an agent. Children traveled half price on the Rhine as well as at sea. Infants traveled for free. The river passage to Rotterdam would account for about a third of the total transportation costs to America.

4. J. Schraver, ed., *Rotterdam: Gateway to Europe* (Rotterdam: A. D. Donker, 1948), 193–94. The Mainz boat guild controlled the Rhine upstream from Mainz.

5. Rosalind J. Beiler, "Searching for Prosperity: German Migration to the British American Colonies, 1680–1780," in *The Atlantic World: Essays on Slavery, Migration, and Imagination*, edited by Wim Klooster and Alfred Padula (Upper Saddle River, NJ: Pearson Prentice Hall, 2005), 103–4; Wokeck, *Trade in Strangers*, 88–89, 123.

6. During his Grand Tour of Europe in 1878, Mark Twain rode down the Neckar on a timber raft. He wrote that they were 50 to 100 yards long, less than 10 logs wide (to accommodate the narrowness of the river and the arches of its bridges), and segmented to bend around curves. They were steered by poling — which was harder than it looked, apparently: Twain jumped off just before his raft collided with a bridge pier and "went all to smash and scatteration like a box of matches struck by lightning." Twain, *A Tramp Abroad* (New York: Harper and Brothers, 1921), 164.

7. The literature (letters, diaries, manumission records, etc.) is filled with examples of emigrants who left under a cloud. The disgraced minister was Moritz Goetschy, who led a group of Swiss emigrants to Rotterdam in 1734. The disastrous journey is described in detail in "The Limping Messenger from Carolina, or Ludwig Weber's (from Wallisellen) Account of his Journey from Zurich to Rotterdam with that certain company which recently from Switzerland to Carolina planned to emigrate," published in Zurich by Johann Jacob Lindinner, 1735 (original in the Zurich Archives). A translation is included in the booklet *The Goetschy Family and the Limping Messenger*, by

Ruth and William Heidgerd, published by the Huguenot Historical Society, New Paltz, New York, 1968. Weber's account (pp. 6–20) gives an excellent description of the Rhine River journey.

8. Hölzer and Wistar had grown up together in the Neckar Valley. In 1717, at the age of twenty-one, Wistar moved to Philadelphia. He supported himself that first year hauling ashes for a soap maker, but over the next decade, he became a brass button maker, a hardware and dry goods retailer, a wholesale merchant, and a land speculator. In 1726 he abandoned his Reformed faith and married a woman from a wealthy and connected Quaker family in Germantown. By the early 1730s, Wistar was on his way to becoming one of the richest men in Pennsylvania, with a handsome, three-storey brick home on High Street, several doors down from the rented dwelling of his friend, the printer Ben Franklin.

9. Beiler, *Immigrant and Entrepreneur*, 144–45; Beiler, "From the Rhine to the Delaware Valley: The Eighteenth-Century Transatlantic Trading Channels of Caspar Wistar," in *In Search of Peace and Prosperity*, edited by H. Lehmann, H. Wellenreuther, and R. Wilson (University Park: Penn State University Press, 2000), 180. See also the correspondence between Wistar and Hölzer housed in the Wistar Family Papers and Morris Family Papers at the Historical Society of Pennsylvania (HSP), Philadelphia.

10. Hölzer to Wistar, May 4, 1732 (NS), Wistar Family Papers, HSP, as cited in Rosalind Beiler, "Smuggling Goods or Moving Households?" in *Menschen zwischen zwei Welten: Auswanderung, Ansiedlung, Akkulturation*, edited by Walter G. Rödel and Helmut Schmahl (Trier: WVT, 2002), 18–19.

11. Wistar had learned about gun technology as the son of a forester and as a former apprentice to the chief huntsman in the Palatinate. Note that air guns date back to 1580. In the seventeenth century they were used to hunt deer and wild boar. They required no gunpowder but instead were charged by pumping air into a reservoir. They were faster to load than conventional firearms, quieter, and could be used in wet weather.

12. Wistar to Hölzer, October 1, 1737 (OS); Wistar to Hölzer, November 17, 1737 (OS); both Morris Family Papers, HSP.

13. The information about what was contained in this shipment was gleaned from the following letters: Wistar to Hölzer, October 1, 1737 (OS); Hölzer to Wistar, April 1, 1739 (NS); Hölzer to Wistar, June 1, 1740 (NS) and June 6, 1740 (NS). Morris and Wistar Family Papers, HSP.

14. Beiler, "Smuggling Goods or Moving Households?" 23; Wokeck, *Trade in Strangers*, 45 (table 2).

15. Wistar to Hölzer, November 20, 1736 (OS), Wistar Family Papers, HSP, as cited in Beiler, "Smuggling Goods or Moving Households?" 22.

16. Wistar to Hölzer, October 1, 1737 (OS), Morris Family Papers, HSP.

17. Gehr is also referred to as "Geer," "Geers," and "Gerr" in the correspondence between Hölzer and Wistar.

18. Wistar to Hölzer, April 6, 1739 (OS), Morris Family Papers, HSP. Wistar refers to a letter Hölzer sent him via Gehr. The letter Gehr carried was dated May 1, 1738 (NS). That translates to April 20 in the Old Style calendar.

19. Wistar to Hölzer (no date, but possibly winter 1731–32), Wistar Family Papers, HSP.

20. Charles R. Haller, *Across the Atlantic and Beyond: The Migration of German and Swiss Immigrants to America* (Bowie, MD: Heritage Books, 1993), 242 (table 6.6).

21. Roy E. H. Mellor, *The Rhine: A Study in the Geography of Water Transport*, O'Dell Memorial Monograph No. 16 (1983): 86, 90–91.

22. Richard Remer, "Toll Stations along the Rhine," *The Palatine Immigrant*, vol. 21, no. 3 (June 1996): 116–17.

23. Remer, "Toll Stations along the Rhine," 117 (fig. 1), 119–25; Mellor, *The Rhine*, 71 (fig. 4.3b).

24. Robert Mark Spaulding, "Anarchy, Hegemony, Cooperation: International Control of the Rhine River, 1789–1848," paper presented to the Consortium on Revolutionary Europe: 1750–1850 (Charleston, SC, 1999), 3.

25. Gottlieb Mittelberger, who traveled to Pennsylvania in 1750, said it took him seven weeks from Heilbronn to Rotterdam, "caused by the many stoppages down the Rhine and in Holland, whereas this journey could otherwise be made swifter." He wrote that "the Rhine-boats from Heilbronn to Holland have to pass by 36 custom-houses, at all of which the ships are examined, which is done when it suits the convenience of the custom-house officials. In the meantime the ships with the people are detained long, so that the passengers have to spend much money. The trip down the Rhine alone lasts therefore 4, 5, and even 6 weeks." *Gottlieb Mittelberger's Journey to Pennsylvania in the Year 1750 and Return to Germany in the Year 1754* (Ithaca, New York: Cornell University Press, 2009), 13–14, 18.

26. Durs Thommen, a Swiss emigrant who made the Rhine journey in 1736, wrote: "As far as illness is concerned, the Mannheim skippers had two of the boats sidewise together; in the one besides ours 7 children died of small pox and a woman of spotted fever, and in our boat 19 people died until

Rotterdam." Letter from October 20, 1736, as cited in Leo Schelbert, "On the Power of Pietism: A Documentary on the Thommens of Schaefferstown," *Historic Schaefferstown Record*, vol. 17, nos. 3 and 4 (July–October 1983): 51.

27. Today the fort is located on the German side of the border.

28. Wokeck, *Trade in Strangers*, 62–63; Wokeck, "Promoters and Passengers," 268.

29. Wust, "The Emigration Season of 1738," 23–24.

30. Letter from Johannes Burckhalter in Geroltzheim to Bartholomeus von Löwring in Amsterdam, May 13, 1738 (New Style calendar; May 2 Old Style). Archives of the Mennonite Congregation at Amsterdam, Gemeentelijke Archifdienst, Amsterdam. Burckhalter wrote: "Most valued friends, I can't refrain from writing to you once again, in order to report that our dear and valued friend and brother in Christ, Henrich Kündtig from Grumbach, was here to visit. He informed me that many people are embarking on their journey to Pennsylvania, and are moving to that country. A skipper from Heidelberg told him that there are about 3000 people in all, children and adults, and also that many of them are being transported to Amsterdam. When I was in Worms on the 10th of this month there were already 12 ships there, and I saw the sad state of affairs with my own eyes. And on the 12th of this month about 20 ships were in Mannheim." Note: According to the Old Style calendar, the dates in his letter translate to April 30 and May 1.

31. Church register of Lichtenau for 1738, 475; as cited in Wust, "The Emigration Season of 1738," 26.

32. "Authentic Open Letter from Pennsylvania in America" ["Glaubhaftes Send=Schreiben aus Pennsylvania in America"]. Published in Frankfurt, 1739. Reprinted in English in *The Brethren in Colonial America*, edited by Donald F. Durnbaugh (Elgin, IL: The Brethren Press, 1967), 49; also Wust, "The Emigration Season of 1738," 28.

33. Wust, "The Emigration Season of 1738," 28, 46.

3. Port of Departure

1. Much of the Netherlands is at or below sea level (*Nederlands* is Dutch for "low lands"). Since ancient times the inhabitants have struggled to hold back river and sea water by building dikes, dams, sea walls, and coastal dunes, and rerouting it with canals, drainage channels, and ditches. To this day the landscape is a patchwork of polders, tracts of sodden turf reclaimed by encircling with a dike and pumping out the water. During the eighteenth century,

more than 10,000 wind-driven pumps — the iconic Dutch windmills — were in use in the lowlands in a continuous battle against flooding.

2. Emigrants who had made arrangements to leave from Amsterdam traveled north on the Ijssel River. The largest and most powerful Dutch city played only a minor role in the emigrant trade, though. Of the more than 530 Palatine voyages made prior to the American Revolution, only 14 are known to have sailed from there. Just one ship was being readied for the 1738 season (Wokeck, *Trade in Strangers*, appendix).

3. Wokeck, *Trade in Strangers*, 60, 114–15, appendix.

4. Arthur L. Jensen, *The Maritime Commerce of Colonial Philadelphia* (Madison: State Historical Society of Wisconsin for the Dept. of History, University of Wisconsin, 1963), 88–90; John H. Andrews, "Anglo-American Trade in the Early Eighteenth Century," *Geographical Review*, vol. 45, no. 1 (January 1955): 100–103.

5. Wokeck, *Trade in Strangers*, 59–60, 67–68, 73.

6. Farley Grubb, "Redemptioner Immigration to Pennsylvania: Evidence on Contract Choice and Profitability," *Journal of Economic History*, vol. 46, no. 2 (June 1986): 409–11, 415.

7. Wokeck, *Trade in Strangers*, xvix–xx. Wokeck's book provides an in-depth examination of the social, economic, and technological forces at work in the Palatine trade. See especially chapter 3.

8. John Stedman commanded the *Pennsylvania Merchant* from 1731–34, and the same ship renamed *St. Andrew* in 1737.

9. Wokeck, *Trade in Strangers*, appendix.

10. Farley Grubb, "The Market Structure of Shipping German Immigrants to Colonial America," *Pennsylvania Magazine of History and Biography*, vol. 3, no. 1 (January 1987): 30–33.

11. *American Weekly Mercury* (Philadelphia), February 14–21, 1738.

12. Grubb, "Market Structure," 31.

13. Ibid., 40.

14. Wokeck, *Trade in Strangers*, 70 (table 3).

15. Ruth and William Heidgerd, *The Goetschy Family and the Limping Messenger* (New Paltz, NY: Huguenot Historical Society, 1968), 17.

16. Wokeck, *Trade in Strangers*, 70 (table 3), 71 (note a), appendix.

17. Wokeck, *Trade in Strangers*, 63–64; Wust, "The Emigration Season of 1738," 24; Wokeck, "Promoters and Passengers," 268.

18. "Emigratie over Rotterdam in de 18ᵉ eeuw" [Emigration from Rotterdam in the 18th Century], in *De Gids* [The Guide], vol. 72 (Amsterdam:

P. N. van Kampen and Son, 1908), 329; *DWL — de Esch Bestemmingsplan*, 13 maart 2013, Hoofdstuk 3, Beschrijving plangebied en ruimtelijke analyse, 3.1 Archeologie [Zoning plan for the waterworks of de Esch, May 13, 2013, chapter 3: Description planning area and spatial analysis, 3.1 Archaeology], 20–24. Online at http://www.betrokkenbijrotterdam.nl/Clusters/RSO/Document %202013/Bekendmakingen/Bestemmingsplannen/DEELGEMEENTE%20 KRALINGEN%20CROOSWIJK/2.%20Bestemmingsplan%20DWL-de %20Esch_oh01.pdf.

19. *Resolutien van de Heeren Staaten van Hollandt ende West Vrieslandt*, 13–5 (1738), 285, as cited in Wust, "The Emigration Season of 1738," 25.

20. "Authentic Open Letter from Pennsylvania in America," 49. The report was written by fourteen prominent men from Philadelphia, based on what they said were about one hundred "unanimous" eyewitness accounts. It's not known if any of those accounts were written down or if they still exist.

21. Extract from the "Resolutions of the Mayors and 'Fabrijkmeesteren' [Department of Public Works] of the City of Rotterdam," dated June 20, 1737 (June 9, OS). Stadsarchief Rotterdam (City Archives of Rotterdam), BNR 33.01, Inventory no. 5139.

22. *Rotterdamse Courant*, June 11, 1738 (May 31, OS). Section begins: "Gisteren arriveerden" (Yesterday arrived).

23. Wokeck, *Trade in Strangers*, 76–77 (including note 45 on p. 76).

24. This is an estimate based on the arrival of the *Princess Augusta* at Hellevoetsluis (May 30, OS) and a power of attorney document from the City Archives of Rotterdam, dated June 24 (June 13, OS), that states that George Long is "now bound for America." It's likely that the ship left Rotterdam in late June, but at the very least the passengers were on board in mid-June. Source: City Archives of Rotterdam, Notarial Records, granting George Long power of attorney for Mary Pillans, ONA 2332–145 (541).

25. E. Wiersum, *Rotterdamsch jaarboekje* [Rotterdam Yearbook] (Rotterdam: W. L. & J. Brusse, 1921), 45.

26. Walter L. Robbins, "Swiss and German Emigrants to America in Rotterdam, 1736: Excerpts from a Travel Journal of Hieronymus Annoni," *The Report* [of the Society for the History of Germans in Maryland], vol. 35 (1972): 46–51.

4. The *Princess Augusta*

1. A tun cask held 252 gallons of wine and weighed approximately 2,240 pounds. A ship's tonnage could vary somewhat from voyage to voyage, based on how the vessel's interior was configured to accommodate a particular cargo. In two earlier voyages, the *Princess Augusta* was rated at 170 tons and 210 tons, respectively. The admiralty issued a Mediterranean pass to the ship for the 1738 voyage. At that time she was rated at 200 tons.

2. Many of the details related to the ship's origin, size, and design; the makeup of the crew; and the ship's prior voyages were provided by Michael Hunt, curator of the Ramsgate Maritime Museum in Ramsgate, England.

3. The master/owners of the *Princess Augusta* paid the seamen's levy in London, at the end of a voyage from Arkhangel'sk that terminated on October 20, 1737. Seamen's Sixpence records, the National Archives (United Kingdom), ADM 68/197.

4. Will of George Long, Mariner of Ramsgate, Isle of Thanet, Kent. The National Archives (United Kingdom), PROB 11/696/62.

5. She may have sailed to North America before 1736 under a different name.

6. Letter from Durs Thommen dated October 20, 1736. Reprinted in Schelbert, "On the Power of Pietism," 50–51.

7. *American Weekly Mercury* (Philadelphia), September 16–23, 1736.

8. Ralph Davis, *The Rise of the English Shipping Industry in the Seventeenth and Eighteenth Centuries* (New York: St. Martin's Press, 1962), 71.

9. Mediterranean Pass 2463, issued May 25, 1738 (OS), to the *Princess Augusta* to make a voyage from London to Philadelphia to the West Indies, the National Archives (United Kingdom), ADM 7.

10. In London newspapers in the 1730s, Coleman advertised himself as a "legal Broker, who buys and sells all Manner of Merchandize, and Ships, at publick and private Sales; enters and clears Ships, &c. at the Custom-House, and takes out Mediterranean Passes, and lets out Ships to Freight."

11. Mediterranean Pass 2463, issued May 25, 1738 (OS). The National Archives (United Kingdom), ADM 7.

12. Jensen, *The Maritime Commerce of Colonial Philadelphia*, 45–46.

13. A hogshead is a sixty-three-gallon cask.

14. There was an Abraham Redwood, a merchant from Newport, Rhode Island, who ran a large sugar plantation on Antigua. It's not known if he was related to John Redwood of Ramsgate, part owner of the *Princess Augusta*.

15. Jensen, *The Maritime Commerce of Colonial Philadelphia*, 45–46.

16. This language is taken from the 1738 charterparty for the 200-ton *Glasgow* (Captain Walter Stirling). City Archives of Rotterdam, Notarial Records: ONA 2332–122 (414–418).

17. Wokeck, *Trade in Strangers*, 130.

18. Numerous letters from America warned against the practice. Leonard Melchior, a German who sailed to Pennsylvania in 1732, wrote a pamphlet some years later containing travel advice for prospective emigrants. Among other tips, he warned travelers to make sure "the water is kept in good casks, which must be specially provided for that purpose (for the merchants often use wine barrels, beer barrels, and the like, to save expenses). If this is not done, the water will acquire a stench and become the cause of much sickness, and cause the death of passengers at sea, which unfortunately happens quite often." See "Well Meant Information as to How the Germans, Who Wish to Travel to Pennsylvania, Should Conduct Themselves" [pamphlet usually referred to by historians as "Melchior's Advice"], written in 1749. Reprinted in *Pennsylvania German Roots Across the Ocean*, edited by Marion F. Egge (Philadelphia: Genealogical Society of Pennsylvania, 2000), 47.

19. Again, this language is from the Hope firm's charterparty for the 200-ton *Glasgow* (1738) and would have been nearly identical to that of the *Princess Augusta*.

20. Michael Schneider, age forty, was a tailor. He traveled with his wife, Anna Elisabeth, age thirty, and two sons, George (twelve) and Johann (six). The family was believed to be from Landau in the Palatinate. They ended up on a ship to Georgia (see chapter 10). Within a year of their arrival in America, Anna Elisabeth died in childbirth. Schneider remarried Anna Elisabeth Sanftleben in April 1740. Frank L. Perry, Jr., *Johannes Michael Schneider Descendants and Allied Families: 1738–1993* (Lilburn, GA: Published by the author), 117.

21. Their fate is revealed in the journals of Martin Boltzius, the minister of the Salzburger community in Ebenezer, Georgia, contained in volumes 5–8 (1738–1741) of *Detailed Reports on the Salzburger Emigrants Who Settled in America*, edited by Samuel Urlsperger (Athens: University of Georgia Press). See also chapter 10.

22. In *Trade in Strangers* (129), Wokeck describes the sizes of Palatine ships at mid-century. One of the smallest, at 100 tons, had a space between decks of four to four-and-a-half feet. One of the largest, at 220 tons, had a space between decks of four feet ten inches.

23. *Boston Gazette*, January 8–15, 1739.

24. One researcher suggests multiplying the number of full freights by 1.28 to approximate the number of people on board. Abbot Emerson Smith, "Some New Facts About Eighteenth-Century German Immigration," *Pennsylvania History*, vol. 10, no. 2 (April 1943): 116.

25. *Boston Gazette*, January 15–22, 1739.

26. This language is taken from a Hope contract dated 1756 (reprinted in Yoder, ed., *Pennsylvania German Immigrants*, 255–58). Except for some minor improvements in the menu and the insertion of an "escape clause," the shipper's contracts had not changed much since the 1730s.

27. The passengers had originally planned to go to South Carolina, where they had family and friends, but were told by the Rotterdam magistrates that it was against King George's orders to transport them there. The emigrants then contracted with the Hopes for passage to Philadelphia. This story is retold in Elizabeth Clarke Kieffer, "The Cheese Was Good," *Pennsylvania Folklife*, vol. 19, no. 3 (Spring 1970): 27–29. Original petition is in the National Archives (United Kingdom): "Report on the Petition of Theobald Kieffer and Others. 9 September, 1737." Record no. SP 42/138.

28. Klaus Wust, "William Byrd II and the Shipwreck of the *Oliver*," *Newsletter* [of the Swiss-American Historical Society], vol. 20, no. 2 (1984): 4–5; Wust, "Palatines and Switzers for Virginia, 1705–1738: Costly Lessons for Promoters and Emigrants," *Yearbook of German-American Studies* 19 (1984): 52. Note: Wust states the Switzers arrived in Rotterdam in early June, which would have been late May according to the Old Style calendar used in this book.

29. Wust, "William Byrd II and the Shipwreck of the *Oliver*," 5.

30. Ibid.

31. Wust, "The Emigration Season of 1738," 29. The four other ships were the *Queen Elizabeth*, *Thistle Galley*, *Winter Galley*, and *Glasgow*. The *Rotterdamse Dingsdaagse Courant* (June 24, 1738, NS) reported that the five ships reached the North Sea on the day before (June 23). That date translates to June 12 (OS). It would have taken the ships several days to reach the sea from Rotterdam, so we can infer that these ships left port in the first week or the beginning of the second week of June.

32. "Authentic Open Letter from Pennsylvania in America," 49.

33. Schraver, ed., *Rotterdam*, 14.

5. Crossing the English Channel

1. Cowes is pronounced "cows." It was apparently named after a pair of cow-shaped sandbanks at the entrance to the harbor.

2. Ralph Beaver Strassburger, *Pennsylvania German Pioneers: A Publication of the Original Lists of Arrivals in the Port of Philadelphia from 1727 to 1808*, edited by William John Hinke (Baltimore: Genealogical Publishing, 1980); Wokeck, *Trade in Strangers*, 241; Wust, "The Emigration Season of 1738," 49.

3. A letter written by Caspar Wistar to Georg Friedrich Hölzer on April 6, 1739 (OS), provides the only known timeline of the ship's passage through the English Channel; Morris Family Papers, HSP. Wistar wrote, "They sailed for 7 days to Cowes."

4. *Rotterdamse Dingsdaagse Courant*, June 24, 1738 (NS).

5. Wust, "The Emigration Season of 1738," 29.

6. Stadsarchief Rotterdam (City Archives of Rotterdam), Notarial Records: ONA 2415–181, C. A. Cantier, July 8, 1738 (NS).

7. Ibid., 515.

8. Ibid., 516–17.

9. Ibid., 515.

10. Deposition of Carlo Toriano, as reprinted in Wust, "William Byrd II and the Shipwreck of the *Oliver*," 6. Original deposition (in French) is housed in the Stadsarchief Rotterdam (City Archives of Rotterdam), Notarial Records: ONA 2415–181, C. A. Cantier, August 4, 1739 (NS).

11. Today, West Cowes is referred to simply as Cowes.

12. Rob Martin, "Carolina, Cowes and the Rice Trade," produced by the Isle of Wight History Center (http://www.iwhistory.org.uk/), 2004.

13. Martin, "Carolina, Cowes and the Rice Trade"; John Medland, "Cowes at Centre of World Trade," *Isle of Wight County Press Online*, March 21, 2014, http://www.iwcp.co.uk/news/wight-living/cowes-at-centre-of-world-trade-54992.aspx.

14. In a petition submitted to the Council of the Province of Pennsylvania, passenger Durst Thome (written in other documents as Durs Thommen) explained that during their journey down the Rhine, the Palatines had sold their old household goods for a small quantity of new, less bulky ones. When the ship stopped at Cowes, "the said Household Goods, Utensils, and other Things belonging to your Petitioners were freely exposed to the View of the Officers of that Port, who suffered them to pass without Molestation or requiring any Rates, Duty, or Customs for the same, they being for the proper use of your Petitioners, and not for Sale." Yet, due to "the Severity" of the inspectors in Philadelphia, all of their property had been seized. As a result, the Palatines were "reduced to very great Straits." *Minutes of the Provincial Council of Pennsylvania*, vol. 4, March 11, 1737, 171–72.

The goods in question included 165 cast-iron chimney backs (weighing nearly 5.5 tons), 596 scythes, 103 straw knives, 276 clasp knives, 24 pairs of scissors, 27 iron stew pans with lids, 81 ladles, 54 worsted caps, 24 printed linen caps, 63 shovels, 13 axes, 5 copper stills, 9 kegs of brandy, and dozens and dozens of other items in suspiciously large quantities and packaged in bundles. The passengers also carried with them a wide variety of luxury goods: umbrellas, black girdles, ivory combs, ivory needle cases, tobacco pipes with brass covers, eyeglasses, mirrors, flutes, and wooden clocks, according to the Writ of Appraisement [of the ship and cargo], October 13, 1736, in *Records of the Court of Vice Admiralty Held in Philadelphia*, vol. 1, 1735–1747, 68–71. It's difficult to read the itemized list — which takes up several pages in the record book — and not conclude that the passengers were smuggling. How they made it past Cowes "unmolested" is anyone's guess.

In a letter to a friend, merchant Caspar Wistar told how the customs officers boarded the ship while the male passengers were at the courthouse taking their oath of allegiance. "Those nasty culprits were so terrible," he wrote, "they even searched people's bags and under women's clothes." (Wistar to Baltzer Langhar, November 25, 1736 (OS), Wistar Family Papers, HSP.) What Wistar didn't say was that inspectors caught some of the passengers sneaking goods off under their coats.

The case was first brought before the Vice Admiralty Court in Philadelphia in October 1736. The presiding judge, Charles Read, ruled in the Palatines' favor. However, Judge Read died before his order to return the goods could be carried out. Customs officials released the ship but held on to the Palatines' property. The passengers petitioned the council again in March 1737, but on July 19 the court ruled that the property had been rightly confiscated.

15. D. Arnold-Forster, *At War with the Smugglers* (London: Conway Maritime Press, 1970), 29–30; "The History of Cowes Customs Until 1750," http://www.customscowes.co.uk//history_of_cowes_customs_until1750.htm.

16. Benson, *Peter Kalm's Travels in North America*, 10.

17. See these eighteenth- and nineteenth-century travel guides: John Sturch, *A View of the Isle of Wight in Four Letters to a Friend* (1780); Richard Worsley, *The History of the Isle of Wight* (1781); John Albin, *A Companion to the Isle of Wight* (1799); and Thomas Barber, *Barber's Picturesque Illustrations of the Isle of Wight* (1834).

18. *Daily Gazetteer* (London), July 25, 1738 (OS).

19. According to the letter from Caspar Wistar to Georg Friedrich Hölzer dated April 6, 1739 (OS), the *Princess Augusta* traveled 5 days from Cowes to Plymouth. According to the Toriano deposition (reprinted in Wust, "Wil-

liam Byrd II and the Shipwreck of the *Oliver*"), it took the *Oliver* "11 or 12 days" to reach Plymouth from Cowes. It's not known if the ships left Cowes together.

20. "Authentic Open Letter from Pennsylvania in America," 50.

21. This account appeared in the obituary of Samuel Suther's son, David Suther, and is based on information contained in Samuel's diary. The obituary was published in the *Reformed Church Messenger*, May 10, 1843. Excerpt reprinted in Wust, "William Byrd II and the Shipwreck of the *Oliver*," 10.

6. Life and Death on the North Atlantic

1. Richard Nicholls Worth, *The History of Plymouth: From the Earliest Period to the Present Time* (Plymouth, England: W. Brenden, 1890), 136–39.

2. In the Northern Hemisphere, the prevailing winds blow in a clockwise direction, with the northeast trade winds blowing from east to west between the equator and 30 degrees north, and the westerlies blowing from west to east between 30 and 60 degrees north. In the Southern Hemisphere, the prevailing winds blow in a counterclockwise direction.

3. Klaus Wust, "Feeding the Palatines: Shipboard Diet in the Eighteenth Century," *The Report* [of the Society for the History of the Germans in Maryland], vol. 39 (1984): 39.

4. Robert A. Selig, "Rats, Maggots, and Hardtack: Transatlantic Travel in the 18th Century," *German Life* (February/March 2000): 29.

5. Wust, "Feeding the Palatines," 39; Wokeck, *Trade in Strangers*, 134.

6. John George Käsebier, who crossed the Atlantic in 1724, described how a young woman fell into the hold while carrying an iron kettle of soup and died after being bedridden for several weeks. Letter reprinted in "Two Early Letters from Germantown," *Pennsylvania Magazine of History and Biography*, vol. 84, no. 2 (April 1960): 220. (Käsebier's letter also appears in Durnbaugh, ed., *The Brethren in Colonial America*, 222.)

David Scholtze recalled a close call on board the *Pennsylvania Merchant* in 1733. At dinnertime a woman spilled butter into the fire, which caused it to flare up. "Had the main-sail been lying on the other rigging it might easily have caught fire and thus between fire and water, the whole ship would have gone to destruction," he wrote. Journal of David Scholtze reprinted in "Narrative of the Journey of the Schwenckfelders to Pennsylvania, 1733," *Pennsylvania Magazine of History and Biography*, vol. 10, no. 2 (July 1886): 177.

7. Regarding the meat, "Every Man was obliged to beat his Share with a Maul to make it tender, with a little stinking Butter for Sauce," wrote one

emigrant in 1729; Susan E. Klepp and Billy G. Smith, eds., *The Infortunate: The Voyage and Adventures of William Moraley, an Indentured Servant* (University Park: Pennsylvania State University Press, 2002), 60. Käsebier discovered the meat he and his shipmates were being served had been in barrels for six or seven years, during which time it had traveled to the East Indies and back; "Two Early Letters from Germantown," 222. Gottlieb Mittelberger wrote of the hardtack that there was scarcely a piece "the size of a dollar that had not been full of red worms and spiders' nests"; *Gottlieb Mittelberger's Journey to Pennsylvania*, 24.

8. Georg Friedrich von Berbisdorff, who sailed on the *Albany* in 1728, wrote about the dolphins caught from his ship: "They were delicious to eat," he claimed, "the broth tasting as good as if from a chicken." "Diary of a Voyage from Rotterdam to Philadelphia in 1728," translated by Julius F. Sachse, *The Pennsylvania-German Society Proceedings and Addresses at Philadelphia, Dec. 8, 1907*, vol. 18 (1909): 10. Note that the author of the diary was unknown at the time it appeared in this journal. He has since been identified as Berbisdorff.

9. Wust, "Feeding the Palatines," 34. Two quarts seemed to be the average, although it could vary from one to four quarts, depending on the ship.

10. Mittelberger wrote that the water he was given was "black, thick and full of worms," and one drinks it "at the risk of his life"; *Gottlieb Mittelberger's Journey to Pennsylvania*, 24. Peter Kalm, a Swede who traveled to America from London in 1748, wrote that his ship got its water from the Thames River, "reputed to have the best of any river." He described how the water had to be aired out for several hours after the casks were opened, to allow the "nauseous smell" to dissipate. If a candle were held too close, the vapors rising from the water would catch fire; Benson, *Peter Kalm's Travels in North America*, 14–15.

11. Letter by Joggi Thommen, reprinted under the heading "Copia," *Schaefferstown Bulletin*, vol. 6, no. 1 (March 1972): 3.

12. In 1742, Lutheran pastor Henry Melchior Muhlenberg wrote in his journal about how their ship had run low on water. "The captain said that he still had a small quantity of olive oil, of which each might drink a little every day and keep alive when the water was gone. He also had left a few bottles of vinegar, of which we took a little occasionally." One week later, their ship obtained several casks of water from a passing English warship. *The Journals of Henry Melchior Muhlenberg*, vol. 1, 1742–1763, translated by T. G. Tappert and J. W. Doberstein (Camden, ME: Picton Press, 1993), 54.

13. After landfall, five of the passengers brought murder charges against the captain, claiming he had purposely delayed the voyage in order to extort

money from the passengers by starving them. He was tried but acquitted. For more on this voyage, see chapter 8.

14. Wokeck, "Promoters and Passengers," 271. Clothing and bedding had to be rinsed in fresh water because the salt in seawater attracts moisture, preventing the fabric from drying.

15. Mittelberger wrote how "the lice abound so frightfully, especially on sick people, that they can be scraped off the body"; *Gottlieb Mittelberger's Journey to Pennsylvania*, 20. "There are such quantities of lice on the people," wrote Swiss emigrant John Naas in 1733, "that many persons are compelled to louse for a whole day at a time, and if one does not do this very frequently they might devour one." Letter by Naas reprinted in Martin Grove Brumbaugh, *A History of the German Baptist Brethren in Europe and America* (Mount Morris, IL: Brethren Publishing House, 1899), 121.

16. Wokeck, "Promoters and Passengers," 271.

17. According to Muhlenberg, the rats "were so numerous on the ship that one could count several thousands. They gave me many a sleepless night and came so near me in bed that I had to shoo them away like flies with a handkerchief." As it was, the Reverend Muhlenberg's accommodations were the best on the ship, as he and several other prominent passengers shared quarters with the captain. *The Journals of Henry Melchior Muhlenberg*, 35.

18. Naas letter in Brumbaugh, *A History of the German Baptist Brethren in Europe and America*, 121.

19. *Boston News-Letter*, January 12, 1739. To convert eighteenth-century British pounds sterling to today's American dollars, go to http://www.uwyo.edu/numimage/currency.htm.

20. Long could find latitude by using a sextant, but to find longitude he needed to know how fast he had traveled in a given direction from a set point over a certain period of time. A log with a knotted rope was used to determine speed (in "knots"); an hourglass measured time. This process, called dead reckoning, was not terribly accurate. The problem of finding longitude would be solved with the invention of the chronometer in 1761.

21. Wokeck, *Trade in Strangers*, 91–92; Wokeck, "Capitalizing on Hope: Transporting German Emigrants across the Atlantic before the American Revolution," *Amerikastudien/American Studies: Transatlantic Migration*, vol. 42, no. 3 (1997): 350.

22. Naas letter in Brumbaugh, *A History of the German Baptist Brethren in Europe and America*, 118–19.

23. "Diary of a Voyage from Rotterdam to Philadelphia in 1728," 11. Note

the eighteenth-century names for flying fish, dolphins, whales, porpoises, sharks, and rays — all of which were commonly seen during the voyage across the North Atlantic.

24. Benson, *Peter Kalm's Travels in North America*, 14. "Blubber" was an eighteenth-century name for jellyfish.

25. Wokeck, *Trade in Strangers*, 135. In 1733, Stedman's *Pennsylvania Merchant* passed a dozen ships at sea, including a French man-of-war; Scholtze, "Narrative of the Journey of the Schwenckfelders to Pennsylvania, 1733," 174.

26. *Belfast New-Letter*, March 20, 1738 (OS).

27. Marcus Rediker, *Between the Devil and the Deep Blue Sea: Merchant Seamen, Pirates, and the Anglo-American Maritime World, 1700–1750* (New York: Cambridge University Press, 1987), 265.

28. Pirate ships would often do the opposite: hide all but a few men, to give the appearance of a harmless merchant ship with a small crew.

29. John Naas described what happened when his ship met another at sea. It is one more example of why Captain Stedman was held in such high regard by the Germans: "Our Captain had a boat lowered into the water and rowed with 4 seamen to their ship. When they had drunk the welcome together, he returned and brought with him half a bag of apples, a goose, a duck, and 2 chickens and distributed the beautiful apples at once among the people. That caused great rejoicing to get such beautiful American apples on the high sea, and those which were still left over he threw among the people to grapple for them, and they fell in heaps over one another for the beautiful apples." Naas letter in Brumbaugh, *A History of the German Baptist Brethren in Europe and America*, 113–14.

30. *Daily Gazetteer* (London), October 19, 1738 (OS). Gravesend was the first port of call on the Thames River leading to the port of London.

31. Wistar to Hölzer, April 6, 1739 (OS), Morris Family Papers, HSP.

32. The most common diseases on eighteenth-century transport ships were the three "fevers": typhus, typhoid, and dysentery. It can be difficult to distinguish among them because they share many of the same symptoms, beginning with an elevated body temperature. Typhus, sometimes referred to as Palatine fever because of its prevalence on board German immigrant ships, is a bacterial infection transmitted by the feces of lice and fleas when crushed into bite sites through scratching, or through inhalation of dust-sized particles. Typhoid and dysentery are intestinal infections spread through oral contact with the feces of an infected person.

33. *The Boston Gazette*, January 15, 1739.

34. Dysentery may be caused by several different infectious agents, including bacteria, protozoa, viruses, and parasites. Bacillary dysentery and amoebic dysentery are the most common forms. Bacillary dysentery is caused by any of four species of the *Shigella* bacterium. Amoebic dysentery is caused by the protozoan *Entamoeba histolytica*.

35. James C. Riley, "Mortality on Long-Distance Voyages in the Eighteenth Century," *The Journal of Economic History*, vol. 41, no. 3 (September 1981): 652; Farley Grubb, "Morbidity and Mortality on the North Atlantic Passage: Eighteenth-Century German Immigration," *Journal of Interdisciplinary History*, vol. 17, no. 3 (Winter 1987): 575.

36. Wust, "The Emigration Season of 1738," 34.

37. Wistar to Hölzer, April 6, 1739 (OS), Morris Family Papers, HSP. According to Wistar, the *Princess Augusta* was on the Atlantic for fourteen weeks. According to Boston newspapers, when the ship grounded on Block Island, 105 of 340 people were still alive. It's not clear if these numbers include crew or account only for passengers.

38. David J. Stewart, "Burial at Sea: Separating and Placing the Dead During the Age of Sail," *Mortality*, vol. 10, no. 4 (November 2005): 277.

39. *Pennsylvania Gazette*, February 15, 1732; *Gentleman's Magazine*, vol. 2 (April 1732): 727.

40. For data on tropical storms and hurricanes, see http://www.aoml .noaa.gov/hrd/tcfaq/E11.html and http://www.weatherexplained.com/Vol-1 /Hurricanes.html.

41. National Oceanic and Atmospheric Administration (NOAA), "Hurricane Basics," May 1999, https://www.hsdl.org/?view&did=34038.

42. Sherry Johnson, "From El Niño to the 'Long La Niña': Early Indicators of Crisis in the Atlantic World, 1730s–40s," presented at the American Historical Association conference in New Orleans, January 5, 2013.

43. *Boston Post-Boy*, April 9, 1739.

44. *Pennsylvania Gazette*, October 19–26, 1738; *Boston Evening-Post*, November 12, 1738.

45. Christopher Schultz, who sailed aboard the *St. Andrew* in 1734, wrote, "This is the most distressing time on board ship . . . on account of being hurled from one side of the ship to the other, one could neither sit nor lie down. This caused a great deal of discomfort to the sick." "Christopher Schultz's Account (1734)," in Alfred T. Meschter, *The Ship St. Andrew, Galley: A Hypothesis* (Pennsburg, PA: Schwenkfelder Library, 1992), 32.

46. Naas letter in Brumbaugh, *A History of the German Baptist Brethren in Europe and America*, 114.

47. "Nitschmann's Diary," in Adelaide L. Fries, *The Moravians in Georgia: 1735–1740* (Raleigh, NC: Edwards and Broughton, 1905), 119.

48. Naas also wrote: "At midnight the waves struck so hard against the portholes aft, that 2 boards sprang away from the windows where part of the people lay in sleep and slumber, and the water rushed in through the window, as big as it was, and straight into the beds, which caused a great terror to those who lay near the window. . . . We took a wool-bag, which was handy, and stopped the window up and the other one with the board, that was made fast again. The ship's carpenter the next morning made a new window board." Naas letter in Brumbaugh, *A History of the German Baptist Brethren in Europe and America*, 115.

49. Letter by John Ulrich Giessendanner, reprinted in H. George Anderson, "The European Phase of John Ulrich Giessendanner's Life," *The South Carolina Historical Magazine*, vol. 67, no. 3 (July 1966): 135.

50. Wust, "The Emigration Season of 1738," 40.

51. Wust, "William Byrd II and the Shipwreck of the *Oliver*," 6.

52. Ibid., 10.

53. "Extracts of Mr. Von Reck's Journal from Dover to Ebenezer," in *An Extract of the Journals of Mr. Commissary Von Reck, Who Conducted the First Transport of Saltzburgers to Georgia: and of the Reverend Mr. Bolzius, One of their Ministers* (London: Society for Promoting Christian Knowledge, 1734), 7.

54. Wust, "The Emigration Season of 1738," 30, 33.

55. *Pennsylvania Gazette*, October 19–26, 1738.

56. "Authentic Open Letter from Pennsylvania in America," 50–51.

57. Ibid., 49.

58. By November, Robert Byrd, the proprietor of the land in Virginia on which the *Oliver*'s passengers were to settle, was concerned about the fate of the ship. In a letter to a friend dated November 30, 1738, he wrote, "I expect every day the arrival of a little ship, with Switzers and Germans, to settle upon part of my land at Roanoke. But they have been now thirteen weeks at sea, so that I am under great apprehensions for them. "Letters of John Clayton, John Bartram, Peter Collinson, William Byrd, Isham Randolph," *William and Mary Quarterly*, second series, vol. 6, no. 4 (October 1926): 307. Byrd was right to be apprehensive but wrong in his calculation: by late November it had been over twenty-four weeks since the *Oliver* left Rotterdam.

59. Grubb, "Morbidity and Mortality on the North Atlantic Passage," 570–71.

7. An Unscheduled Stop

1. The city was known as "Charles Town" until 1783, when its name was shortened to "Charleston." The Carolina territory was divided into two colonies — North Carolina and South Carolina — in 1729. The colony of Georgia was carved from South Carolina in 1732 and named for King George II.

2. "Charles Town: Descriptions of Eighteenth-Century Charles Town before the Revolution," National Humanities Center, 2009; http://national humanitiescenter.org/pds/becomingamer/growth/text2/charlestowndescrip tions.pdf.

3. *Pennsylvania Gazette*, December 6–13, 1738; *South-Carolina Gazette*, October 12, 1738.

4. "Letter from Samuel Dyssli, Charleston, South Carolina, to His Mother, Brothers and Friends in Switzerland," *South Carolina Historical and Genealogical Magazine*, vol. 23, no. 3 (July 1922): 90.

5. *American Weekly Mercury*, October 5–12, 1738.

6. This is according to Dr. John Lining, a resident of Charleston, who made the first systematic weather observations with instruments between 1738 and 1753. See David Ramsay, *History of South-Carolina, from Its First Settlement in 1670, to the Year 1808*, vol. 2 (Charleston: David Longworth, 1809), 65.

7. Sherry Johnson, "Climate Cycles as Agents of Historical Processes along the Southern Frontier: 1738–1739," presented at the American Historical Association conference in New Orleans, January 5, 2013.

8. Marion Strange, *Vital Negotiations: Protecting Settlers' Health in Colonial Louisiana and South Carolina, 1720–1763* (Göttingen, Germany: V & R Unipress, 2012), 7–8.

9. Letter from Robert Pringle to James Hunter & Co. in London, dated December 22, 1738, in *The Letterbook of Robert Pringle*, vol. 1: April 2, 1737–September 25, 1742, edited by Walter B. Edgar (Columbia, SC: University of South Carolina Press, 1972), 52.

10. Ibid., 52–53.

11. Act No. 593: "An Act to Provide a Full Supply for Subsisting Poor Protestants Coming from Europe and Settling in His Majesty's New Townships in This Province . . . ," in *The Statutes at Large of South Carolina, Volume 3, Containing the Acts from 1716, Exclusive, to 1752, Inclusive*, edited by Thomas Cooper (Columbia, SC: A. B. Johnston, 1838), 409–11.

12. Wust, "The Emigration Season of 1738," 23.

13. *Gottlieb Mittelberger's Journey to Pennsylvania*, 40.

14. "It is further agreed that the Said George Fraser shall during the Voyage, not touch with his Said Ship at any Port whatsoever, but by the Leave and direction of the Said John Stedman, who shall direct him during the whole Course of the Said Voyage"; from the charterparty between John Stedman and Captain George Fraser of the ship *John*, July 19, 1736, City Archives of Rotterdam, Notarial Records: ONA 2330-125 (693).

15. "Karlin" is translated either as "Charleston" or "Carolina."

16. Samuel T. Livermore, *History of Block Island, Rhode Island* (Block Island Historical Society, 2003), 122. Lignum vitae was valued for its medicinal qualities, hence the Latin name meaning "wood of life."

8. Shipwreck!

1. Quoted in Ron Redfern, *Origins: The Evolution of Continents, Oceans and Life* (Norman: University of Oklahoma Press, 2001), 241.

2. *Depositions of Officers of the Palatine Ship "Princess Augusta": Wrecked on Block Island 27th December 1738 and which was apparently the "Palatine" of Whittier's Poem* (Providence, RI: E. L. Freeman, 1939), 6–8.

3. The deposition says the ship was anchored "in 10^f [fathoms] water near Cape James in Lat. 38°:57' . . . the said Cape bearing from the N. W. by N. dist^a [distance] about 4 Leagues." The latitude measurement was probably several minutes off, but it can be assumed the ship was at the entrance to Delaware Bay and not off Cape Cod, as previous researchers of the legend have claimed. Both Cape Cod and Cape Henlopen were referred to in colonial times as Cape James, but the latitude measurement places the ship at Cape Henlopen.

4. Wearing, also called jibing, required all hands on deck and placed great strain on the masts and rigging, causing them to "wear." The opposite of wearing is tacking, whereby the ship turns by swinging the bow through the wind.

5. *Depositions of Officers of the Palatine Ship "Princess Augusta,"* 6–7.

6. Ibid., 7.

7. Ibid.

8. Ibid., 7–8.

9. Wistar to Hölzer, April 6, 1739 (OS), Morris Family Papers, HSP.

10. "Pennsylvania Weather Records, 1644–1835," *The Pennsylvania Magazine of History and Biography*, vol. 15, no. 1 (1891), 111. Record reads: "1739. Jan 25, river now open; fast since Dec 18." See also the *Pennsylvania Gazette* for

the months of December 1738 and January 1739. There are no Philadelphia Customs House entries during the weeks in which the port was closed due to ice. An entry in the January 18–25 issue (p. 3), dated January 25, states: "Our River is now intirely clear of Ice, and some Vessels are this Day gone down." For more information on the river conditions that winter, see the merchants' correspondence (especially John Reynell's in the Coates and Reynell Family Papers) at the Historical Society of Pennsylvania.

9. Rescue and Recovery

1. Les Sirkin, *Block Island Geology* (Watch Hill, RI: Book & Tackle Shop, 1996), 83 (fig. 15), 84, 108; "Block Island Sound and Approaches," NOAA Chart 13205, http://ocsdata.ncd.noaa.gov/BookletChart/13205_BookletChart.pdf. Today, foreign vessels are required to carry a local pilot when passing through Block Island Sound.

2. The letter to the *Boston Gazette*, written on March 2 by a committee of islanders that included Simon Ray, John Dickens, Ackurs Tosh, Thomas Dickens, and Nathanial Littlefield, was published in the March 12–19, 1739, issue.

3. Wistar wrote that at the time of the wreck, "92 people were still alive. Thereafter they immediately sent a boat load of them on land, where it was so cold, that 8 of those 92 people froze." Letter from Caspar Wistar to Georg Friedrich Hölzer, April 6, 1739 (OS).

4. Livermore, *History of Block Island, Rhode Island*, 290.

5. According to Livermore, John Revoe Paine lived in the house built by Edward Sands. An 1870 map of Block Island shows Paine's house located about halfway between Fresh Pond and Sands Pond. Robert M. Downie, *Block Island: The Land* (Block Island, RI: Book Nook Press, 2001), vii.

6. The Ray letter states: "the next Day the Ship was a-drift with all the Palatines Goods and Money &c. and by several we are informed with two living Souls."

7. *Boston Post-Boy*, January 15, 1739. Note that the *Boston News-Letter* also included the full version of the article in its January 11–18 issue, while abbreviated versions of the article appeared on January 15 in the *Boston Evening Post* and the *Boston Gazette*, and on January 16 in the *New England Weekly Journal*.

8. *Diary of Joshua Hempstead of New London, Connecticut* (New London: County Historical Society, 1901), 343–48. His entries for December 1738 to April 1739 are the source of weather information on Block Island, which is

located twenty-seven miles across Block Island Sound from New London, Connecticut. Note that Block Island's weather is moderated somewhat by the surrounding ocean.

9. January 22, 1739: *Boston Evening Post, Boston Post-Boy,* and *Boston Gazette*; January 23: *New England Weekly Journal.*

10. Between 1706 and 1734, John Wanton held the offices of deputy to the General Assembly, speaker of the House of Deputies, and deputy governor. He became the governor of Rhode Island in 1734 following the death of his brother William, who had been governor of the colony the previous two years. Wanton went on to serve six consecutive terms as governor, and died in office in 1740 at the age of sixty-eight.

11. Edward Sands's grandfather, James, also had been friends with Roger Williams as well as with religious exile Anne Hutchinson. James Sands began building a house for Hutchinson in what is now the Bronx, but abandoned the project due to Indian hostilities. Hutchinson was killed by Indians shortly after, in 1643.

12. Livermore, *History of Block Island,* 289.

13. Letter from Simon Ray to Benjamin Colman, September 22, 1734; letter from Ray to Colman, April 29, 1735. Benjamin Colman Papers: 1641–1806, Massachusetts Historical Society, Boston.

14. Among the famous Quaker merchants in Philadelphia were the Reynell, Logan, Norris, Drinker, Pemberton, Shippen, Morris, Shoemaker, Baynton, and Wistar families.

15. *Depositions of Officers of the Palatine Ship "Princess Augusta,"* 8–9.

16. Ibid., 9.

17. Ibid.

18. *Daily Gazetteer* (London), April 30, 1739 (OS).

19. The allegation of mutiny is made by one of the passengers, Carlo Toriano, who returned to Rotterdam after the wreck. He provided favorable testimony about the voyage at the request of the Hope firm. See Wust, "William Byrd II and the Shipwreck of the *Oliver,*" 7, 12.

20. *Boston Post-Boy,* February 19, 1739.

21. The first newspaper reports of the *Oliver* wreck were published in the *Virginia Gazette* on January 12 and January 19, 1739. Subsequent reports appeared in the *New York Weekly Journal* (January 22), the *New York Gazette* (January 22–29), the *American Weekly Mercury* (January 23–30), the *Pennsylvania Gazette* (January 25–February 1), the *Boston News-Letter* (February 15–22), the *Boston Post-Boy* (February 19), the *Boston Evening Post* (February 19), the *New England Weekly Journal* (February 20), and the *Pennsylvania Ga-*

zette (March 22–29). Reports appeared in Europe in April and May (*Gentleman's Magazine, Daily Gazetteer, Belfast News-Letter*).

22. William Byrd, the proprietor of the land in Virginia on which the *Oliver*'s passengers were to settle, wrote to a friend in March of 1739: "We have had the misfortune, lately, to lose a ship, either by the villany or stupidity of the master, which had 250 Switzers and Germans on board, which effects to a considerable value. These were to seat on part of my land, . . . [but] most of the people [perished], and very little of their effects is saved. Some few of these unhappy wretches are gone upon my land to make a beginning, and will soon be followed by more." "Letters of John Clayton, John Bartram, Peter Collinson, William Byrd, Isham Randolph," 313–14.

23. For a detailed explanation of the incident, see Nancy E. Schanes, "Voyage of the *Love and Unity*," a booklet published by the author in 2003.

24. Letter from Benjamin Colman to Governor John Wanton, undated (but likely written in late January or early February, 1739), Massachusetts Historical Society, Boston.

25. *Boston Gazette*, March 12–19, 1739.

26. Wistar to Hölzer, April 6, 1739 (OS). Emphasis mine.

27. Of the hundreds of Palatine ships that sailed in the eighteenth century, less than a dozen ever carried more than 500 passengers, and all but one of those sailed between 1749 and 1754, the peak years of German migration. Wokeck, *Trade in Strangers*, 44, 45 (table 2), appendix.

28. *Daily Gazetteer* (London), February 23, 1739; *London Evening Post*, February 22, 1739; *The Kentish Post, or Canterbury NewsLetter*, May 2–5, 1739 (all dates OS).

29. *Diary of Joshua Hempstead*, 344.

30. Livermore, *History of Block Island*, 290.

31. *Boston Post-Boy*, March 19, 1739.

10. On to Pennsylvania

1. *Diary of Joshua Hempstead*, 347; *Boston Post-Boy*, March 19, 1739.

2. *American Weekly Mercury*, March 29–April 5, 1739.

3. Letter from J. Reynell to N. Cooper, January 23, 1739, HSP.

4. The following notice appeared in the March 27, 1739, issue of the *New England Weekly Journal*: "*Rhode Island*, March 23 . . . Last Tuesday Night sail'd from hence 30 of the Palatines bound to Philadelphia, and last Night sail'd about 30 more bound to the same Port." A notice also appeared in the *Boston Evening-Post*, March 26, 1739.

5. Upon entering the bay, the captain would raise a flag and fire a cannon, and if no pilot came he would send several sailors ashore to find one. A pilot was no guarantee against grounding, however. The *Princess Augusta* had taken on a pilot at the end of her 1736 voyage, and still hit bottom so hard that passengers and crew alike thought she would break in half and sink. See letter from Durs Thommen dated October 20, 1736, reprinted in Schelbert, "On the Power of Pietism."

6. To prevent the spread of disease from "sickly vessels" to the city's population, immigrant ships were required by law to anchor one mile from the city and obtain a "bill of health," or license, from the government-appointed health inspector before landing passengers. Sick passengers and crew had to either remain on board until they recovered or be quarantined in houses outside the city at the captain's expense. Officials had been forced to crack down the previous fall, when all but a few Palatine ships arrived with diseased passengers on board. (The captains of two ships from the 1738 fleet were arrested for landing sick passengers in the city.) *Minutes of the Provincial Council of Pennsylvania*, vol. 4, 306–307, 315; *Address Delivered Before the Philadelphia County Medical Society, January 28, 1857, by Wilson Jewell, M.D.* (Philadelphia: T. K. and P. G. Collins, 1857), 8–25, 31–32; Frank Reid Diffenderffer, *The German Immigration in Pennsylvania Through the Port of Philadelphia from 1700 to 1775* (Baltimore: Genealogical Publishing, 2003), 77–78.

7. Palatines who arrived on the large ships were not allowed to disembark until they had settled their passage debts. Those who still owed part or all of their fare (relatives were liable for the debts of loved ones who died at sea) had several weeks to come up with the money before they were sold into indentured servitude. They might be "redeemed" by friends or family who were already there. Or they could post bond or leave their baggage on the ship as collateral while they ventured into the city to sell wares they had brought from Europe or find an employer who would advance money to pay off their debt. The last resort for indebted passengers was the servant auction. But not all immigrants could be sold. "The sick always fare the worst," wrote Mittelberger, "for the healthy are naturally preferred and purchased first; and so the sick and wretched must often remain on board in front of the city for 2 or 3 weeks, and frequently die, whereas many a one, if he could pay his debt and were permitted to leave the ship immediately, might recover and remain alive" (*Gottlieb Mittelberger's Journey to Pennsylvania*, 25).

8. Letters of Administration (for Sebastian Dieter), Archives of Philadelphia at the City Hall, Office of the Register of Wills, Book D, 1737–1743 (April 3, 1739), 71.

9. Letter written by Peter Lohrman of Germantown, October 1739, City Archive of Schwaigern; translation by Wust in "The Emigration Season of 1738," 42. An alternate translation by Dr. Esther Bauer reads that "Jerg Gebert's wife is on her own and still alive."

10. Dr. Bauer's translation of this passage reads as follows: "The ship's captain, that rogue, brought them to Carolina, and thereafter to Rhode Island. They had barely left the ship, when it sank after two days and everything perished. But they all arrived in the following year safe and sound." By "they all," Lohrman must be referring to the surviving castaways, as we know that the families from Schwaigern (except for Elisabetha Gebert) had died at some point during the voyage.

11. Hölzer to Wistar, April 1, 1739, NS (March 21, 1739, OS), Wistar Family Papers, HSP.

12. Wistar to Hölzer, April 6, 1739 (OS), Morris Family Papers, HSP. See the excerpts of the letter included in chapters 5, 8, and 9.

13. Hölzer to Wistar, February 20, 1740, NS (February 9, 1740, OS), Wistar Family Papers, HSP.

14. Tragically, this letter no longer exists. It is alluded to in the letter Hölzer wrote to Wistar, dated June 1, 1740, NS (May 21, 1740, OS).

15. Hölzer to Wistar, June 1, 1740, NS (May 21, 1740, OS), Wistar Family Papers, HSP.

16. *The Journals of Henry Melchior Muhlenberg*, 352; A. E. Reiff, "Conrad Gehr's Peccadilloes," *Pennsylvania Fathers of the Eighteenth Century* (blog), May 26, 2009, http://pennsylvaniafathers.blogspot.com/2009/05/outlaw-reiffs-and-lawless-religion.html.

17. *The Journals of Henry Melchior Muhlenberg*, 352–53.

18. *The Journals of Henry Melchior Muhlenberg*, 353. Conrath Gehr married Anna Maria Reiff. Entries about Gehr also appear in Fred J. Riffe, *Reiff to Riffe Family in America: Descendants of John George Reiff* (Published by the author, 1995), 21–22.

19. Letter reprinted in Lucius Manlius Sargent, *Dealings with the Dead*, vol. 2 (Boston: Dutton and Wentworth, and Ticknor and Fields, 1855), 519. Burgess Hall, age thirty-nine, was captain of the sloop *Swan*.

20. In *Detailed Reports on the Salzburger Emigrants Who Settled in America*, vol. 7, 1740, edited by Samuel Urlsperger, translated and edited by George Fenwick Jones and Don Savelle (Athens: University of Georgia Press, 1983), 277. The Schneider family is mentioned a number of times in volumes 5–8.

21. Wust, "The Emigration Season of 1738," 50. This figure is derived by adding Wust's 3,350 arrivals in Philadelphia with the approximately 60 *Princess Augusta* survivors who landed there in March 1739.

11. The Witch and the Slave

1. Long Kate also was referred to as "Tall Kate" and "Dutch Kattern." I have chosen to use "Long Kate" because that is the name her sixth-great-granddaughter, Gloria Hazard Miller, uses.

2. William P. Sheffield, *A Historical Sketch of Block Island* (Newport: John P. Sanborn & Co., 1876), 40. Sheffield was born on Block Island in 1820 and later moved to Newport, where he served as a member of the Rhode Island state legislature. In his *Sketch* he writes that Short Kattern [Kate] was supported by the town and "billeted about among the inhabitants," and that "she is said to have been buried in the corner of a private burying ground, lately belonging to the late Josiah S. Peckham."

3. I have chosen to refer to him as "New Port," to distinguish between the man and the city of Newport, Rhode Island. He also is referred to this way in other sources.

4. Maizie, *Block Island Scrapbook*, 259.

5. New Port may have been owned by Sands and hired out to Littlefield, a common practice.

6. Note that there were a number of Edwards in different branches of the Sands family. See Land Evidence records, vol. 4, 1761–1781, 341. These records, which include wills, are housed at the Town Hall on Block Island.

7. Thomas Williams Bicknell, *History of the State of Rhode Island and Providence Plantations*, vol. 2 (New York: The American Historical Society, 1920), 502.

8. Obituary of Mrs. Violet Hazard, *Narragansett Times*, December 18, 1903. Hazard was the great-granddaughter of Long Kate and New Port and the daughter of Benjamin Port. Block Island resident Benjamin Sprague, who was born on the island in 1789, knew one of the daughters of Long Kate and New Port and also heard his parents talk about the couple. He claims they married shortly after Long Kate arrived on the island. As cited in Livermore, *History of Block Island*, 119.

9. Ibid.

10. "Mr. Benjamin Sprague's Recollections About the Palatine," in Livermore, *History of Block Island*, 119.

11. Jeffrey Howe, *The History and Genealogy of Descendants of Slaves and Indians from the Island of "Manissee"—Block Island* (Riverside, RI: the author, 1997), 92.

12. Ghost Ship in the Sound

1. John Kobler, "The Mystery of the Palatine Light," *Saturday Evening Post,* June 11, 1960, 54–58. The original source for the incident and quote are not given.

2. For the twentieth-century sightings, I've included only those that initiated a formal search and were reported in newspapers. There may have been other, unreported sightings.

3. Wiley [Willey], "Metheoric Appearance Called the Palatine Light," 408–409.

4. Ibid., 409.

5. Ibid., 410.

6. Willey's account appeared in 1827 in *The Parthenon*, a literary and scientific newspaper. It was picked up by the *Rhode Island Republican* in 1833, and appeared in that paper again in 1836. According to Samuel Greene Arnold (in *History of the State of Rhode Island and Providence Plantations*, vol. 2, 1700–1790), as well as numerous other sources, the sightings stopped in 1832. Chapter 14 of this book offers an explanation for this date.

7. *Boston Post,* July 28, 1879.

8. Letter to the editor of the *Narragansett Times,* February 28, 1879. Northup's letter was in response to a letter submitted two weeks earlier (February 14, 1879) by a Palatine Light enthusiast named Benjamin Congdon. Congdon, a former Rhode Island resident who had moved to upstate New York, claimed that only two people living had ever seen the light: he and Benjamin S. Knowles of Point Judith.

9. "Block Island Legends: Folk Lore of the 'Lazy Man's Paradise,'" *New York Times,* October 19, 1884.

10. "A Seaside Spook: Narragansett Pier's Ghost Story," *St. Louis Globe-Democrat,* September 2, 1880. An excerpt of Hazard's letter also appeared in *Lippincott's Magazine,* December 1882, 542.

11. *Narragansett Historical Register,* 1882–1883, 152.

12. De Forest, *Poems: Medley and Palestina* (New Haven, CT: Tuttle, Morehouse & Taylor, 1902) x–xi.

13. "Burning of the Palatine . . . The Eerie Blaze Appears to a Philadelphian," *New York Times,* August 15, 1885.

14. *The Day*, New London, Connecticut, January 6, 1913.

15. *Newport Daily News*, June 13, 1958 (mentions 1933 and 1958 sightings); April 29, 1963 (mentions 1920s and 1963 sightings).

16. Howard M. Chapin, "The Discovery of the Real Palatine Ship," *Rhode Island Historical Society Collection*, vol. 16, no. 2 (April 1923): 33–38; *Depositions of Officers of the Palatine Ship "Princess Augusta,"* 6.

17. Henry T. Beckwith, *The History of Block Island* (Providence: n.p., 1858), 7; Arnold, *History of the State of Rhode Island*, 68–69.

18. Wiley [Willey], "Metheoric Appearance Called the Palatine Light," 410.

19. Livermore, *History of Block Island*, 120, 122.

20. Ibid., 120–21, 123.

21. *Phosphorescence* is the light produced when energy from an external light source is absorbed by a substance and immediately re-emitted. *Bioluminescence* is the light produced from a chemical reaction that occurs inside an organism. Welcome A. Greene, "A New Theory Regarding the Origin of the Palatine Light," *The Narragansett Historical Register*, vol. 5 (1886–87): 253–57.

22. C. Edwin Barrows, ed., *The Diary of John Comer*, vol. 8 (Providence: Rhode Island Historical Society, 1893), 55–56.

13. The Dancing Mortar

1. It would have been rare to find lignum vitae logs much larger than that because the wood was so heavy and the trees so small. A lignum vitae tree typically grows to between fifteen and thirty feet tall, with the trunk ranging from six to sixteen inches in diameter. One cubic foot of lignum vitae wood weighs about eighty pounds — twice as much as oak and three times as much as pine.

2. Livermore, *History of Block Island*, 120, 122.

3. Ibid., 197–99.

4. Ibid.; Samuel T. Livermore, *Block Island* (Hartford, CT: Press of the Case, Lockwood & Brainard Co., 1882 [abridged]), 89–92.

5. *New York Times*, October 19, 1884, and August 15, 1885.

6. Known today as the Lewis-Dickens farmhouse.

7. Livermore, *History of Block Island*, 121, 199; Livermore, *Block Island* (abridged), 91–92.

8. *The Transformation of Rhode Island Hall*, chapter 3, "History of Rhode Island Hall." Joukowsky Institute for Archaeology and the Ancient World, Brown University, www.brown.edu/Departments/Joukowsky_Institute/about /rihalltransform/6996.html.

14. "The Wreck of a People's Character"

1. See the 1869 letter from Benjamin Congdon to John Greenleaf Whittier, in Samuel T. Pickard, *Life and Letters of John Greenleaf Whittier*, vol. 2 (Boston: Houghton Mifflin, 1894), 527. The ninety-two-year-old Congdon had lived along the Rhode Island coast when he was a child (in the late 1700s) and claimed to have seen the ghost ship eight or ten times. He believed that the islanders had murdered the castaways. "That was a little more than the Almighty could stand," he wrote, "so He sent the Fire or Phantom Ship to let them know He had not forgotten their wickedness."

2. The poem also appeared in the *Boston Daily Evening Transcript* on December 13, 1866.

3. Joseph A. Citro and Diane E. Foulds, *Curious New England: The Unconventional Traveler's Guide to Eccentric Destinations* (Hanover, NH: University Press of New England, 2004), 237; Melanie Saunders, "Historical Society to Host Tour of Former Hazard Property," *The Independent*, June 11, 2015, http://www.independentri.com/independents/arts_and_living/article _c248856d-0ef2–5f4d-8a4c-4b7d52b7aa42.html.

4. We can infer what was in this letter from a letter Hazard sent to the *New York Times*, published on January 13, 1867. He wrote: "The Palatine had the misfortune, some 150 years ago, to fall into the hands that are ever ready to plunder where wrecks are plenty. . . . The horrors of the scene were unusual, but no more than might be expected, as at that day Newport itself was a nest of distillers of rum and stealers of negroes, . . . with a pretty fair admixture of pirates, who, by some strange idiosyncrasy of the times, were considered more worthy of the gallows than the others. The unfortunate ship was plundered and fired, and a man named Ball, passing in a boat among the struggling crew, refused succor to the drowning, and cut off with his sword the arm of a lady who desperately seized the gunwale of his boat."

5. Richard Henry Dana, *Poems and Prose Writings* (New York: Baker and Scribner, 1849), ix–x.

6. Palmer's poem appeared in the *Narragansett Times* on August 20, 1880, and was included in his 1884 collection *Psalms of Faith and Songs of Life* (Hartford, CT: Press of the Case, Lockwood & Brainard Co., 1884), 24–36.

7. J. W. De Forest, "The Phantom Ship," *Harper's New Monthly*, vol. 66, no. 394 (March 1883): 519–20; De Forest, *Poems: Medley and Palestina*, x–xi, 29–30.

8. Because this volume of *The Lady's Book* has been digitized, the origi-

nal story can be read in its entirety online at http://babel.hathitrust.org/cgi
/pt?id=mdp.39015034631443;view=1up;seq=233.

9. "The Palatine," *The Lady's Book*, vol. 5 (1832): 224.

10. The story spells the name *Vanderlin* (without the final *e*). In the legend,
the name is spelled *Vanderline* or *Van der Line*. Interestingly, the wife of the
Dutch shipper Isaac Hope was named Maria Vanvlierden (1710–1731).

11. "The Palatine," *The Lady's Book*, vol. 5 (1832): 217.

12. "The Palatine" was reprinted in the *Rhode Island Republican* (February 26 and March 5, 1833), the *Providence Patriot* (January 12, 1833), and *The
Monthly Traveller* (Boston, February, 1833). An abridged version appeared in
Chambers' Edinburgh Journal, June 4, 1836, 147–48, and in *Tales for the Grave
and the Gay*, vol. 1 (Paris: A. and W. Galignani, 1837), 171–81.

13. Poet and novelist William Gilmore Simms of Charleston wrote "The
Ship of the Palatines," published in July 1843 in the *Ladies' Companion* and
reprinted in Simms's *Poems: Descriptive, Dramatic, Legendary and Contempla-
tive*, vol. 1 (New York: Redfield, 1853). This poem is based on a similar Palatine legend that exists along the North Carolina coast, where approximately
650 Palatines established the settlement of New Bern in 1710. For a modern
retelling of the North Carolina legend, see Charles Harry Whedbee, *The
Flaming Ship of Ocracoke and Other Tales of the Outer Banks* (Winston-Salem:
John F. Blair, 1971), 13–20.

14. In fact, Higginson was the only spiritualist among them. Whittier said
of Spiritualism, "There is a fascination in it, but the fascination is blended
with doubt and repulsion. I am disgusted with the tricks and greed of these
mediums." In Pickard, *The Life and Letters of John Greenleaf Whittier*, vol. 2,
677.

15. Whittier, the "Quaker poet," was a founding member of the Anti-
Slavery Society. Palmer, pastor of the First Baptist Church in Stonington,
CT, was said to have "detested slavery." He approved a petition by his black
congregants to form their own church. De Forest, a captain in the Union
Army, wrote about the bloody reality of war for *Harper's Monthly*. After the
war he was a member of the Freedmen's Bureau, the government agency established to help refugees of the Civil War. The Bureau helped former slaves
obtain an education, health care, and jobs, reunite with their families, and
establish churches. Hale was a Unitarian minister and the founder of numerous charitable societies. He has been called the "pioneer in the modern movement for social work" (*The Christian Register*, vol. 96, no. 51 [December 20,
1917]: 1214). Higginson, also a Unitarian minister, was a militant abolitionist

and colonel of the first black regiment during the Civil War. Philip Godey, publisher of *The Lady's Book*, was a poor French immigrant. He supported women's education and women's rights by hiring them as artist and writers. Sarah Josepha Hale was the magazine's editor from 1837 to 1877.

16. Downie, *Block Island — The Sea*, 46–53.

17. The *Dolphin* was carrying a cargo of molasses, rum, wine, and "stores" consigned to Boston merchant Peter Faneuil, who would later take in several of the shipwrecked Palatines.

18. *Records of the Colony of Rhode Island and Providence Plantations in New England*, vol. IV, 581.

19. Livermore, *History of Block Island*, 120–21.

20. "The Rage for Old China," *New York Times*, August 26, 1877. The article's author (unnamed) purchased several relics believed to be from the Palatine ship: "three or four pieces off this 'Wrack,' as the aborigines term it. On one plate is a view, evidently Dutch, the others have sprays of blue flowers spread over the entire surface." Whittier also claimed to have a plate from the ship, while other nineteenth-century articles describe silver cups in the possession of island residents.

21. Preface to "The Palatine," *The Writings of John Greenleaf Whittier, in Seven Volumes*, vol. 4 (Boston: Houghton Mifflin, 1888), 274.

22. Maizie, *Block Island Scrapbook*, 251–62.

Epilogue

1. Wust, "The Emigration Season of 1738," 50.

2. The number given for survivors is derived from the sixty-or-so Palatines who were ferried to Newport in March 1739, the two women who chose to remain on the island after the others left (Short Kate and Long Kate), and the two women convalescing at Peter Faneuil's home in Boston until 1740. The figure does not take into account surviving crewmembers.

3. "Authentic Open Letter from Pennsylvania in America," 41.

4. Ibid., 51–52.

5. Wistar to Hölzer, April 6, 1739 (OS), Morris Family Papers, HSP.

6. Wokeck, *Trade in Strangers*, 45 (table 2).

7. Wust, "The Emigration Season of 1738," 34.

8. Wust, "The Emigration Season of 1738," 34; Wokeck, *Trade in Strangers*, appendix.

9. Wust, "The Emigration Season of 1738," 34.

10. Ibid., 34–35.

11. For a comprehensive overview of the Hope family's many business interests, see Marten G. Buist, *At Spes non Fracta: Hope & Co. 1770–1815: Merchant Bankers and Diplomats at Work* (The Hague: Martinus Nijhoff, 1974). William Threipland Baxter, *The House of Hancock: Business in Boston* (Boston: Harvard University Press, 1945), 84–86, 94.

12. *A Catalogue of the Collection of Pearls and Precious Stones formed by Henry Philip Hope, Esq., Systematically Arranged and Described by B. Hertz* (London: William Clowes and Sons, 1839), 25. The Hope Diamond (as it is called today) passed out of the Hope family in 1901. Over the next half century, it passed through several owners and ended up in the hands of an American heiress who was known on occasion to fix it to her dog's collar. After she died, the diamond was purchased by jeweler Harry Winston. In 1958 he donated it to the National Gem Collection at the Smithsonian Institution. Said to be worth perhaps $250 million today, it resides in the Smithsonian's National Museum of Natural History. For a history of the Hope Diamond, see http://www.si.edu/Encyclopedia_SI/nmnh/hope.htm.

BIBLIOGRAPHY

Famous Poems and Stories Inspired by the Palatine Legend

Dana, Richard Henry, Sr. "The Buccaneer." In *The Buccaneer and Other Poems*. First edition. (Publisher unknown), 1827. [Reprinted in *Harper's New Monthly*, vol. 45, no. 269 (October 1872): 641–51.] See also "Preface to the First Edition of the Poems," in Dana's *Poems and Prose Writings*, ix–x. New York: Baker and Scribner, 1849.

De Forest, J. W. "The Phantom Ship." *Harper's New Monthly*, vol. 66, no. 394 (March 1883): 519–20. [Also included in *Poems: Medley and Palestina*. New Haven, CT: The Tuttle, Morehouse & Taylor Company, 1902.]

Hale, Edward Everett. *Christmas in Narragansett*. New York: Funk and Wagnalls, 1884.

Higginson, Thomas Wentworth. "The Last Palatine Light." In *Afternoon Landscape: Poems and Translations*, 59–63. New York: Longmans, Green, and Co., 1889.

"The Palatine." *The Lady's Book*, vol. 5 (November 1832): 217–24. Available online at http://babel.hathitrust.org/cgi/pt?id=mdp.39015034631443 ;view=1up;seq=233.

Palmer, Albert G. "The Phantom Ship." *Narragansett Times*, August 20, 1880. [Also included in Palmer's *Psalms of Faith and Songs of Life*. Hartford, CT: Press of the Case, Lockwood & Brainard Co., 1884. Quoted in Samuel T. Livermore's abridged *Block Island*, 106–13.]

Whittier, John Greenleaf. "The Palatine." *Atlantic Monthly*, vol. 19, no. 111 (January 1867): 51–53. [Also included in *The Writings of John Greenleaf Whittier, in Seven Volumes*, vol. 4. London: Macmillan, 1888, and Boston: Houghton Mifflin, 1893.]

Primary Sources

HISTORICAL NEWSPAPERS AND PERIODICALS

American Weekly Mercury (Philadelphia)
Belfast New-Letter (Ireland)

Boston Daily Evening Transcript
Boston Evening Post
Boston Gazette
Boston News-Letter
Boston Post
Boston Post-Boy
Daily Gazetteer (London)
The Day (New London, Connecticut)
Gentleman's Magazine (London)
The Kentish Post, or Canterbury NewsLetter (Kent, England)
London Evening Post
Meriden Daily Republican (Connecticut)
Narragansett Times
New England Weekly Journal (Boston)
New Haven Register
New York Evening Telegram
New York Evening World
New York Gazette
New York Post
New York Times
New York Weekly Journal
Newport Daily News
Newport Mercury
Oprechte Haerlemsch Courant (Haarlem, the Netherlands)
The Parthenon (New York)
Pennsylvania Gazette (Philadelphia)
Philadelphia Enquirer
Providence Patriot
Rhode-Island Republican (Newport)
Rotterdamse Courant
Rotterdamse Dingsdaagse Courant
South-Carolina Gazette (Charleston)
St. Louis Globe-Democrat
Virginia Gazette (Williamsburg)

MUNICIPAL AND OTHER ARCHIVES

Germany
Gemeindearchiv Schwaigern (City Archive of Schwaigern, District of
    Heilbronn)

A Series: Mixed Content Files, Karl Wagenplast Notes
B Series: Inventories and Settlements

The Netherlands
Gemeentelijke Archifdienst, Amsterdam (Municipal Archives of
    Amsterdam)
    Archives of the Mennonite Congregation at Amsterdam
Stadsarchief Rotterdam (City Archives of Rotterdam)
    ONA (Notarial Records)
    BNR (Manuscript Collection)

United Kingdom
The National Archives of the United Kingdom
    ADM (Admiralty)
    PROB (Probate)
    SP (State Papers)

United States
Archives of Philadelphia at the City Hall, Office of the Register of Wills
    Letters of Administration
    Historical Society of Pennsylvania (Philadelphia)
    Coates and Reynell Family Papers
    Morris Family Papers
    Wistar Family Papers
Library of Congress, Manuscript Division (Washington, D.C.)
    Records of the Vice-Admiralty Court Held at Philadelphia
Massachusetts Historical Society (Boston)
    Benjamin Colman Papers
New Shoreham, Block Island, Town Hall
    Land Evidence Records
Rhode Island State Archives
    Notarial Records

BOOKS AND OTHER PUBLICATIONS

*Address Delivered before the Philadelphia County Medical Society, January
    28, 1857, by Wilson Jewell, M.D.* Philadelphia: T. K. and P. G. Collins,
    1857.
Anderson, H. George. "The European Phase of John Ulrich Giessendan-
    ner's Life." *The South Carolina Historical Magazine*, vol. 67, no. 3 (July
    1966): 129–37.
Annual Report of the United States Life-Saving Service for the Fiscal Year End-

ing June 30, 1912. Treasury Department. Washington, D.C.: Government Printing Office, 1913.

"Authentic Open Letter from Pennsylvania in America" ["Glaubhaftes Send=Schreiben aus Pennsylvania in America"]. Published in Frankfurt, 1739. Reprinted in English in *The Brethren in Colonial America*, edited by Donald F. Durnbaugh, 41–53. Elgin, IL: The Brethren Press, 1967.

Barrows, C. Edwin, ed. *The Diary of John Comer.* Vol. 8. Providence: Rhode Island Historical Society, 1893.

Benson, Adolph B., ed. *Peter Kalm's Travels in North America. The English Version of 1770.* Vol. 1. New York: Dover Publications, 1987.

Brumbaugh, Martin Grove. *A History of the German Baptist Brethren in Europe and America.* Mount Morris, IL: Brethren Publishing House, 1899. [Contains letter by Swiss emigrant John Naas.]

A Catalogue of the Collection of Pearls and Precious Stones formed by Henry Philip Hope, Esq., Systematically Arranged and Described by B. Hertz. London: William Clowes and Sons, August 1839.

"Charles Town: Descriptions of Eighteenth-Century Charles Town before the Revolution." National Humanities Center, 2009. http://national humanitiescenter.org/pds/becomingamer/growth/text2/charlestown descriptions.pdf.

"Christopher Schultz's Account (1734)," in Alfred T. Meschter, *The Ship St. Andrew, Galley: A Hypothesis.* Pennsburg, PA: Schwenkfelder Library, 1992.

"Copia" [Copy of a letter by Joggi Thommen]. *Schaefferstown Bulletin*, vol. 6, no. 1 (March 1972): 1–3.

Depositions of Officers of the Palatine Ship "Princess Augusta": Wrecked on Block Island 27th December 1738 and which was apparently the "Palatine" of Whittier's Poem. Providence: E. L. Freeman, 1939. Original in the Rhode Island State Archives, Notarial Records, vol. 4, 1721–1741, 392–94.

"Diary of a Voyage from Rotterdam to Philadelphia in 1728," translated by Julius F. Sachse. *The Pennsylvania-German Society Proceedings and Addresses at Philadelphia, Dec. 8, 1907,* vol. 18 (1909): 8–25.

Diary of Joshua Hempstead of New London, Connecticut. New London: County Historical Society, 1901.

Edgar, Walter B., ed. *The Letterbook of Robert Pringle. Vol. 1: April 2, 1737– September 25, 1742.* Columbia: University of South Carolina Press, 1972.

"Extracts of Mr. Von Reck's Journal from Dover to Ebenezer." In *An Extract of the Journals of Mr. Commissary Von Reck, Who Conducted the First Transport of Saltzburgers to Georgia: and of the Reverend Mr. Bolzius, One of their Ministers*, 5–16. London: Society for Promoting Christian Knowledge, 1734.

Heidgerd, Ruth, and William Heidgerd. *The Goetschy Family and the Limping Messenger*. New Paltz, NY: Huguenot Historical Society, 1968.

Jones, George Fenwick, and Don Savelle, eds. *Detailed Reports on the Salzburger Emigrants Who Settled in America*. Vol. 7, 1740. Athens: University of Georgia Press, 1983.

The Journals of Henry Melchior Muhlenberg, Vol. 1, 1742–1763. Translated by T. G. Tappert and J. W. Doberstein. Originally published by the Evangelical Lutheran Ministerium of Pennsylvania and Adjacent States and the Muhlenberg Press, Philadelphia, 1942. Reprinted by Picton Press, Camden, ME, 1993.

Klepp, Susan E., and Billy G. Smith, eds. *The Infortunate: The Voyage and Adventures of William Moraley, an Indentured Servant*. University Park: Pennsylvania State University Press, 2002.

"A Letter from Dr. John Lining to C. Mortimer M.D. Sec. R.S. Concerning the Weather in South-Carolina; with Abstracts of the Tables of His Meteorological Observations in Charles-Town." *Philosophical Transactions (1683–1775)*, vol. 45 (1753): 336–44.

"Letter from Samuel Dyssli, Charleston, South Carolina, to His Mother, Brothers and Friends in Switzerland." *South Carolina Historical and Genealogical Magazine*, vol. 23, no. 3 (July 1922): 89–91.

"Letters of John Clayton, John Bartram, Peter Collinson, William Byrd, Isham Randolph." *William and Mary Quarterly*, second series, vol. 6, no. 4 (October 1926): 303–25.

Melchior, Leonard, "Well Meant Information as to How the Germans, Who Wish to Travel to Pennsylvania, Should Conduct Themselves, Written 19 Oct. 1749." In *Pennsylvania German Roots across the Ocean*, edited by Marion F. Egge, 45–53. Philadelphia: Genealogical Society of Pennsylvania, 2000.

Minutes of the Provincial Council of Pennsylvania, from the Organization to the Termination of the Proprietary Government, Vol. 3 [1717–1735/6]. Harrisburg: Theo Fenn & Co., 1840.

Minutes of the Provincial Council of Pennsylvania, from the Organization to the Termination of the Proprietary Government, Vol. 4 [1735/6–1745]. Harrisburg: Theo Fenn & Co., 1851.

Mittelberger, Gottlieb. *Gottlieb Mittelberger's Journey to Pennsylvania in the Year 1750 and Return to Germany in the Year 1754*. Ithaca, New York: Cornell University Press, 2009.

"Nitschmann's Diary." In Adelaide L. Fries, *The Moravians in Georgia: 1735–1740*, 101–21. Raleigh, NC: Edwards and Broughton, 1905.

Penn, William. *A Further Account of the Province of Pennsylvania*. London, 1685. Reprinted in Albert Cook Myers, ed., *Narratives of Early Pennsylvania, West New Jersey and Delaware, 1630–1707*, 255–78. New York: C. Scribner's Sons, 1912. Online at https://archive.org/stream/narratives ofearlo3myer#page/259/mode/2up.

———. *Some Account of the Province of Pennsilvania in America*. London: Benjamin Clark, 1681. Reprinted in Albert Cook Myers, ed., *Narratives of Early Pennsylvania, West New Jersey and Delaware, 1630–1707*, 197–215. New York: C. Scribner's Sons, 1912. Online at https://archive.org/stream /narrativesofearlo3myer#page/202/mode/2up.

"Pennsylvania Weather Records, 1644–1835." *The Pennsylvania Magazine of History and Biography*, vol. 15, no. 1 (1891): 109–21.

Records of the Colony of Rhode Island and Providence Plantations in New England, Vol. IV, 1707–1740. Edited by John Russell Bartlett. Providence: Knowles, Anthony & Co., State Printers, 1859.

Robbins, Walter L. "Swiss and German Emigrants to America in Rotterdam, 1736: Excerpts from a Travel Journal of Hieronymus Annoni." *The Report* [of the Society of the History of Germans in Maryland], vol. 35 (1972): 46–51.

Sargent, Lucius Manlius. *Dealings with the Dead*. Boston: Dutton and Wentworth and Ticknor and Fields, 1855. [Contains letter by Peter Faneuil.]

Schelbert, Leo. "On the Power of Pietism: A Documentary on the Thommens of Schaefferstown." *Historic Schaefferstown Record*, vol. 17, nos. 3 and 4 (July–October 1983): 43–74.

Scholtze, David. "Narrative of the Journey of the Schwenckfelders to Pennsylvania, 1733." *The Pennsylvania Magazine of History and Biography*, vol. 10, no. 2 (July 1886): 167–79.

The Statutes at Large of South Carolina, Volume 3, Containing the Acts from 1716, Exclusive, to 1752, Inclusive. Edited by Thomas Cooper. Columbia, SC: A. B. Johnston, 1838.

Strassburger, Ralph B. *Pennsylvania German Pioneers: A Publication of the Original Lists of Arrivals in the Port of Philadelphia from 1727 to 1808*. Vol. 1. Edited by William J. Hinke. Baltimore: Genealogical Publishing, 1980.

Sturch, John. *A View of the Isle of Wight in Four Letters to a Friend*. London: Printed for W. Goldsmith, No. 24 Paternoster Row, 1780.

"Two Early Letters from Germantown." *Pennsylvania Magazine of History and Biography*, vol. 84, no. 2 (April 1960): 219–27. [Contains letter by John George Käsebier.]

Wiley [Willey], Aaron C. "Metheoric Appearance Called the Palatine Light." In *The Medical Repository of Original Essays and Intelligence Relative to Physic, Surgery, Chemistry, and Natural History*, edited by Samuel L. Mitchill, Felix Pascalis, and Samuel Akerly, vol. 1, no. 1 (1813): 408–10.

Secondary Sources

An Abridgment of Mr. Edwards's Civil and Commercial History of the British West Indies. In Two Volumes. Vol. II. London: Printed for J. Parsons, Paternoster-Row: And J. Bell, Oxford-Street, 1794.

Albin, John. *A Companion to the Isle of Wight.* Newport, Isle of Wight: Printed for, and sold by J. Albin, 1799.

Alton, John L. "The Princess Augusta." *The Irish Palatine Association Newsletter*, no. 4 (December 1993): 16–17. Rathkeale, County Limerick, Ireland: Irish Palatine Heritage Center.

Andrews, John H. "Anglo-American Trade in the Early Eighteenth Century." *Geographical Review*, vol. 45, no. 1 (January 1955): 99–110.

Arnold, James N., ed. "Historical Notes: The Palatine Light." *The Narragansett Historical Register*, vol. 1, no. 2 (October 1882): 152–53.

Arnold, Samuel Greene. *History of the State of Rhode Island and Providence Plantations.* Vol. 2, 1700–1790. New York: D. Appleton and Co., 1860.

Arnold-Forster, D. *At War with the Smugglers.* London: Conway Maritime Press, 1970.

Ball, Beatrice. *Block Island: An Illustrated Guide.* New York: Norman Pierce Co., 1909.

Barber, Thomas. *Barber's Picturesque Illustrations of the Isle of Wight.* London: Simpkin & Marshall, Stationers Court, 1834.

Bass, George F., ed. *Ships and Shipwrecks of the Americas.* London: Thames and Hudson, 1988.

Bathurst, Bella. *The Wreckers: A Story of Killing Seas and Plundered Shipwrecks, from the 18th Century to the Present Day.* New York: Houghton Mifflin, 2005.

Baxter, William T. *The House of Hancock: Business in Boston 1724–1775.* New York: Russell & Russell, 1965.

Beckwith, Henry T. *The History of Block Island.* Providence: Publisher unknown, 1858.

Beiler, Rosalind J. "From the Rhine to the Delaware Valley: The Eighteenth-

Century Transatlantic Trading Channels of Caspar Wistar." In *In Search of Peace and Prosperity*, edited by Hartmut Lehmann, Hermann Wellenreuther, and Renate Wilson, 172–88. University Park: Pennsylvania State University Press, 2000.

———. *Immigrant and Entrepreneur: The Atlantic World of Caspar Wistar*. University Park: Pennsylvania State University Press, 2008.

———. "Searching for Prosperity: German Migration to the British American Colonies, 1680–1780." In *The Atlantic World: Essays on Slavery, Migration, and Imagination*, edited by Wim Klooster and Alfred Padula, 91–106. Upper Saddle River, NJ: Pearson Prentice Hall, 2005.

———. "Smuggling Goods or Moving Households?" In *Menschen zwischen zwei Welten: Auswanderung, Ansiedlung, Akkulturation*, edited by Walter G. Rödel and Helmut Schmahl, 9–23. Trier: WVT, 2002.

Benson, Frederick J. *Research, Reflection and Recollections of Block Island*. New Shoreham, RI: Published by the author, 1977.

Bicknell, Thomas Williams. *History of the State of Rhode Island and Providence Plantations*, Vol. 2. New York: The American Historical Society, 1920.

"Block Island Sound and Approaches — NOAA Chart 13205." Published by the National Oceanic and Atmospheric Administration; http://ocsdata.ncd.noaa.gov/BookletChart/13205_BookletChart.pdf.

Brown, Arthur W. "New England Cities and Towns: XIX — Block Island." *New England Magazine*, vol. 6, no. 2 (February 1888): 107–25.

Buist, Marten G. *At Spes non Fracta: Hope & Co. 1770–1815: Merchant Bankers and Diplomats at Work*. The Hague: Martinus Nijhoff, 1974.

Byrnes, Garrett D. "Palatine Legend Debunked" [a four-part article]. *The Evening Bulletin, Providence*, September 11–14, 1933.

Carlson, Robert W. *The Palatine Ship: Ghost Ship of Block Island*. College Park, MD: Archaeoastronomy Press, 1994.

Chamberlain, J. P. *The Regime of the International Rivers: Danube and Rhine*. New York: AMS Press, 1968.

Chapin, Howard M. "The Discovery of the Real Palatine Ship." *Rhode Island Historical Society Collections*, vol. 16, no. 2 (April 1923): 33–38.

———. "Whittier's 'Palatine' Discovered." *The American Collector: A Monthly Magazine for Collectors' Lore*, edited by Charles F. Heartman, vol. 3, no. 3 (December 1926): 118–22.

Chapman, Fredrik Henrik af. *Architectura Navalis Mercatoria: The Classic of Eighteenth-Century Naval Architecture*. Mineola, NY: Dover Publications, 2006 (reprint). Originally published by Holmiæ in Stockholm, 1768.

Citro, Joseph A., and Diane E. Foulds. *Curious New England: The Unconventional Traveler's Guide to Eccentric Destinations.* Hanover, NH: University Press of New England, 2004.

Clapp, Edwin J. *The Navigable Rhine.* Boston: Houghton Mifflin, 1911.

Cobb, Sanford H. *The Story of the Palatines: An Episode in Colonial History.* New York: G. P. Putnam's Sons, 1897. Reprinted by Forgotten Books, 2012.

Coughtry, Jay. *The Notorious Triangle: Rhode Island and the African Slave Trade, 1700–1807.* Philadelphia: Temple University Press, 1981.

D'Amato, Donald A., and Henry A. L. Brown. *Images of America: Block Island.* Charleston, SC: Arcadia Publishing, 1999.

Davis, Paul. "The Unrighteous Traffic: Rhode Island's Slave Trade." http://res.providencejournal.com/hercules/extra/2006/slavery/.

Davis, Ralph. *The Rise of the English Shipping Industry in the Seventeenth and Eighteenth Centuries.* New York: St. Martin's Press, 1962.

Deutsch, Sarah. "The Elusive Guineamen: Newport Slavers, 1735–1774." *The New England Quarterly,* vol. 55, no. 2 (June 1982): 229–53.

Diffenderffer, Frank Reid. *The German Immigration in Pennsylvania Through the Port of Philadelphia from 1700 to 1775.* Baltimore: Genealogical Publishing, 2003.

Downie, Robert M. *Block Island — The Land.* Block Island, RI: Book Nook Press, 2001.

———. *Block Island — The Sea.* Block Island, RI: Book Nook Press, 1998.

Drake, Samuel Adams. *New England Legends and Folk Lore, in Prose and Poetry.* Boston: Little, Brown, and Co., 1901.

Drury, Tom. "Past Tense Clandestine Actions." *Providence Journal,* August 6, 1989.

Duffy, John. *Epidemics in Colonial America.* Port Washington, NY: Kennikat Press, 1972.

———. "The Passage to the Colonies." *Mississippi Valley Historical Review,* vol. 38, no. 1 (June 1951): 21–38.

Dunn, Richard S. "William Penn and the Selling of Pennsylvania, 1681–1685." *Proceedings of the American Philosophical Society,* vol. 127, no. 5 (October 14, 1983): 322–29.

DWL — de Esch Bestemmingsplan, 13 maart 2013, Hoofdstuk 3, Beschrijving plangebied en ruimtelijke analyse, 3.1 Archeologie [Zoning plan for the waterworks of de Esch, May 13, 2013, chapter 3: Description planning area and spatial analysis, 3.1 Archaeology], 20–24. http://www.betrokken bijrotterdam.nl/Clusters/RSO/Document%202013/Bekendmakingen /Bestemmingsplannen/DEELGEMEENTE%20KRALINGEN%20 CROOSWIJK/2.%20Bestemmingsplan%20DWL-de%20Esch_0h01 .pdf.

Edwards, Mary K. Bercaw. "'The Slack Eend of a Lyin' Tale,'" *Log of the Mystic Seaport*, vol. 51 (Autumn 1999): 38–43.

Faust, Albert Bernhardt. "Increase in German Immigration in the Eighteenth Century, and Its Causes," in *The German Element in the United States*, vol. 1. Boston: Houghton Mifflin Company, 1909. Online at https:// archive.org/stream/germanelement01fausrich#page/n9/mode/2up.

Fogleman, Aaron Spencer. *Hopeful Journeys: German Immigration, Settlement, and Political Culture in Colonial America, 1717–1775*. Philadelphia: University of Pennsylvania Press, 1996.

Gardiner, Robert, ed. *The Heyday of Sail: The Merchant Sailing Ship, 1650–1830*. London: Conway Maritime Press, 1992.

Gemming, Elizabeth. *Block Island Summer*. Riverside, CT: The Chatham Press, 1972.

"God's Little Acre — America's Colonial African Cemetery: Slave Life." http://www.colonialcemetery.com/newport-slavery/.

Green, Welcome A. "A New Theory Regarding the Origin of the Palatine Light." *Narragansett Historical Register*, vol. 5 (1886–1887): 253–58.

Groot, Irene de, and Robert Vorstman, eds. *Sailing Ships: Prints by the Dutch Masters from the Sixteenth to the Nineteenth Century*. New York: Viking Press, 1980.

Grubb, Farley. "The Market Structure of Shipping German Immigrants to Colonial America." *Pennsylvania Magazine of History and Biography*, vol. iii, no. 1 (January 1987): 27–48.

———. "Morbidity and Mortality on the North Atlantic Passage: Eighteenth-Century German Immigration." *Journal of Interdisciplinary History*, vol. 17, no. 3 (Winter 1987): 565–85.

———. "Redemptioner Immigration to Pennsylvania: Evidence on Contract Choice and Profitability." *Journal of Economic History*, vol. 46, no. 2 (June 1986): 407–18.

Haberlein, Mark. "German Migrants in Colonial Pennsylvania: Resources, Opportunities, and Experience." *William and Mary Quarterly*, vol. 50, no. 3 (July 1993): 555–74.

Haley, John Williams. "The Palatine Light." *The Old Stone Bank History of Rhode Island*, vol. 7 (1931): 3–9.

Haller, Charles R. *Across the Atlantic and Beyond: The Migration of German and Swiss Immigrants to America.* Bowie, MD: Heritage Books, 1993.

Harper, Douglas. "Slavery in the North: Slavery in Rhode Island." http://slavenorth.com/rhodeisland.htm.

Harrison, Shirley. *The Channel.* Glasgow: William Collins Sons and Co., 1986.

Hawes, Alexander Boyd. *Off Soundings: Aspects of the Maritime History of Rhode Island.* Chevy Chase, MD: Posterity Press, 1999.

Hazard, Thomas. *Recollections of Olden Times.* Newport, RI: John P. Sanborn, 1879.

Hazewinkel, H. C. *Geschiedenis van Rotterdam / Deel 2.* [History of Rotterdam, Vol. 2]. Zaltbommel: Europese Bibliotheek, 1974.

Herman, H. *Abbildungen der verschiedenen Gattungen von Fahrzeugen, wie man sie auf dem Rheine sieht* [Pictures of Different Types of Vehicles, as Seen on the Rhine]. Mainz: Müller, 1820.

"The History of Cowes Customs Until 1750." http://www.customscowes.co.uk/history_of_cowes_customs_until%201750.htm.

Hostetler, John A. *Amish Society.* Baltimore: Johns Hopkins University Press, 1993.

Howe, Jeffrey. *The History and Genealogy of Descendants of Slaves and Indians from the Island of "Manissee"— Block Island.* Riverside, RI: the author, 1997.

Hurricane Research Division, Atlantic Oceanographic and Meteorological Laboratory, National Oceanographic and Atmospheric Administration. http://www.aoml.noaa.gov/hrd/tcfaq/E11.html.

"Hurricanes." *Weather Explained,* http://www.weatherexplained.com/Vol-1/Hurricanes.html.

Jensen, Arthur L. *The Maritime Commerce of Colonial Philadelphia.* Madison: State Historical Society of Wisconsin for the Department of History, University of Wisconsin, 1963.

Johnson, Sherry. "Climate Cycles as Agents of Historical Processes along the Southern Frontier: 1738–1739." Presented at the American Historical Association conference in New Orleans on Saturday, January 5, 2013.

———. "From El Niño to the 'Long La Niña': Early Indicators of Crisis in the Atlantic World, 1730s–40s." Presented at the American Historical Association conference in New Orleans, January 5, 2013.

Jones, George Fenwick. *The Georgia Dutch: From the Rhine and Danube to the Savannah, 1733–1783*. Athens: The University of Georgia Press, 1992.

Kieffer, Elizabeth Clarke. "The Cheese Was Good." *Pennsylvania Folklife*, vol. 19, no. 3 (Spring 1970): 27–29.

Klein, Herbert S., Stanley L. Engerman, Robin Haines, and Ralph Shlomowitz. "Transoceanic Mortality: The Slave Trade in Comparative Perspective." *William and Mary Quarterly*, vol. 58, no. 1 (January 2001): 93–118.

Klein, P. W. "'Little London': British Merchants in Rotterdam During the Seventeenth and Eighteenth Centuries." In *Enterprise and History: Essays in Honour of Charles Wilson*, edited by D. C. Coleman and Peter Mathias, 116–34. Cambridge, England: Cambridge University Press, 1984.

Knittle, Walter Allen. *Early Eighteenth-Century Palatine Emigration*. Baltimore: Genealogical Publishing, 2004.

Kobler, John. "The Mystery of the Palatine Light." *Saturday Evening Post*, June 11, 1960, 54–58.

Kyriakodis, Harry. *Philadelphia's Lost Waterfront*. Charleston, SC: The History Press, 2011.

Lanman, Charles. "Block Island." *Harper's New Monthly Magazine*, vol. 53, no. 314 (July 1876): 168–78.

Leary, Lewis. *John Greenleaf Whittier*. New York: Twayne Publishers, 1961.

Lehmann, Hartmut, Hermann Wellenreuther, and Renate Wilson, eds. *In Search of Peace and Prosperity: New German Settlements in Eighteenth-Century Europe and America*. University Park: Pennsylvania State University Press, 2000.

Lemon, James T. *The Best Poor Man's Country: A Geographical Study of Early Southeastern Pennsylvania*. New York: W. W. Norton & Co., 1976.

Livermore, Samuel T. *Block Island* [abridged]. Hartford, CT: Press of the Case, Lockwood & Brainard Co., 1882.

———. *History of Block Island, Rhode Island*. Originally printed in 1877 and reprinted by the Block Island Historical Society in 2003.

Maizie [Rose, Mary]. *Block Island Scrapbook*. New York: Pageant Press, 1957.

Martin, Rob. "Carolina, Cowes and the Rice Trade." Produced by the Isle of Wight History Center (http://www.iwhistory.org.uk/), 2004.

Marvin, William. *A Treatise on the Law of Wreck and Salvage*. Boston: Little, Brown and Co., 1858.

McGowan, Alan. *The Ship: The Century before Steam — The Development of the Sailing Ship, 1700–1820.* London: Crown, 1980.

Medland, John. "Cowes at Centre of World Trade." *Isle of Wight County Press Online,* March 21, 2014. http://www.iwcp.co.uk/news/wight-living/cowes-at-centre-of-world-trade-54992.aspx.

Mellor, Roy E. H. *The Rhine: A Study in the Geography of Water Transport.* O'Dell Memorial Monograph No. 16. Department of Geography, University of Aberdeen, 1983.

Mendum, Samuel W. "Block Island." In *Tales of the New England Coast,* compiled by Frank Oppel, 265–78. Edison, NJ: Castle Books, 1984.

Meschter, Alfred T. *The Ship St. Andrew, Galley: A Hypothesis.* Pennsburg, PA: Schwenkfelder Library, 1992.

Migliaccio, Fran. *Ghosts of Block Island.* Block Island, RI: Frances Huggard Migliaccio, 2005.

Mitchell, Edwin Valentine. *It's an Old New England Custom.* New York: Bonanza Books, 1946.

Müller-Alfeld, Theodor, Willy Eggers, and Harald Busch, eds. *Portrait of a River: The Rhine.* New York: Hastings House Publishers, 1956.

Nash, R. C. "Trade and Business in Eighteenth-Century South Carolina: The Career of John Guerard, Merchant and Planter." *South Carolina Historical Magazine,* vol. 96, no. 1 (January 1995): 6–29.

"NOAA: Hurricane Basics." Homeland Security Digital Library, https://www.hsdl.org/?abstract&did=34038.

Oehler, Dorothee. "Hexen und Hexenverfolgung im Zabergäu und Umgebung" [Witches and witch hunting in Zabergäu and surroundings]. *Zeitschrift des Zabergäuvereins,* no. 4 (2000): 57–78.

"The Palatine Light." *Lippincott's Magazine,* vol. 17, no. 97 (January 1876): 132.

Perry, Charles E. "Block Island's Story." *New England Magazine,* vol. 30, no. 5 (July 1904): 515–24.

Perry, Frank L. *Johannes Michael Schneider Descendants and Allied Families: 1738–1993.* Lilburn, GA: Published by the author, 1993.

"Phantom Lights at Sea." *Scientific American,* vol. 47, no. 4 (July 22, 1882): 56.

Pickard, Samuel. *The Life and Letters of John Greenleaf Whittier,* Vol. II. Cambridge, MA: The Riverside Press, 1894.

Post, John D. "Climatic Variability and the European Mortality Wave of the Early 1740s." *Journal of Interdisciplinary History,* vol. 15, no. 1 (Summer 1984): 1–30.

Powell, Noel. "Block Island's Fiery Ghost." *Yankee Magazine*, vol. 20, no. 7 (July 1956): 58–60.

Price, Kenneth M., and Susan Belasco Smith, eds. *Periodical Literature in Nineteenth-Century America*. Charlottesville: University Press of Virginia, 1995.

Ramsay, David. *History of South-Carolina, from Its First Settlement in 1670, to the Year 1808*, Vol. 2. Charleston: David Longworth, 1809.

Rebok, Barbara, and Doug Rebok, eds. *Early Days in Block Island and South Kingston, Rhode Island, Compiled from Early Historical Records*. [City unknown]: A Plus Printing Company, 2001.

Redfern, Ron. *Origins: The Evolution of Continents, Oceans and Life*. Norman, OK: University of Oklahoma Press, 2001.

Rediker, Marcus. *Between the Devil and the Deep Blue Sea: Merchant Seamen, Pirates, and the Anglo-American Maritime World 1700–1750*. New York: Cambridge University Press, 1987.

Reiff, A. E. "Conrad Gehr's Peccadilloes." *Pennsylvania Fathers of the Eighteenth Century* (blog). May 26, 2009, http://pennsylvaniafathers.blogspot.com/2009/05/outlaw-reiffs-and-lawless-religion.html.

Remer, Richard. "Toll Stations Along the Rhine." *The Palatine Immigrant*, vol. 21, no. 3 (June 1996): 116–17.

Riffe, Fred J. *Reiff to Riffe Family in America: Descendants of John George Reiff*. Marathon, FL: the author, 1995.

Riley, James C. "Mortality on Long-Distance Voyages in the Eighteenth Century." *The Journal of Economic History*, vol. 41, no. 3 (September 1981): 651–56.

Ritchie, Ethel Colt. *Block Island Lore and Legends*. Block Island, RI: Mrs. Frances M. Nugent, 1955.

Saunders, Melanie. "Historical Society to Host Tour of Former Hazard Property." *The Independent*. Posted June 11, 2015, http://www.independentri.com/independents/arts_and_living/article_c248856d-0ef2-5f4d-8a4c-4b7d52b7aa42.html.

Schanes, Nancy E. "Voyage of the *Love and Unity*." Booklet published by the author in 2003.

Scheer, Teva J. *Our Daily Bread: German Village Life, 1500–1850*. North Saanich, BC: Adventis Press, 2010.

Schraver, J., ed. *Rotterdam: Gateway to Europe*. Rotterdam: A. D. Donker, 1948.

Schuessler, Anne, and Helmut Schuessler. "Scharfrichter und Wasenmeister im Dienst der Gemeinschaft, aber sozial ausgegrenzt — mit einer Kurzbiographie des Kraichgauer Nachrichters Ostertag" [Executioner and knacker in the service of the community, but socially excluded — a short biography of the Kraichgauer Nachrichters Ostertag]. *Bad Rappenauer Heimatbote*, vol. 16, no. 17 (2006): 27–33.

Selig, Robert A. "Rats, Maggots, and Hardtack: Transatlantic Travel in the 18th Century." *German Life* (February/March 2000): 26–31.

Sheffield, William P. *A Historical Sketch of Block Island*. Newport: John P. Sanborn & Co., 1876.

Shepard, Birse. *Lore of the Wreckers*. Boston: Beacon Press, 1961.

Simons, Richard B. "The Achievements of Our German Peasant Ancestors." *The Palatine Immigrant*, vol. 20, no. 2 (March 1995): 64–77.

Sirkin, Les. *Block Island Geology*. Watch Hill, RI: Book & Tackle Shop, 1996.

Smith, Abbot Emerson. "Some New Facts About Eighteenth-Century German Immigration." *Pennsylvania History*, vol. 10, no. 2 (April 1943): 105–17.

Snow, Edward Rowe. *Strange Tales from Nova Scotia to Cape Hatteras*. New York: Dodd, Mead & Co., 1949.

Spaulding, Robert Mark. "Anarchy, Hegemony, Cooperation: International Control of the Rhine River, 1789–1848." Paper presented to the Consortium on Revolutionary Europe: 1750–1850, Charleston, SC, 1999.

Steele, Ian K. *The English Atlantic, 1675–1740: An Exploration of Communication and Community*. Oxford, England: Oxford University Press, 1986.

Stewart, David J. "Burial at Sea: Separating and Placing the Dead During the Age of Sail." *Mortality*, vol. 10, no. 4 (November 2005): 276–85.

Strange, Marion. *Vital Negotiations: Protecting Settlers' Health in Colonial Louisiana and South Carolina, 1720–1763*. Göttingen, Germany: V & R Unipress, 2012.

Te Lintum, C. "Emigratie over Rotterdam in de 18ᵉ eeuw" [Emigration from Rotterdam in the eighteenth century]. *De Gids*, vol. 72 (1908): 323–35.

Thomas, Hugh. *The Slave Trade: The Story of the Atlantic Slave Trade: 1440–1870*. New York: Simon Schuster, 1997.

Todd, Charles Burr. "The Island of Manisees." *Lippincott's Magazine*, vol. 4, no. 8 (December 1882): 529–43.

Tolles, Frederick B. *Meeting House and Counting House: The Quaker Merchants of Colonial Philadelphia, 1682–1763*. New York: W. W. Norton & Co., 1948.

"The Transformation of Rhode Island Hall." Joukowsky Institute for Archaeology and the Ancient World, Brown University, www.brown.edu
/Departments/Joukowsky_Institute/about/rihalltransform/6996.html.

Turnbaugh, William A. "The Palatine." *Tidings* (July 1992): 16–19.

Weigley, Russell F., ed. *Philadelphia: A 300-Year History.* New York: W. W.
Norton & Co., 1982.

Whedbee, Charles Harry. *The Flaming Ship of Ocracoke and Other Tales of
the Outer Banks.* Winston-Salem, NC: John F. Blair Publisher, 1971.

Whiteman, Herbert S. *Exploring Old Block Island.* Old Greenwich, CT:
Chatham Press Books, 1980.

Wiersum, E. *Rotterdamsch jaarboekje* [Rotterdam yearbook]. Rotterdam:
W. L. & J. Brusse, 1921.

Williamson, J. A. *The English Channel.* London: Readers Union Collins,
1961.

Wilson, Malcolm Sands. *Descendants of James Sands of Block Island.* New
York: Privately printed, 1949.

Wokeck, Marianne. "Capitalizing on Hope: Transporting German Emigrants across the Atlantic before the American Revolution." *Amerika-
studien/American Studies: Transatlantic Migration*, vol. 42, no. 3 (1997):
345–56.

———. "The Flow and the Composition of German Immigration to Philadelphia, 1727–1775." *Pennsylvania Magazine of History and Biography*,
vol. 105, no. 3 (July 1981): 249–78.

———. "German and Irish Immigration to Colonial Philadelphia." *Proceedings of the American Philosophical Society*, vol. 133, no. 2 (June 1989):
128–43.

———. "Promoters and Passengers: The German Immigrant Trade, 1683–
1775." In *The World of William Penn*, edited by Richard S. and Mary
Maples Dunn, 259–78. Philadelphia: University of Pennsylvania Press,
1986.

———. "A Tide of Alien Tongues." PhD diss., Temple University, 1982.

———. *Trade in Strangers: The Beginnings of Mass Migration to North
America.* University Park: Penn State Press, 1999.

Wood, Peter H. *Black Majority: Negroes in Colonial South Carolina from
1670 Through the Stono Rebellion.* New York: Alfred A. Knopf, 1974.

Woodward, William McKenzie. *Historic and Architectural Resources of
Block Island, Rhode Island.* Providence: Rhode Island Historical Preser-
vation Commission, 1991.

Worsley, Richard. *The History of the Isle of Wight*. London: Printed by A. Hamilton; And sold by R. Dodsley, T. Cadell, G. Robinson, R. Faulder, and G. Nicol: Collins and Co. Salisbury; and Burdon, at Winchester, 1781.

Worth, Richard Nicholls. *The History of Plymouth: From the Earliest Period to the Present Time*. Plymouth, England: W. Brenden, 1890.

Wust, Klaus. "The Emigration Season of 1738: Year of the Destroying Angels." *The Report*, [of the Society for the History of the Germans in Maryland], vol. 40 (1986): 21–56.

———. "Feeding the Palatines: Shipboard Diet in the Eighteenth Century." *The Report*, vol. 39 (1984): 32–42.

———. "Palatines and Switzers for Virginia, 1705–1738: Costly Lessons for Promoters and Emigrants." *Yearbook of German-American Studies*, vol. 19 (1984): 43–56.

———. "William Byrd II and the Shipwreck of the *Oliver*." *Newsletter* [of the Swiss-American Historical Society], vol. 20, no. 2 (1984): 3–19.

Wust, Klaus, and Heinz Moos. *Three Hundred Years of German Immigrants in North America: 1683–1983*. Baltimore: Heinz Moos Publishing Co., 1983.

Yoder, Don, ed. *Pennsylvania German Immigrants: 1709–1786*. Baltimore: Genealogical Publishing, 1980.